THE TERRIBLE ALTERNATIVE

Whoever he be that is willing to suffer for his faith, whether he be little lad or man grown, Jew or Gentile, Christian or Infidel, man or woman, it matters not at all: who dies for justice dies a martyr, a defender of the cause of Christ.
John of Salisbury (c. 1115–80)

THE TERRIBLE
ALTERNATIVE

Christian Martyrdom
in the Twentieth Century

EDITED BY
ANDREW CHANDLER

CASSELL

Cassell
Wellington House, 125 Strand, London WC2R 0BB
370 Lexington Avenue, New York, NY 10017-6550

Website: www.cassell.co.uk

© The editor and contributors 1998

First published 1998

British Library Cataloguing-in-Publication Data
A catalogue record for this book is available from the British Library.

ISBN 0-304-70287-0

The translation of the quotation from John of Salisbury on page i comes from a
letter by Helen Waddell: D. Felicitas Corrigan, *Helen Waddell: A Biography*
(London, 1986), p. 316.

Typeset by BookEns Ltd, Royston, Herts.
Printed and bound in Great Britain by
Biddles Ltd, Guildford and King's Lynn

Contents

Illustrations

The Authors

Anthony Harvey is Sub-Dean of Westminster Abbey. His many publications include *A Companion to the New Testament*, *Jesus and the Constraints of History*, *Strenuous Commands: The Ethic of Jesus* and *Promise or Pretence? A Christian's Guide to Sexual Morals*.

Andrew Chandler is Director of the George Bell Institute and Senior Research Fellow at Queen's, Birmingham. His publications include *Brethren in Adversity: Bishop George Bell, the Church of England and the Crisis of German Protestantism 1933–1939* and *New Soundings: Essays on Developing Tradition* (with Graham James and Stephen Platten).

Philip Berryman is a leading authority on Christianity in Central and South America. His books include *Liberation Theology*, *Christians in Guatemala's Struggle* and *The Religious Roots of Rebellion*. He lives in Philadelphia.

Georgii Chistyakov is a priest serving at the church of SS Cosmas and Damian in Moscow. He also works as Rector of the Alexander Men Open University and cares for children with leukaemia at the First Children's Republic Hospital in the city. Before his ordination he was Professor of Classics at Moscow University.

Mandy Goedhals is Head of the Department of History at the University of Durban-Westville. Her publications include *Change and Challenge*, a volume of essays, edited with John Suggit, marking the 150th anniversary of Robert Gray's arrival as first Bishop of Cape Town in 1848 (1998) and 'From paternalism to partnership? The CPSA and mission 1848–1988' in T. Paterson and F. England (eds), *Bounty in Bondage* (1989).

Sehon Goodridge is Bishop of the Windward Islands. His publications include *A Companion to Liberation Theology* and *Facing the Challenge of Emancipation*.

Errol Hodge is a Senior Lecturer in journalism in the School of Media and Journalism at Queensland University of Technology, Australia.

Klemens von Klemperer is L. Clark Seelye Professor of History (Emeritus) at Smith College, Massachusetts. His many publications include *The German Resistance Against Hitler: The Search for Allies Abroad 1938-1945* and *A Noble Combat: The Letters of Shiela Grant Duff and Adam von Trott zu Solz 1932-1939*.

Roman Komaryczko OFM Conv is a Franciscan Conventual from Cracow, where he studied theology. He is currently working on his doctorate in philosophy at the Catholic University of Lublin, Poland.

John Sentamu was born in Uganda. He is Bishop of Stepney, London.

Patrick Sookhdeo is Director of the Institute for the Study of Islam and Christianity in London. His publications include *The Asian in Britain*.

Philip Wickeri is Professor of Evangelism and Mission at San Francisco Theological Seminary. He has lived and worked in Asia for more than twenty years.

Preface

Westminster Abbey and the twentieth-century martyrs

T
HIS BOOK is one of the fruits of a major project at Westminster Abbey that was brought to completion in 1998. The project was that of filling ten niches on the west front of the Abbey with statues of twentieth-century martyrs. It arose in the first instance out of the restoration of the entire exterior of the Abbey which began in 1973. There were strong grounds for believing that the niches, which were built in the fifteenth century and remodelled by Hawksmoor early in the eighteenth century, were always intended for statues — as was normally the case in the later Middle Ages: Henry VII's Chapel (completed in 1519) has nearly a hundred statues in niches inside, and the niches outside were certainly filled until their contents disappeared in the mid-eighteenth century. There seemed therefore to be a strong architectural case for regarding the restoration as incomplete until these niches were filled.

Accordingly, in 1990–92, the six niches high up on the Hawksmoor towers were filled with conventional subjects: four New Testament saints (the Blessed Virgin Mary, St John, St Peter and St Paul) and two medieval ones closely connected with the Abbey (St Edward the Confessor and St Faith). Being so high, these attracted little notice, though they undoubtedly enhance the appearance of the towers. The remaining fourteen niches (ten over the door and two on either side) presented a greater challenge. They would attract more attention when filled, and the choice of subject was more difficult, given that most of the eligible historical figures were already represented somewhere inside or outside the Abbey. It was then that the idea was born to use these niches to convey a message — one that is of great contemporary significance but by no means sufficiently well known: that the twentieth century has seen not only more innocent suffering but also more Christian martyrdoms than any other period in history, greatly exceeding, for example, those of the great persecutions of the early centuries of the Church.

The choice of these ten from among the thousands who have lost their lives through their fidelity to Christian beliefs and values this century involved prolonged research, discussion with local churches and the exercise of a collective judgement informed so far as possible by knowledge of the circumstances in each case. There could be no question of choosing by merit or popularity: each martyr must be capable of representing all the other victims of a particular area of persecution, and recognized as such both by compatriots and by the world at large. Standing together in their niches, the statues are intended to represent the whole gamut of this ultimate Christian witness across a wide range of denominations, cultures and continents.

For the statues themselves, it was a deliberate decision, approved (after much discussion) by the Architectural Advisory Panel of Westminster Abbey, to employ mason-carvers trained in a manner that continued the medieval tradition. Vital experience had been gained during repairs to the Henry VII Chapel in 1992-95, when more than 300 pieces of sculpture (mainly heraldic beasts and devices) were re-carved by a team of a dozen or so mason-carvers, thereby creating a veritable school of modern architectural statuary. By way of a trial, it was decided to use Abbey funds to fill the two niches on each side of the door with allegorical gothic figures representing the four traditional 'virtues', or values, for which the martyrs might be said to have died – mercy, truth, justice and peace. These were modelled and carved by Tim Crawley, chief sculptor of Rattee and Kett, and again attracted little notice: most visitors assumed they had always been there. But the ready acceptance of them by the public encouraged the Panel, and on their advice the Dean and Chapter, to authorize the same traditional method for the ten statues of martyrs, the completion of which had now been made possible by a generous private donation. Tim Crawley was joined by two other sculptors with the same training and experience (Neil Simmons and John Roberts) but remained in overall control, having himself carried out considerable research both on comparable medieval statuary and on the biography and appearance of each martyr. The Panel deputed a small committee to monitor the work at every stage – from small clay models through plaster casts to the finished sculptures. The Surveyor of the Fabric (Donald Buttress), who had originally pressed for the project to be carried forward on architectural grounds, provided technical and aesthetic advice throughout and carried the ultimate responsibility for the successful completion of the project in time for the statues to be unveiled by the Archbishop of Canterbury in the presence of the Queen and the Duke of Edinburgh and church leaders and representatives from many parts of the world on 9 July 1998.

The publication of the list of martyrs in October 1997 evoked considerable interest and some anxious questioning. Why was no British martyr being commemorated? Was there not a slight suspicion of anti-Semitism attaching to one of them? Was not the private life of another too beset by ambiguities for his inclusion to be justified? Were not the reasons for the death of a third more political than religious? These questions in turn raised deeper issues concerning the nature of martyrdom in the twentieth century, given that the circumstances which precipitated it are so different from those which obtained in the early centuries of the Church. It is both the particular questions and the more general issues which are the subject of these essays and to which the authors have striven to make a significant contribution.

The Dean and Chapter of Westminster owe a debt of gratitude to the distinguished international group of scholars who have willingly submitted to the rigid time limit imposed on their work and to the freedom required by the editor to give the book a consistent style and unity of purpose. In particular they are indebted to the editor, Andrew Chandler, who, with substantial support from the George Bell Institute, successfully completed the daunting task of gathering these diverse contributions into a handsome book ready for publication at the time of unveiling. The full extent of his contribution to the success of the entire project can be known and appreciated only by those who have been privileged to work on it with him.

December 1997   Anthony Harvey
                                                        Sub-Dean of Westminster

The editor wishes to thank Gillian Paterson, Diana Smallshaw and Fiona McKenzie of Cassell for their assistance in the preparation of this book.

Introduction

ANDREW CHANDLER AND ANTHONY HARVEY

I N 1929, 30 young Russian nuns were taken from their convent at Sharmordino and transported to the labour camps of the Solovki Islands. Their warders were embarrassed by their presence there. The fact that the nuns refused to comply even with their most modest demands exasperated them. They gave only their names in religion, and answered no further questions. They would not work. The government of the country was, they insisted, Antichrist. A doctor visited them and, moved by their plight, said that he would register them as unfit for labour so that they could not be beaten. This the nuns also rejected. They were fit to work, but they would not. The doctor assured them that there were already Christians in the camp who did co-operate: a bishop worked as an accountant, another in the fisheries department. This did not persuade them. Later, the little group was moved on again. Nobody knew what became of them. One catches only a glimpse of a few tenacious women, resisting the directives of a massive totalitarian state, moving off with now inaudible psalms into the vast landscape, the oblivion, of the Soviet Union.[1]

The sufferings of faithful predecessors are much invoked in each Christian generation. In many traditions much has been done to organize them into categories, or systems, of witnesses and martyrs. But the sense of order that such formulations bring to religious history rests uneasily on the untidiness of human experience. Christianity has never presented a uniform reality. To begin with, the Church is not merely an institution, although most churches have acquired powerful institutional characteristics in their pursuit of order. When we come to think of the churches of history as diffuse, difficult realities, embracing men and women with no position or authority, all of them living out their faith in various spheres of life and work, our image fragments. Our perception of what stands at the heart of Christian life, and what is on the fringe, begs its own questions. Who do we remember, and why? Moreover we know that churches were conceived in different terms in different places, and even in opposition to one another. This affects the issue of martyrdom all too clearly. Just as doctrines were in conflict, the martyrs of one church were, for another, simply heretics.

We also find that the Christian understanding and experience of the world fractures in our hands as soon as we look closely at it. Religious institutions, ideas and lives are in any age entangled in a complex fabric of politics, social currents and cultural forces. Their demands have from the first troubled Christians, as the writings of St Paul testify.[2] Most of the faithful have sought to reconcile a resolve to be distinct from the wider environment with a wish to be a part of it, and to redeem it. Once Christians assured themselves that the whole world was the creation of God, that it was good, that it lived in his care and under his judgement, they found themselves participants, not abstainers, in its great questions. Some observed that the ways of the world may corrupt. Later critics of the Roman Church judged that the papacy secularized itself by imposing its will with methods that spoke more of political authority than Christian faith. The reformers of the sixteenth century argued that if the Church of Rome was strong, it was because it oppressed its followers. If it was rich, it was because it was worldly. The European Reformation, however, often attached the Protestant churches more firmly to the power of princes and politicians than ever. Christians in every age have made of the world quite different things, and when they have tried to uphold their faith, they have been seen to disappear in a variety of directions. In the modern era, many sanctioned imperialism, promoted socialism and applauded fascism. At the same time, others questioned empires, contradicted the politics of the left, and resisted dictators. It is in the midst of such complicated realities that the phenomenon of Christian martyrdom in the twentieth century must be viewed. The subject demands much of us. In pursuing it, we must expect to be pulled in unsettling directions and into unexpected regions.

THE PROBLEM OF MARTYRDOM: JESUS HIMSELF

'The martyr', writes the historian P. W. Gooch, 'dies as a testimony to the over-riding importance of some belief or commitment greater than life itself.'[3] Christianity itself may be said to be in part an expression, and a development, of this theme. That Christ died as a martyr was not doubted by the Christians of the first three centuries: if called to martyrdom themselves they looked to Jesus as their model and inspiration. They were consoled and strengthened by the sense of being privileged to share in the torments endured by Jesus on the cross. Yet a certain ambivalence is betrayed even by the terminology that we have inherited from that age. The Christian calling was to a life of 'witness' — *martyria* — which might or might not lead to death (it was at least a century before the word was narrowed down to denote 'red martyrdom'); and this witness was to faith in Jesus Christ as the Son of God. In what sense, then, could Jesus himself have been a martyr? What did he 'witness' to? Significantly it was Stephen, not Jesus, who became the 'proto-martyr' of Christian tradition: he was the first to have borne witness, to the point of death, to the lordship of Jesus and his exaltation to the right hand of God. Yet no one wished to deny that Jesus himself was a martyr, indeed the martyr who inspired all who followed him on the road that could lead to death.

To grasp the significance of this word 'witness', we need to bear in mind a significant difference between ancient Jewish legal procedures and our own.[4] To establish the facts of a case today in the West, we are accustomed to assembling evidence that is factual and verifiable: in the stories of the English writer Arthur Conan Doyle, it is the exceptional powers of observation shown by the detective Sherlock Holmes that provide the vital clues for reconstructing the train of events leading up to the crime. But two thousand years ago Jewish procedure set little store by such practical investigation; the question was simply 'Whose story can we trust?' Everything depended on the reputation of the witness. If he was known to be a trustworthy witness (women were not qualified to testify) then his statement should be accepted. In the case of Jesus the question was whether certain claims were true. Was he the prophet who was to come (Deuteronomy 18:15ff.)? Was he the promised Messiah? Was he the Son of God? Signs and miracles might point in this direction; but the question would depend on who was making the claim, the 'witnesses'. These witnesses were not, in the early years at least, persons of widely known probity and respectability. They could not command assent simply by their reputation and the respect in which they were held. They could establish their trustworthiness only by the consistency of their lives and their activities with what they proclaimed. The ultimate test of this consistency might be their willingness to endure death.

The issue is clearest in John's Gospel, though implicit in the others. Jesus makes some very large claims: to be the light of the world, to have been sent by God, to be the good shepherd, to speak the truth. None of these can be *proved*; and since Jesus appears to be the only witness to

them (two witnesses being required to establish the truth) his evidence
can be regarded as not valid (John 5:1). But in fact there is another
witness: God himself. Now to call God to witness is to swear a solemn
oath. To disbelieve a statement made on oath is to disbelieve God and
incur his punishment. By disbelieving Jesus his enemies were seriously
at fault: they were rejecting the testimony of God. But it is in the nature
of evidence that it leaves options open. The most reputable and
authoritative witness may fail to persuade. So it was with Jesus; in John's
theological terms, 'he came unto his own and his own received him not'.
Yet there would always be witnesses who would challenge the world to
believe and respond to the truth.

To what, then, did Jesus 'witness'? Or (to put the question in its
simplest form) for what did Jesus die? It is true that in St John's Gospel,
on which much of the above exposition is based, Jesus' claims are
mainly centred upon himself: he makes statements about his origin, his
authority and his mission which are regarded by 'the Jews' as so
offensive or blasphemous that on several occasions they attempt to
exact the prescribed penalty of death. But in the Synoptic Gospels the
focus is strikingly different. Instead of drawing attention to himself and
his status in relation to God, it is as if he instinctively and systematically
deflects attention from himself on to God and his kingdom, inviting his
hearers to discern signs of the Spirit's activity in his own miraculous
works of healing and exorcism and challenging them to participate in
the realization of God's kingdom through the adoption of new spiritual
and moral priorities. Precisely what circumstances and what legal
charges led to his death is a subject for continuing scholarly debate; but
the more general question of what he died *for* can be answered (at least
on the basis of the Synoptics) with less difficulty. His mission was to
proclaim the kingdom, with all that it entailed in terms of the remission
of debt, the espousal of the poor and the marginalized, the casting out of
evil spirits and the release of those resources of love, generosity and
compassion which are so easily repressed by social convention and
misguided religious scrupulosity. This mission incurred his death, a
sacrifice he freely accepted, almost certainly sensing that it would have
redemptive value within the community of his followers and beyond.
That God had not rejected this mission and its performance, but had, on
the contrary, confirmed Jesus' divinely appointed status, was proved by
the totally unexpected sequel of the resurrection. It was to this, above
all, that his followers were to be 'witnesses'; but in witnessing to the
reality of the resurrection they were witnessing also to the person who
had been resurrected, his values, his priorities and his moral demands.

THE CULTURE OF MARTYRDOM IN THE EARLY CHURCH AND NOW

It is evident that this account of the 'witness' borne by the immediate followers of Jesus might authorize a considerably broader sense of Christian martyrdom than that which became the norm under both Jewish and Roman persecutions. In the West, Christian martyrdom has traditionally been regarded as a phenomenon of the first three centuries of Christian history. It was the direct consequence of vigorous opposition to the Christian religion, first from the Jews, and then from the authorities of the pagan Roman empire, which unleashed a series of official persecutions, reaching their climax at the beginning of the fourth century of our era; it resulted in a theology of martyrdom, and a widespread cult of individual martyrs, that marked a particular phase in Christian witness and devotion. The very notion of Christian martyrdom, as of Jewish martyrdom before it, evolved in a framework of assumptions and beliefs which are virtually obsolete in the modern world. There was, for example, both in later Judaism and in Christianity, an expectation of life after death so fervent that suffering for one's faith even to the point of death seemed amply compensated for by the certainty of the reward which awaited the martyr in heaven. The deaths of the Maccabean martyrs were to be avenged by God in a heavenly scenario according to which the persecutors would suffer eternal torments in the sight of their now exalted victims. The Christian martyr, according to explicit promises of Jesus and the equally explicit reasoning of St Paul, could expect to be united with his Lord by virtue of suffering for the Name. 'I reckon that the sufferings we now endure bear no comparison with the glory, as yet unrevealed, which is in store for us' (Romans 8:13).

Faith of this intensity in a life of blessedness after death was what lent to the martyrs of the early centuries a courage, a serenity and at times a radiance which impressed their contemporaries, sometimes to the point of converting them to the new faith. It is not, of course, that the Church of today has abandoned belief in 'the resurrection of the body and the life everlasting'. But it is probably true to say that for the majority of Christians these doctrines have become, if not theoretical, at least somewhat secondary to those which motivate their style of life and discipleship. For most, death remains inherently unwelcome. 'I have written no letters of farewell', wrote the Jesuit Alfred Delp, who, in 1944, was in prison awaiting trial for involvement in a conspiracy to assassinate Hitler, 'since everything within me resists doing it.'[5] The apparent emphasis placed by Jesus on 'rewards in heaven' finds less resonance in the modern Christian than his insistence on being ready to seize the present moment for action, to respond to one's neighbour when in need and to discern the signs and work for the establishment of God's kingdom here on earth.

In the second place, the early martyrs had inherited, both from the Jewish Maccabean martyrs and from the apocalyptic expectations of New Testament Christianity, a profound conviction that the forces of paganism responsible for their persecution were in their last throes and would shortly be overthrown by God — a dénouement that would be hastened by their own martyrdom. A similar conviction that we are living in the last days of the present world order is of course to be found today among members of certain fundamentalist Christian sects; but it is far from the world-view of the mainstream churches, or indeed of any of the martyrs in this book. Those who died at the hands of a tyrannical regime may not have doubted that the rule of their persecutors would in due course come to an end; but they expected it to be overthrown, not by an apocalyptic act of God, but by a historical evolution fuelled by the courageous resistance of people such as themselves. Those who, as in the Americas, were caught up in the struggle for the rights of the poor, the oppressed and the victims of racial discrimination certainly risked their lives in a cause they believed would ultimately prevail, and their deaths have arguably empowered others to work for the universal recognition of human rights. But none of them had the simple faith of the early martyrs that God would shortly intervene to establish his kingdom of justice and peace.

The alternatives perceived by the early martyrs were either to incur the shame and eternal damnation which would follow denial of the Name, or to win the glory of the martyr's crown in heaven. Dietrich Bonhoeffer faced other alternatives: the survival of Christianity in Europe by the defeat of his own nation in war, or the victory of Germany and the destruction of the Church. In a situation of tyrannical oppression, did the path of Christian faithfulness consist of patient endurance and self-sacrificial care for the victims of evil policies or of outright opposition that might involve complicity in acts of violence against those set in authority? The former gave some assurance of safety; the latter declared its dangers all too clearly — it was the fundamental, decisive and fatal alternative. Certainly, it could not be regarded as a qualification for the highest Christian honours. Bonhoeffer's death was seen by many not as a martyrdom for the faith, but as a political death. In pursuing his Christian conscience he had moved beyond the moral sanctuary of the Church and into the company of politicians, soldiers and men of affairs.

With the Christianization of the Roman Empire in the West the Christian Church became at once dubious in the eyes of the governing powers of the East, in the lands that are now called Syria, Persia, India, China and Mongolia. For them, Rome was the great enemy. The fact that Christians had been persecuted by it ensured their safety in Persia. But now, as Constantine gathered his forces to attack Persia, the Church there was suspected as his ally, a fifth column even. Around the year 340 the emperor Shapur II inaugurated a great persecution of Christians, one that was far greater than anything that had been seen in the West. Christians were taxed. Churches were destroyed and priests who refused to participate in Zoroastrian ritual killed. In 344 Simon, Bishop of Seleucia-Ctesiphon, was taken outside the walls of the city of Susa to see the execution of 500 bishops and 100 priests of his church. Then he, too, was beheaded. To follow Simon as Bishop of Seleucia-Ctesiphon was to bring death upon oneself almost immediately. Yet such men were to be found. By the fifth century, as many as 190,000 may have died.

Shapur II had warred against the Church, but not because its doctrines or practices offended him. He did so because he perceived that it had a political significance. What the Christians believed of themselves was unimportant.[6]

In the early centuries, the deliberate targeting of Christians, either as scapegoats for instances of public disorder or as objects of fear, envy or revulsion, meant that a martyr's death was one defined by faithful adherence to the Christian profession in the face of insult, calumny and active persecution. In due course this developed into the dogmatic requirement that for a death to be truly a martyrdom there must be evidence of a specific *odium fidei*, or opposition to the Christian faith. This somewhat restrictive definition of 'martyr' has in fact continued with little in the way of challenge until recent times. But in the twentieth century certain Christian cultures have progressively identified the churches with the Enlightenment values of freedom, democracy and human rights. The biblical foundations of such ideas are to be found in the humanitarian legislation and the insistent prophetic demand for justice in the Hebrew Scriptures, and in the implications of Jesus' teaching in the Synoptic Gospels on the kingdom of God. This shift in theological priorities has produced a different set of conditions for possible martyrdom. Christians are now threatened and attacked, not because they profess the Christian religion, but because they show solidarity with those whose rights, dignity and livelihood are diminished by an uncaring or dictatorial regime. In the midst of oppression in El

Salvador, the Jesuit Jon Sobrino has written, 'The Church is being persecuted because it defends the life of the poor, denounces the unjust destruction of life and promotes the historical practice of justice'.[7] Even the cautious and highly respected Roman Catholic theologian Karl Rahner pleaded for a wider definition of martyrdom that would include death incurred in the struggle for Christian moral values,[8] finding support for his view in Thomas Aquinas himself.[9] If the self-sacrifice of a Bonhoeffer, a Martin Luther King, a Luwum, or a Romero appears to share with that of many others the motivation of a this-worldly commitment to human freedom and dignity in the face of tyranny, it has also been nourished and strengthened by an authentically twentieth-century Christian spirituality.

The culture of Christian martyrdom in the early Church was quite different from that of later Christian experience. Yet the stories that Christians tell of martyrdom in each age are often found to bear striking comparison with each other. The construction of martyrdom narratives is often intricate, emphasizing the dignity of the martyrs, their proclamation, and their power to convert even those who persecuted them.[10] In many of them, an important moment of decision arises, and it is resolved when the prospective martyr takes, not the road to safety, but its alternative, knowing that death awaits. To Jesus himself, such a moment occurred when he 'turned his face towards Jerusalem'. After him, Paul went to Rome and met his death there. Centuries later, Thomas Becket travelled back across the English Channel towards martyrdom: a picture in the medieval *Becket Leaves* shows him facing the coastline and seeing there a crowd of men and women trying to turn him back. In another age, the same journey was made, but to a Protestant England, by the Jesuit Edmund Campion. In the twentieth century, Dietrich Bonhoeffer made his way back to Germany on the eve of war in 1939. He had turned aside from the prospect of security and eminence in the United States and decided, instead, to resist the tyranny of his own government. The dilemma may take the opposite form. Christ stayed in the Garden of Gethsemane when he might have fled to safety. As described in this book, the Grand Duchess Elizabeth of Russia remained at her convent in Moscow as the threats against her mounted. When the danger of Japanese invasion loomed, the martyrs of New Guinea chose not to leave their mission stations but to stay.

A CULMINATION OF DANGEROUS CURRENTS

The roots of the persecution of the churches in the twentieth century are deep. In many societies, men and women had moved away from Christian life, or even come to distrust the Church. Intellectual pursuit, for so many centuries sustained by the fertile premises of Christian faith and cultivated by the institutions of the Church, moved outwards beyond its teachings. The world of the mind was more and more a secular realm. The new ideal was rational logic: tangible cause and material effect. The mystical view appeared, to some minds, archaic. It was heard that religion was obsolete.

Churches were increasingly suspected as sources of reaction. In many societies their authority was sustained by a relationship with a political order which was now seen to be oppressive. This exposed them to danger. When he looked with sceptical eyes at the world of the *ancien régime*, the French writer Voltaire found the Roman Catholic Church hypocritical, corrupt, superstitious, tyrannous, even absurd. Justice, the great theme of the Enlightenment, was logical. In Voltaire's eyes, Christianity seemed utterly illogical. The new thinking advocated toleration. The Church was the sponsor of persecution. Voltaire was unimpressed by its history of martyrs: he perceived that the martyrs of the Roman Empire died, not because they were Christians, but because they had become fanatical and intolerant themselves.[11]

In many societies the churches were pillars of political legitimacy. Religion often sanctified authority. The churches owned land, and much of it. The poor owned little or nothing. Christians in most ages believed that existing political authorities governed under God. Against authority were ranged the forces of anarchy, and these were to be feared. In 1776 the American Revolution established a new, rational state, in which the Church was simply disestablished. Shortly afterwards, the French Revolution sought to abolish Catholicism with violence. The Church was not merely disestablished but dispossessed and looted. Priests were forced to flee abroad. By the later nineteenth century the Roman Catholic Church saw in secular modernity a threat to all that it affirmed. Rather than concede and slide down a slope to no one knew where, in 1864 the Vatican published the *Syllabus of Errors*, condemning rationalism of all kinds, indifferentism, toleration and socialism, and attaching a list of attendant errors to boot.[12] This placed Catholics in opposition to the ideals of the moment. In countries where the Church was strong, the politics of the Left were vehemently anticlerical. Revolutionary ideologues spread a hatred of Christianity across Europe.

In Russia, Orthodoxy was detested as a conspiracy to keep the people in a condition of ignorance and obedience. They could be free only when religion itself was extinct. The ability of radical writers to portray the Church in ways that would seldom, if ever, have occurred to Christians themselves could present an alarming spectacle:

> The Christian catechism teaches that the Church is a society of the faithful who are united by a common creed, by the sacraments, etc. For the communist, the church is a society of persons who are united by definite sources of income at the cost of the faithful, at the cost of their ignorance and lack of true culture. It is a society united with the society of other exploiters such as the landlords and the capitalists, united with their State, assisting that State in the oppression of the workers, and reciprocally receiving from the State help in the business of oppression.[13]

These were the words of the Bolshevik theorist Nikolai Bukharin. In the new totalitarian regimes of the twentieth century the very idea of religion was challenged by the absolute claims of the political state. In the Soviet Union the Christian Church was devastated. In Nazi Germany it was confined and undermined.

These were European matters. But by the twentieth century the Christianity of Europe had spread far into other hemispheres in an age of mission and empire. The reality of imperialism was, of course, complex, and the various strands of the enterprise often coalesced uneasily. Christian missions were often, and increasingly, independent of the political and commercial realities of empire. But they could still be suspected in historic cultures as new and alien forces. Converts to Christianity could face a persecution that was born out of fear or incomprehension. Although some missionaries were deeply sensitive to indigenous life, a sense of cultural superiority often underlay the missionary achievement.

It was a testimony to the success and humanity of the missions that the new nationalist movements of the southern hemisphere were rarely antagonistic towards the churches. Many of their leaders were themselves devout Christians. But Christianity could all too easily become a target for anger in the minds of bitter men. In April 1919 British soldiers fired into a crowd of protesters at the holy city of the Sikhs, Amritsar. Officially 379 people died and 1,560 were wounded. The general who was responsible then imposed martial law in the Punjab. Shortly afterwards a woman missionary was attacked and badly beaten there. Afterwards, Indians were ordered to make their way past the scene of the crime, crawling on all fours. Soon after the independence of India in 1947, the Kikuyu rose against British rule in Kenya. In the so-called Mau Mau revolt, many Christians who refused to join the struggle were brutally murdered. When the Communists came to power in China in 1948 they saw in the missionaries agents of Western imperialism. The mission stations were closed down almost at once, and the missionaries expelled.

The twentieth century has been an age of world war. In such a turbulent context Christians of all nations have found themselves divided by different political claims or trapped by violent circumstances. Many believed that the causes for which their governments contended in war were Christian. Accordingly, Christian men slaughtered each other on the battlefields of Europe in the Great War of 1914-18. Nationhood, not religious confession, was the dominant language of identity in such a world. The Japanese soldiers who murdered missionaries in New Guinea in 1942 saw no reason to distinguish a priest from a soldier. What mattered to them was the fact that they were Australian.

THIS BOOK

It is a rarely acknowledged truth that in the twentieth century more Christians have died for their faith than in any other age. The awful dimensions of that fact defy the imagination. How, then, can we begin to understand what this really tells us about the nature of religious faith in a violent world of suspicion, ideology and conflict? The martyrologies of the early Church exalted the triumphant faith of the Christian individual. But such stories also spoke of the many whose names were lost to history and known only to God. In this book, ten writers have sought to interpret ten lives which concluded, some might say culminated, in an act of martyrdom for their Christian faith. Together they develop some distinctive approaches, exploring their own experiences and insights as scholars and participants in Christian life. But they have also sought to examine those lives in the midst of the great social and political contexts in which they arose, contexts in which countless others, of different faiths or none, were similarly trapped. For the revolution that murdered the Grand Duchess Elizabeth also took the lives of hundreds, and it established a new state in which millions would perish. The political powers of El Salvador murdered thousands with impunity, and one of them was the Archbishop of San Salvador, Oscar Romero. It is in such crowded landscapes that individual witnesses emerge. Most are unrecorded, scattered, forgotten. This book is not merely a study of remembered lives. It seeks to retrieve something of the immensity of the tragedy of this age, and to analyse historically and theologically the terrible alternatives that men and women of faith have faced and are still facing today.

Notes

1   Pierre Pascal, *The Religion of the People*, trans. Rowan Williams (London, 1976), pp. 130–6.
2   Paul wrote to the Christians of Rome 'Be not conformed to this world' (12:2).
3   P. W. Gooch, *Reflections on Jesus and Socrates* (Yale, 1996), p. 19.
4   For an extended treatment of this difference see A. E. Harvey, *Jesus on Trial* (London, 1976), pp. 46ff.
5   Helmut Gollwitzer, Käthe Kuhn and Reinhold Schneider (eds), *Dying We Live: The Final Messages and Records of Some Germans Who Defied Hitler* (London, 1956), p. 114.
6   Samuel Hugh Moffett, *A History of Christianity in Asia,* Volume I: *Beginnings to 1500* (London, 1992), pp. 136–47.
7   Jon Sobrino, *The True Church and the Poor* (Maryknoll, NY, 1981), p. 173.
8   *Concilium,* 163 (3/1983), pp. 9–11.
9   Aquinas notes that the Church reveres John the Baptist as a martyr, who died, not because he confessed Christ, but because he protested against adultery. Similarly, 'the works of all the virtues', when directed towards God, may be regarded as a form of profession of faith leading to martyrdom: *Summa Theologiae* IIa-IIae, q. 124, n. 5.
10 For a lively discussion of martyrdom narratives, see Robin Lane Fox, *Pagans and Christians in the Mediterranean World from the Second Century to the Conversion of Constantine* (London, 1986), pp. 419–92.
11 Voltaire, *The Calas Affair: A Treatise on Tolerance*, trans. Brian Masters (London, 1994), pp. 48–62. It is striking to find how much in tune with Voltaire is Robin Lane Fox in the above.
12 See Henry Bettenson, *Documents of the Christian Church* (Oxford, 1973), pp. 379–80.
13 Nikolai Bukharin and Evgenii Preobrazhensky, *The ABC of Communism* (published 1920; English edition, London, 1969), p. 301.

Orthodoxy, monarchy and revolution: The Grand Duchess Elizabeth of Russia

GEORGII CHISTYAKOV

O N 5 AUGUST 1914 the French ambassador in St Petersburg, Maurice Paléologue, attended a service in the cathedral of that city:

> At the end of the nave opposite the iconostasis the three Metropolitans of Russia and twelve archbishops stood in line. In the aisles on their left was a group of one hundred and ten bishops, archimandrites and abbots. A fabulous, indescribable wealth of diamonds, sapphires, rubies and amethysts sparkled on the brocade of their mitres and chasubles. At times the church glowed with a supernatural light.

As the Russian imperial family processed round the cathedral he observed Grand Duchess Elizabeth, and admired her elegance as she bowed or knelt. At the end of the service, Paléologue spoke to the Tsar and Tsarina, and during the conversation the Grand Duchess approached them. Beneath her long white woollen veil he found her face 'alive with spirituality': 'Her delicate features and white skin, the deep, far away look in her eyes, the low, soft tone of her voice and the luminous glow round her brow all betrayed a being in close contact with the ineffable and divine.'[1]

Elizabeth of Hesse-Darmstadt was born on 1 November 1864 and was a grand-daughter of Queen Victoria. She was named after Elizabeth of Hungary (1207–31), a Catholic saint and one of the founders of the house of Hesse as well as of Saxony. St Elizabeth of Hungary had been renowned for her acts of charity; she built hospitals near her castle, spent enormous sums of money on the poor, for which she was constantly reprimanded by her mother-in-law, and, in the end, sold all her jewellery and dresses so that she could give the money to those in misfortune. After the death of her husband, Landgrave Ludwig IV of Thuringia, she had joined the Franciscan Third Order and, following the example of St Francis, she took care of lepers. Six centuries later, the mother of Elizabeth of Hesse-Darmstadt, Princess Alice, was also a woman who was deeply involved in charitable work. She visited hospitals, orphanages and homes for the disabled, and often she took her daughter with her. From early childhood Elizabeth learned to care for those in need, and it was this compassion that later led her to become one of the few women saints in the history of the Russian Orthodox Church.

Although she was named after a Catholic saint, Elizabeth was baptized into the Lutheran Church and then brought up in a distinctly Anglican Christian culture. At the age of 14 she lost her mother and came to live in England with her grandmother, Queen Victoria. Later in life she would become a dedicated religious, but by this time within the Orthodox Church. Accordingly, she combined in her own life four Christian traditions and, while being totally faithful to the path she had chosen within Orthodoxy, she did not disown the ideals of her childhood and the way of practical Christianity associated with her patron saint. 'All Christians are the children of Christ', she once wrote in a letter to her younger brother, Ernst.

In 1884 Elizabeth married Grand Duke Sergei Alexandrovich, the fifth son of Alexander II, and so became the aunt of the last Tsar. According to Grand Duke Alexander Mikhailovich, a nephew of Alexander II, 'everybody fell in love with "Aunt Ella" the very first moment she arrived in St Petersburg'; he found her a ravishing beauty, intelligent, with a sense of humour, great patience and a generous heart.[2] In 1894, when Nicholas II married Elizabeth's younger sister, Princess Alice of Hesse, the future Empress Alexandra, Elizabeth was linked for a second time to the Romanovs. She was to become one of the most striking figures within the Tsar's family. But to the end of her days Elizabeth remained in many ways an Englishwoman. In her letters, even those sent to Nicholas II, she always wrote in English, and she compared the countryside where she lived in Russia with the English countryside. According to the accounts of her contemporaries, the authors she read were almost exclusively English. Among her new relatives she was particularly close to the first cousin once removed of the Tsar, Grand Duke Konstantin Konstantinovich (whose father had been a brother of Alexander II), a well-known poet who wrote under the pseudonym of K. R. Hee, and also the author of a play in verse, *The King of Judea*, about Christ's final days.

When Elizabeth married she remained a Lutheran, something that was possible in nineteenth-century Russia. But she also began to take an interest in Orthodoxy and to study its special features. In 1888 she and her husband travelled to the Holy Land, where she was present at the consecration of the Russian Church of St Mary Magdalen above Gethsemane, the church where she was later to be buried. She also visited monasteries and churches and read many books on Orthodox spirituality. However, she finally took the decision to convert to Orthodoxy after a period of more than six years, by then feeling that inwardly she already belonged to the Orthodox faith. When Elizabeth told her father in Darmstadt of her decision he was hurt by the news and even angry; other members of the family did not support her either. But her grandmother, Queen Victoria, was more sympathetic. 'My very dearest Grandmama', Elizabeth wrote on 7/19 February 1891 from St Petersburg,

> You cannot think how intensely and deeply touched I was by all you say. I was afraid you might not understand this step and the comforting joy your dear lines gave me I shall never forget ... The Greek [Orthodox] Church reminds me so of the English Church, and that is why I understood it differently from those who have been brought up in the German Protestant Church.[3]

Her German relations were afraid that she would be baptized again when she became a convert to Orthodoxy. Elizabeth reassured them that this would not happen: another baptism was forbidden according to tradition as this sacrament in the Lutheran Church was recognized as valid by the Russian Orthodox Church, and the rite for a new convert only consisted in being anointed and in receiving communion. Her brother suspected that she had simply been fascinated by the external glitter of the Orthodox Church. 'In that you are mistaken', wrote Ella. 'Nothing in the outer signs attracted me, not the service – the foundation of the belief. The outer signs are only to remind us of the inner things.'[4]

When she joined the Orthodox Church, Elizabeth refused to give up her name: for her St Elizabeth of Hungary remained a model of a devout life and of love for others. This showed a certain courage; a devotion to Catholic saints was not welcomed by Orthodox clergy in Russia. However, as her saint had lived after the schism of 1054 and was not recognized by the Orthodox Church, her official patron saint was declared to be Elizabeth, the mother of John the Baptist.

Until 1904 Elizabeth's life was peaceful and surrounded by luxury, like that of any other member of the Tsar's family. She was meticulous about her appearance and dress. According to Grand Duchess Maria Pavlovna, 'Even when in the country my aunt gave a great deal of time and attention to her appearance. She designed most of her dresses herself, sketching and painting them in water-colours, planning them with care, and wearing them with art and distinction. My uncle, who had a passion for jewels, gave her many – so that she had a different set to harmonize with almost every costume that she wore.' When dressing she made sure that her maids organized her clothes carefully; she had a triple mirror so that she could see herself from all angles, and once dressed she would allow Maria Pavlovna to choose her jewellery.[5]

It was the outbreak of the Russo-Japanese war in 1904 that immediately revealed her practical nature. Because her husband, Grand Duke Sergei Alexandrovich, was governor of Moscow, she enjoyed authority and influence in that city. All the main rooms of the Kremlin were turned by her into workshops where women from all parts of Moscow worked at sewing machines, producing clothes for the troops, blankets and dressings for the wounded. These Kremlin rooms also became collection points for medicines, presents, warm clothing and other such items. In addition, Elizabeth organized a number of well-equipped hospital trains which were sent to the Far East. She also established special committees to provide for widows and orphans. There is considerable evidence about her work during these years; although it may not have gone beyond what was normal at the time for a *grande dame* involved in charity during a time of danger for her country, it remained highly effective.

The other face of such public commitment was, however, an increasingly introverted private identity. Her marriage to Grand Duke Sergei Alexandrovich was difficult. Grand Duchess Maria Pavlovna, who was brought up by Elizabeth, recalled in her memoirs 'Their relations towards each other were distinguished by a strained fondness that rested on my aunt's serene acceptance of my uncle's decision in all matters great and small'.[6] She also perceived 'It was as if she were being driven deeper and deeper within herself for refuge' in the face of a husband who did not understand her devout nature:

> Converted to the Orthodox religion, my aunt had become each year more devoutly attached to its forms and practices. Although himself pious and scrupulous in observance of all the rites of Orthodoxy, Uncle Sergei regarded with anxiety his wife's increasing absorption in things spiritual and ended by regarding it as immoderate.[7]

Then, on 18 February 1905, the Grand Duke Sergei Alexandrovich was killed by a revolutionary terrorist. When she heard the news Elizabeth was at the Nikolsky Palace with Maria Pavlovna and her brother Dmitri. She took charge at the scene of the assassination. It was she who gathered up the remains of her husband's dismembered corpse in the snow and placed them on an army stretcher. This was taken to the Chudov Monastery, which was linked to the Nikolsky Palace by a covered passage. Maria Pavlovna wrote:

> My aunt was on her knees beside the litter. Her bright dress shone forth grotesquely amid the humble garments surrounding her. I did not dare look at her. Her face was white, her features terrible in their stricken rigidity. She did not weep, but the expression of her eyes made an impression on me I will never forget as long as I live.

Later, after praying in the chapel of the Chudov Monastery, Elizabeth was led away by Maria Pavlovna and her brother:

> Dmitri and I succeeded in leading her back towards her rooms. She let herself fall weakly into an arm-chair. Her eyes dry and with the same peculiar fixity of gaze, she looked straight into space, and said nothing.[8]

During the following days Maria Pavlovna watched her aunt closely: 'Always shut up in herself, she became more so.'[9] Grand Duke Konstantin Konstantinovich also noted the deep impression that Elizabeth made on him at the time: 'Her calmness, her goodness, her submission to the will of God, and her lack of anger are striking and deeply moving.'[10] When he heard that she had visited the murderer of her husband, talked with him and offered him an icon, he remarked that she was a saint. Some did not believe the story, and even laughed.[11]

In the summer of 1905 Elizabeth organized a hospital for the wounded on her Ilinskoe estate outside Moscow, where she had lived with her husband. She opened another in Moscow, not far from the Kremlin, in premises rented at her own expense. At this time she decided to part with all her jewellery including her wedding ring. On the proceeds of the sale of her jewellery, her pictures and other works of art including furniture and china (Grand Duke Sergei Alexandrovich was an assiduous collector), Elizabeth decided to build a home, an *obitel'*, for prayer, work and charity. She named it after Martha and Mary. Her younger brother, Grand Duke Ernst Ludwig, later wrote in his memoirs that, after studying life in Russia's convents, his sister had observed that Russian nuns, apart from needlework, did no practical work. In fact such work in hospitals, among the poor and homeless, the care for orphans and the elderly, was hardly ever undertaken by convents in Russia. On the other hand by the beginning of the twentieth century many institutes for training nurses had been founded, where the staff often held atheistic and incendiary views and even led lives that were deliberately and provocatively disordered. Public reaction to these institutes varied, but it was often negative. They came to be associated less with charitable service than with revolutionary movements. Elizabeth decided that her task was to avoid extremes and to take all that was positive within women's monasticism and within the nursing tradition. Her intention was to combine the two. According to her close friend, Countess Alexandra Olsufeva, Elizabeth respected the traditions of Russian monasticism, but also took the view that constant prayer and inner contemplation should be put aside as the final reward for those who had already given their all in the service of God through serving their neighbour. Work itself was the basis of religious life, whereas prayer was part of the rest which followed. Often she invoked words from the Gospel of Matthew, where Christ says: 'For I was an hungered, and ye gave me meat: I was thirsty, and ye gave me drink: I was a stranger, and ye took me in; naked, and ye clothed me: I was sick, and ye visited me: I was in prison, and ye came unto me.' By naming her new community after Martha and Mary, Elizabeth emphasized that she wished to combine in her labours the service of Martha who was 'careful and troubled about many things' and Mary who 'sat at Jesus' feet, and heard his word' (Luke 10:38-42). She stressed that there was nothing wrong in the way Martha was 'careful and troubled'. Was it not Martha who received Christ 'into her house'? Elizabeth called her followers to add to such service that sense of listening and contemplation that was epitomized by Mary.

She believed that she and her sisters were called not to the monastic life but to the diaconate, that is to the service of God and of neighbour. She suggested the restoration of the ancient order of the female diaconate, which had been quite widespread in Byzantium, especially in the fourth century. St Olympias, whose ministry had paralleled that of her close friend St John Chrysostom, St Macrina, Nonna, Melania, Theosebia, Gorgonia and others were all deacons (*ai diakonoi* as distinct from *oi diakonoi*). They offered themselves for service within the diaconate, in an order like the diaconate for men. As for their place within the Church, they were not only involved in pastoral care, in distributing alms and caring for the sick, but also took as significant a part in the Church's liturgical life as male deacons. The diaconate for women was not discontinued intentionally or seen as alien to the Orthodox faith: it was simply forgotten and disappeared from church practice in a medieval world in which institutions increasingly taught the inferiority of women.

In the nineteenth century the idea of a women's diaconate was again in the air. The Siberian missionary Archimandrite Makarii Glukharev believed that deaconesses could contribute greatly in the missionary field. Later, in 1860, Fr Aleksandr Gumilevskii claimed that it was essential to re-establish the diaconate of women. But the statutes which he drew up for the Krestovozdvizhenskii Sisters of Charity failed to win acceptance, and he was removed from St Petersburg. At the beginning of the twentieth century several Russian bishops spoke out in support of the diaconate of women. But it was in Greece that Bishop Nektarios (now honoured as a saint and much loved by the people) ordained two nuns as deacons in 1911. The nuns had helped him in his ministry, and he allowed them to wear the vestments normally used by deacons. His example was followed by Archbishop Chrysostom in Athens. These currents did not express liberal tendencies, or moves towards modernism, or even secularization, but a desire to return to an ancient Christian ideal and to the Church's practice of the first centuries.

Elizabeth tried not to damage relations with the Holy Synod, the ruling body in the church, and conservative at that. She did not raise the question of the ordination of women deacons. The diaconate of women, in her understanding, should be confined to serving the sick and suffering as sisters of charity and consolation. It was an interpretation which was still suspected by many as excessively liberal and Protestant. As a result the women and girls who joined the Martha and Mary community came to be called Sisters of the Cross, rather than deaconesses.

But Elizabeth was encouraged by the eminent. Metropolitan Vladimir of Moscow (he was killed by the Bolsheviks in Kiev in 1918, and subsequently canonized) enthusiastically supported her enterprise from the outset. At his request Bishop Trifon of Turkestan created an official order of service in accordance with which Elizabeth and 17 sisters were dedicated as Sisters of the Cross of Love and Mercy in April 1909. To avoid accusations of carrying out an unauthorized ordination to the diaconate, the service of dedication did not take place during the eucharistic liturgy when men are normally ordained to the diaconate and priesthood, but in the evening before the end of vespers. Prince Yusupov observed that it was with 'a last touch of worldliness' that Elizabeth asked a famous Muscovite painter, Nesterov, to design the habit for her order: 'a long pearl-grey robe of fine wool, a lawn wimple which framed the face and a white woollen veil that fell into long classical folds'.[12] Afterwards, both Elizabeth herself and her sisters hardly ever wore black habits. For feast days they wore white, and on ordinary days light grey.

The new community included young women from very different backgrounds, ranging from that of a princess to that of a peasant. On the day of their dedication Elizabeth spoke to them: 'I am leaving a glittering world where I had a glittering position, but with all of you I am descending into a greater world – the world of the poor and the suffering.' Metropolitan Vladimir invested each sister with a pectoral cross of cypress wood, and appointed Elizabeth as mother superior of the *obitel'*.

Elizabeth acknowledged that because she was a close relation of the Tsar, she was in a privileged position to achieve what she wanted. She perceived how fragile the enterprise was, and sensed that it was important to define clearly the meaning and particular purpose of the new order independently of herself. In a private letter to Nicholas II, she wrote:

> This work must have a 'particular place' in the Church else it will be always vacillating and after my death, who knows, more than likely be made into a convent or 'secular commune'. We are based on a strictly Church foundation, in all details Orthodox as we are blessed by our metropolitan who of course knows all our life.

A convent and a secular commune were the two extremes which she wished to avoid in order to create something fundamentally different: it was her new approach which had to be developed. In no way should they go backwards, or return to what should be left behind. The task of the Christian was not merely to reproduce forms approved by tradition and time. Rather should the Christian meet the challenge of a particular time by searching for answers which were rooted in the spirit of the gospel and the teaching of Jesus.

The Grand Duchess now led the life of a dedicated ascetic. She slept on a wooden bed without a mattress and on a hard pillow. The search for new spiritual paths which were in harmony with the guidance of the elders and ascetics of the past was one of the basic characteristics of her spirituality. Sometimes she slept for no more than three hours. Instead she prayed at night and patrolled the wards of the hospital for the poor which had been built within the Martha and Mary foundation for the poor. In 1910 Prince Felix Yusupov described her way of life in his memoirs:

> The Mother Superior lived in a small, simply furnished three-room house; her wooden bed had no mattress and her pillow was stuffed with hay.

The Grand Duchess slept little, a few hours at most, when she was not spending the whole night by a sick bed, or praying over a coffin in the chapel. Hospitals and nursing homes sent her their worst cases, and she nursed them herself.[13]

She would assist in the operating theatre at the hospital and she qualified as a theatre nurse. All the sisters in the community had to take a basic medical course. Elizabeth considered this essential not so much for their work in the hospital, which employed doctors and specialists, as for the work of the diaconate beyond. The sisters often visited the shelters for the poor and destitute where first aid might be urgently needed. Elizabeth's hospital included an out-patients' department where medical specialists in various fields saw patients on a daily basis. There was a dental surgery and a pharmacy as well. Elizabeth also organized a library with free membership, a feeding centre for the poor, a building with flats for young women factory-workers and for needy students. A clinic for women with tuberculosis was also opened. In 1913 she provided clothes for over 1,800 children. She believed that such work might set a pattern in other parts of Russia. At the very least she wanted to set up a few branches outside Moscow. This never happened.

Every Sunday after vespers discussions were organized in the sisters' church. There were bishops who took part, sometimes coming specially to Moscow for this purpose. Large numbers of people were attracted, since it was unusual to discuss matters of faith in Russia at that time. In general, people were expected to keep all the fasts strictly, to say their prayers and attend church services. But they were not expected to think about their faith. Here, too, Elizabeth boldly broke new ground. Some condemned her work as a Protestant deviation.

Elizabeth wrote little. There appeared in 1914 a small pamphlet entitled *The Martha and Mary Home of Mercy* which was certainly largely compiled by her, though her name is absent from the title page. In her spirituality, inner honesty was important above all things; it was what brought a person closer to God. It was essential to awaken a sense of God in the social outcasts whom she and her sisters encountered each day, to touch their hardened hearts and speak to them as equals, affirming their human dignity. 'The image of God can sometimes be obscured by darkness but it can never be destroyed', she remarked. She is said to have entrusted her bag containing a considerable amount of money more than once to vagrants she met with the request that they take it to the community's home. No one ever tried to rob her.

The Khitrovka market, close to the centre of Moscow, attracted a heaving mass of humanity: thieves, vagrants, homeless children, people who had recently been freed or escaped from prison. It became a place of particular concern to Elizabeth. Here she built a special hostel for boys, which provided a team of messenger-boys (before the telephone spread their work was indispensable to Muscovites). It soon acquired an excellent reputation in the city. She regularly visited the basement slums and filthiest areas of the market, though it was with some difficulty that she understood the underworld slang used by the locals. The simplicity with which she always spoke to people was neither forced nor artificial, and was part of the very essence of her faith in the one who called all who laboured and were heavy laden. She would gather up orphans; when parents were still in evidence she would persuade them to let her take care of their destitute children. It was an extraordinary sight to see a close relative of the emperor in dirty boots amidst the mud, stench and filth. She had no protection; police did not venture into the area as a rule. At the same time, she did not for a moment forget her position in society when she was dealing with the city authorities, from whom she could extract certain privileges. Some of the wealthy were prepared to help her financially because she was the sister of the empress. But Grand Duke Konstantin Konstantinovich observed in his diary for 1910: 'There is a holiness without a hint of hypocrisy about her; so much simplicity and sincerity.'[14]

In August 1914 war broke out between Russia, France and Great Britain and Germany. German on her father's side, English on her mother's, and Russian by adoption, all the more did Elizabeth experience the conflict as an immense personal tragedy. During the first weeks of the war she visited hospitals and comforted the wounded. She collected medicines, presents and warm clothing for them. But she visited not only Russian soldiers; German and Austrian prisoners also found her attending to their needs. It soon led to criticism from the public. There were rumours that she sympathized with the Germans; that when she visited the Russians she only gave them icons, whereas she gave money to her own people. It was heard that she was a spy for the enemy. Her visits to prisoners had to cease. Once she had walked through the streets of Moscow to her convent alone and unobserved in her monastic habit; in May 1915 she returned from the funeral of Grand Duke Konstantin Konstantinovich in a motor car through a crowd which began to throw stones at her, spit, and shout and swear at her.[15] A new period in her life began. Gossip in Moscow made out that the Martha and Mary community was a centre for espionage where Germans were hidden. There were demonstrations outside its walls. On one such occasion the Grand Duchess herself came out to find crowds trying to break down the gates. She warned them that inside there were many seriously ill people who needed peace and quiet. The attack ended.

In December 1915 Grand Duchess Maria Pavlovna visited the community. She wrote later:

> My aunt had greatly changed during the last few years. In spite of the fact that she was living in a nunnery, she came now into contact with a greater number and variety of people. This had broadened her outlook, made her softer, more human. Not only did she come face to face with phases of life of which previously she had known nothing, but she had now to take into account opinions and viewpoints entirely at variance with her own.[16]

Relations between Elizabeth and the Tsar's family had become strained during these last years. She considered the new focus of the court, Grigori Rasputin, to be 'a dreadful person', a threat to the authority of Nicholas and a source of public hostility. She warned Alexandra against him, but this only created a coldness between the sisters. When Rasputin was murdered Elizabeth sent a congratulatory telegram to Felix Yusupov, who was partly responsible. She also praised his parents for the patriotic act of their son.

But the Tsarist state was crumbling under the pressures of war. In March 1917 Nicholas II was forced to abdicate. Now, revolutionaries regularly visited the Martha and Mary foundation. Sometimes they searched the community for German weapons. At other times they came simply to demonstrate that Elizabeth was no longer to be treated as royalty, or to foment some scandal among the sisters, or else to provoke a conflict between the sisters and those who supported the revolutionaries outside. They tried to arrest the Grand Duchess a number of times. There were threats to kill her, but nothing happened. 'Clearly we are not yet worthy of a martyr's crown',[17] Elizabeth said to her sisters. On 1 March 1917 a troop of revolutionary soldiers surrounded the convent, shouting 'Where is the German spy?' The Grand Duchess came forward and told them 'There is no German spy; this is a convent, of which I am the Mother Superior'.[18] The new Provisional Government treated her with great respect and suggested to her more than once that she move to the Kremlin. 'I left the Kremlin', she said 'with the intention of leaving secular life and founding an *obitel*', and not in order to be driven back there by the revolution.' The Swedish government tried to engineer her transfer to Stockholm. Later, Felix Yusupov recalled in his memoirs that the Kaiser of Germany offered repeatedly to shelter her in Germany: 'but she sent him word that she would never leave her convent, or Russia, of her own free will.'[19]

All during the summer of 1917 she was seriously ill. Grand Duchess Maria Pavlovna visited the community again in the autumn and found her aunt very weak and passing much of her time with a piece of embroidery, or knitting, upon a wicker chaise-longue.[20] In October the Bolsheviks, a small revolutionary party which enjoyed mass support in the city, took advantage of the prevailing confusion and seized power. These were dangerous new days. The Revolution was followed by months of bitter civil war. The new regime pursued peace with Germany and secured a severe settlement. Immediately afterwards, the German ambassador, Count Mirbach, tried to persuade Elizabeth to leave Russia, but she refused even to meet him. There were also ordinary Russians who wanted to help her; one of them, a shoemaker, suggested that she escape abroad by sledge. Some Christians of the Church of the Old Believers, who were often antipathetic towards representatives of the official Church, suggested that she go into hiding in one of their sketes in the Urals.

The landscape in which she lived had changed, utterly. In April 1918, Elizabeth wrote to Countess Alexandra Olsufeva: 'Holy Russia cannot perish. But great Russia no longer exists.' On 7 May 1918, Tuesday in Holy Week, she was arrested and taken away from Moscow with two sisters from the convent, Varvara Yakovleva and Ekaterina Yanysheva. Ekaterina later returned from exile. But Varvara remained with Elizabeth until the last moment of her life, and died with her. Almost nothing is known about Varvara's life or background or even where she was born. Now she proved the most virtuous and faithful of companions.

The Patriarch of Moscow and All Russia attempted to save Elizabeth.[21] Her family received only one further letter from her, sent while she was on her journey. She wrote 'I live in the hope of soon being reunited with you and I would like to find you all together. Apart from the Gospels, read the Epistles together. I have a Bible with me; let us read and pray and hope.' The remaining facts about her are known only from the records that lie in the investigation case file. With a number of other prisoners she was sent to Perm. On the journey her guards refused even to give her a cup of hot water. The little group was then taken to Ekaterinburg where they spent a few days. In this town Nicholas II and his family were confined. One of the sisters attempted to get in touch with them, managing to find the house where the Romanovs were being held, and even glimpsing the Tsar through a gap in the fence. But she was unable to give him any signal. The final destination for Elizabeth and her companions lay 150 km away, in Alapaevsk. They arrived there on 20 May 1918, and were housed in a school on the edge of the town with other members of the Romanov family, including the elderly Grand Duke Sergei Mikhailovich; Konstantin, Igor and Ioann, the three sons of Grand Duke Konstantin Konstantinovich; and Prince Vladimir Paley, the younger son of Grand Duke Pavel Alexandrovich.

Under Elizabeth's supervision they created a kitchen garden in the school yard, planting rows of vegetables and laying flowerbeds. Prince Vladimir Paley wrote to his mother that Aunt Ella knew more than anyone about such things.[22] In the evenings they would all read the Bible and pray together. Elizabeth would usually ask Ioann to read out loud to them. On 21 June the prisoners' personal possessions were confiscated and they were confined to the school building. All those accompanying the members of the royal family, except for Fyodor Mikhailovich Remez, former secretary of Grand Duke Sergei Mikhailovich, and Varvara Yakovleva, were released. Those who remained understood that they had not long left to live.

On 17 July 1918 the Tsar and his immediate family were murdered in Ekaterinburg. During the night of 18 July the prisoners in the school building in Alapaevsk were woken up. According to an account written by one of the assassins, Ryabov, the women were first roused and told to get dressed; their hands were tied behind their backs, they were blindfolded and put in a cart which took them off to a mineshaft twelve kilometres away. Grand Duke Sergei Mikhailovich resisted, and 'barricaded himself behind a cupboard'. Ryabov shot him in the arm and he gave himself up. As light was beginning to break, Ryabov and his collaborators began to hurry. Grand Duke Sergei Mikhailovich asked why they should be killed. He had never been involved in politics, but had only played billiards and other sports. 'I reassured him as best I could', Ryabov remembered later, 'although I was myself very agitated by everything I had been through that night.' His account continues:

> First we led Grand Duchess Elizabeth up to the mine. After throwing her down the shaft, we heard her struggling in the water for some time. We pushed the nun lay-sister Varvara down after her. We again heard the splashing of water and then the two women's voices. It became clear that, having dragged herself out of the water, the Grand Duchess had also pulled her lay-sister out. But, having no other alternative, we had to throw in all the men also. None of them, it seems, drowned, or choked in the water and after a short time we were able to hear almost all their voices again. Then I threw in a grenade. It exploded and everything was quiet.

But not for long. We decided to wait a little to check whether they had all perished. After a short while we heard talking and a barely audible groan. I threw another grenade. And what do you think – from beneath the ground we heard singing! I was seized with horror. They were singing the prayer: 'Lord, save thy people!' We had no more grenades, yet it was impossible to leave the deed unfinished. We decided to fill the shaft with dry brushwood and set it alight. Their hymns still rose up through the thick smoke for some time yet. When the last signs of life beneath the earth had ceased, we posted some of our people by the mine and returned to Alapaevsk by the first light and immediately sounded the alarm in the cathedral bell tower. Almost the whole town came running. We told everyone that the grand dukes had been taken away by persons unknown![23]

In October 1918 the district was occupied by counter-revolutionary forces under the command of Admiral Kolchak. On 11 October the bodies were brought out of the mineshaft on his orders. An investigation revealed that Elizabeth had not fallen right to the bottom of the mineshaft but had landed on a ledge 15 metres below. Local residents later related how they had heard liturgical singing coming from the mineshaft the day after the execution. Seriously wounded herself (a haematoma the size of a child's palm was discovered in her head), Elizabeth had evidently made a bandage out of her handkerchief and tended Prince Ioann, who had fallen onto the same ledge. She died later.

The dead were placed in the burial vault of the Holy Trinity Cathedral in Alapaevsk. Then they were transferred to Chita, until finally they were taken to the Russian Spiritual Mission in Peking. From there two coffins with the bodies of Elizabeth and Varvara Yakovleva were sent to Jerusalem at the direction of Elizabeth's younger sister Princess Victoria, the Marchioness of Milford Haven. They were finally buried in the crypt below the church of St Mary Magdalen, the church which Elizabeth had once attended as a young woman with her new husband. It was many years later that Elizabeth and Varvara were acknowledged as saints, first by the Russian Orthodox Church Abroad in 1984, and then by the Moscow Patriarchate in 1992.

(Translated and prepared by Xenia Dennen.)

NOTES

1   Andrei Maylunas and Sergei Mironenko, *A Lifelong Passion: Nicholas and Alexandra, Their Own Story* (New York, 1997), pp. 399–400 (entry dated 5

August 1914). See also Maurice Paléologue, *An Ambassador's Memoirs* (London, 1923-25).

2 Maylunas and Mironenko, *A Lifelong Passion*, pp. 266-7.

3 Lubov Millar, *Grand Duchess Elizabeth of Russia* (Redding, CA: Nikodemos Orthodox Publication Society, 1991), p. 64.

4 Ibid., p. 63. Letter dated 11/23 January 1891.

5 Maylunas and Mironenko, *A Lifelong Passion*, pp. 265-6.

6 Ibid., p. 264 (entry for 1905 in Maria Pavlovna's memoirs).

7 Ibid.

8 Ibid., pp. 262-3 (entry for 1905 in Maria Pavlovna's memoirs).

9 Ibid., pp. 271-2.

10 Ibid., pp. 263-4.

11 Ibid., p. 268.

12 Ibid., p. 333.

13 Ibid.

14 Ibid.

15 Ibid., p. 492 (entry for 1916 in Maria Pavlovna's memoirs).

16 Ibid., p. 443 (entry for 1915 in Maria Pavlovna's memoirs).

17 E. M. Almedingen, *An Unbroken Unity: A Memoir of Grand-Duchess Serge of Russia 1864-1918* (London, 1964), p. 116.

18 Maylunas and Mironenko, *A Lifelong Passion*, p. 541 (entry for 1917).

19 Ibid., p. 623.

20 Ibid., p. 577.

21 Ibid., p. 623.

22 Almedingen, *An Unbroken Unity*, p. 126.

23 Maylunas and Mironenko, *A Lifelong Passion*, pp. 638-9.

Bibliography

E. M. Almedingen, *An Unbroken Unity: A Memoir of Grand-Duchess Serge of Russia 1864-1918* (London, 1964).

Andrei Maylunas and Sergei Mironenko, *A Lifelong Passion: Nicholas and Alexandra, Their Own Story* (New York, 1997).

Lubov Millar, *Grand Duchess Elizabeth of Russia* (Redding, CA: Nikodemos Orthodox Publication Society, 1991).

Imperialism, mission and conversion: Manche Masemola of Sekhukhuneland

MANDY GOEDHALS

MANCHE MASEMOLA spent her short life in Sekhukhuneland.[1] She died as a martyr in 1928, fifty years after the British defeat of the Pedi paramount Sekhukhune swung the balance of power in the Transvaal decisively in favour of colonial society. But the Pedi did not easily submit to the colonial order,[2] and any understanding of Manche's life and death is rooted in the struggle for political, economic and cultural autonomy in the northern Transvaal.

In the early nineteenth century, Pedi hegemony extended over much of the land to the north and east of what is now Johannesburg, but was then open veld and a place of no importance. In the 1820s, depredations from other African chiefdoms and advance commandos from white Boers had forced the Pedi to withdraw from their capital in the productive Steelpoort river valley and move northwards to the mountain fortresses, between the Steelpoort and Olifants rivers. Here they regrouped under their chief, Sekwati. But the nature of the new location cast a shadow on the future of the Pedi kingdom. The land was not fertile, and the mountains which provided military defence acted as a barrier to rain, so the Pedi were impelled to search for wealth beyond the borders of their heartland, while the devastating storms and fearful lightning which periodically struck the Pedi domain helped to shape the culture and outlook of its people.[3]

From the 1840s, white trekkers began to settle on the perimeter of the Pedi kingdom, a development which Sekwati initially viewed with a degree of tolerance, as the Pedi polity was really a loose confederation accustomed to incorporating new groups. Boers and Pedi, both pastoralists, entered into treaties about land, but with different perceptions of ownership. Here lay the seeds of future conflict: among the Pedi, a chief could grant usufruct but land was communally owned, whereas the trekkers assumed that a transfer of ownership had taken place. Sekwati died in 1862, and although Sekhukhune inherited the chiefdom without a succession dispute, the change in leadership and the existence of external challenges to Pedi rule encouraged some subchiefs to assert their independence of the new Pedi paramount. By the 1870s, the Pedi had unknowingly signed away much of their land to the Boers of the South African Republic (ZAR)[4] while the Kimberley diamond diggings attracted workers away from the Transvaal, creating a shortage of farm labour. The Pedi were determined to oppose ZAR demands for land and labour which threatened their independence, and by 1876 the two groups were at war. Although the Boers sent a large army into the field, they did not break Sekhukhune's resistance. But afterwards, the ability of the Pedi to rival the Boers as a focus of power and authority in the north-eastern Transvaal declined.[5]

In the last quarter of the nineteenth century, the profits of the diamond fields and the potential wealth of alluvial gold deposits in the Transvaal led to a reformulation of imperial policy for southern Africa. Political control of the subcontinent, long avoided as too expensive, was now clearly in Britain's interests. The mineral revolution required a cheap labour supply, for which the hitherto independent African chiefdoms provided an obvious source. Economic imperatives super-seded philanthropic notions of protectorate: a steady labour force would be unlocked through the imposition of taxes on African peoples, taxes which would conveniently cover the costs of colonial administration. This policy was clearly incompatible with the continued autonomy of African chiefdoms, including the Zulu and the Pedi. Britain had been critical of the attack made by the ZAR against the paramountcy in 1876, but in 1879, Sir Garnet Wolseley, in alliance with the Swazi, defeated the Pedi and captured Sekhukhune. In the wake of this defeat, small parcels of the Pedi heartland were set aside for African occupation, the notion of private property as opposed to communal tenure was entrenched, and taxes which Pedi had always resisted were system-atically collected. These legacies remained when the Transvaal reverted to the ZAR in 1881, although ZAR administration was then carried out by and in the interests of local white farmers.[6]

British rhetoric implied that the South African War (1899–1902) was fought in the interests of the indigenous peoples, but Britain's post-war policy in South Africa was designed mainly to conciliate the defeated Boers. To ensure that the Pedi did not regain their independence, there was no change in land settlement, while the Pedi were confronted with confiscation of their arms and increased demands for rent. British officials, owing allegiance to empire rather than local farmers, took responsibility for what was called 'native administration'. Major D. R. Hunt, prepared by education in an English public school and then service in the Cape Mounted Rifles, was native commissioner in Sekhukhuneland from 1908 to 1931. His views combined notions of racial supremacy and benevolent paternalism. Senior officials made it clear to him that a strong paramount should not be allowed to emerge, and Hunt administered his vast territory with the assistance of a few chiefs, to whom the government paid a salary, subject to their co-operation with the authorities. Hunt spent most of his time collecting taxes and issuing passes. Although there was no overt resistance from the Pedi, neither were they craven victims. Within the Pedi polity, subordinate chiefs had always enjoyed regional autonomy, and under British and then Union administration, this assertion of an independent existence continued. Beyond the ken of native commissioners, the chiefs held court, allocating land and settling disputes. They received cash or cattle fines, tribute paid in labour, agricultural produce or beer, and a proportion of bridewealth payments as well. They also presided over seasonal ceremonies of rainmaking, sowing and reaping, and their maintenance of community life, through mediation with the ancestors and through initiation rites for young men and women, kept traditional customs and values alive in the popular consciousness.[7]

The Pedi way of life, with its values deeply rooted in a rural existence, was financially maintained by labour migrancy. From the 1840s, young men had travelled south, first to the eastern Cape, and then, from the 1870s, to the diamond fields: at this stage of Pedi dominance, their object was cash to buy guns for defence. But as Pedi territory shrank and became impoverished, labour migrancy became a matter of economic survival. Soil in their locations was poor, the rainfall erratic, and by the late 1920s overcrowding due to population growth and expulsion of Pedi from white farms placed further pressure on the land. The Pedi herds had been decimated by rinderpest[8] and then East Coast fever, and in the drought of 1924–29, over ten thousand cattle died of starvation. There was seldom a crop surplus, even when drought-resistant crops like millet and sorghum were planted, and, by 1930, the Pedi had had to bear the cost of imported mealies as part of their staple diet through six years of drought. In 1930, nine thousand migrants, mostly young men, left the Pedi enclaves for the mines and domestic service in towns while the conservatism of Pedi society ensured that very few women left their homes as labour migrants. Migrancy remained only the means to an end: a way to pay taxes, to build a home, to provide for a wife and family and to save for old age, but the outside world and urban life was regarded as immoral and corrupt and time spent there was a necessary evil to preserve the rurally based social and moral order of the Pedi.[9]

Pedi society was not egalitarian. Members of the royal house enjoyed wealth and status not available to commoners, and although all men were still able to obtain access to land and stock, there was a gulf between the prosperous Pedi and those whose economic resources were slight. The deepest breach in Pedi society was not primarily economic, but occurred between the *bakristi* (the name given to the minority Christian community) and those who adhered to Pedi religious practices, whom Christian converts called *baheitene*, from the word 'heathen' so often employed pejoratively by European mission-aries. Other names given to the two groups further illustrate this division. Christians were called *majakane*, a word which implied that they had chosen to live in a foreign country, while those who preferred the established ways of their people were called *baditsaba* or 'those of the community'.[10] This separation from and suspicion of Christians, which was deeply rooted in Pedi society and which was to shape the course of Manche Masemola's life, had its origins in the role which Christian missionaries had played in Pedi history in the nineteenth century.

Often echoing the views of colonial authorities, missionary apologetic from the nineteenth and early twentieth century presented the Pedi as heathen savages, and the Pedi chiefs, in particular Sekhukhune, as persecutors of Christianity.[11] There is another perspective on the past. First Pedi contacts with Christianity came through the Transvaal Boers, and through Pedi who travelled to work in Natal and the Cape, and encountered missions there. Some Pedi were baptized, and a few proved diligent evangelists when they returned home. Their initial impression of the missionaries was probably favourable: to the south, in the territory of the Sotho paramount Moshoeshoe, agents of the Paris Evangelical Missionary Society acted as advisers and channels of communication with Free State Boers and colonial officials, and supported Moshoeshoe against threats to his authority from both inside and outside the chiefdom.[12] Sekwati, too, was interested in acquiring such counsellors and, in 1861, Alexander Merensky and Albert Nachtigal of the Berlin Missionary Society established the first mission on Pedi land.[13] The society, founded in 1824, combined piety and the ethos of Prussian nationalism: trained as artisans, the missionaries emphasized discipline and hard work, and created an atmosphere of authoritarian paternalism. Wishing to retain their political usefulness and medical knowledge, Sekwati smoothed the way for the missionaries, and his successor, Sekhukhune, allowed them to remain until it became clear that their presence threatened his own position and undermined the independence of the Pedi. Not only were his rivals for the paramountcy forming alliances with the missionaries, but he was forced to act by popular belief that Christian rejection of traditional values and practices endangered the kingdom, rendering it vulnerable to enemies and exposing land and people to drought and disease. The first steps were taken against Pedi Christians, but, in 1866, the Berlin missionaries were expelled from the chiefdom. Sekhukhune described the mission as wounds through which his people bled away.[14] Nor was this a figment of his imagination. The missionaries regarded African traditional custom as anathema and sought to eradicate it. They also realized that while the Pedi kingdom remained intact their efforts would gain no foothold, and they therefore had an interest in undermining the political independence of the Pedi. In 1863, Merensky accepted appointment as ZAR agent with the Pedi, thus allying himself with the land and labour interests of white farmers which were diametrically opposed to those of the Pedi.

After the 1866 exclusion, numbers of converts followed Merensky to Botshabelo, the mission he established outside the Pedi kingdom. Here he further showed his true colours, demanding that African Christians acknowledge ZAR authority and exacting payment of taxes to the Boer republic, at a time when the Boers themselves had no efficient means of enforcing revenue collection. The Berlin missionaries also had a role in encouraging the ZAR war against the Pedi in 1876. BMS partisanship was not forgotten, and the past, in which Christians were associated with undermining Pedi values and with the process of colonial conquest, became an integral part of the Pedi outlook on contemporary events.

Anglican perspectives on Sekhukhuneland were shaped by the Boers and the Berlin Missionary Society. T. E. Wilkinson, the Bishop of Zululand, who visited the Transvaal regularly from 1872, was warned that Sekhukhune was 'hostile and cruel'. Of the Berlin missionaries he wrote: 'Most glad I am to see them here.'[15] A bishop, Henry Bousfield, was consecrated for the Transvaal in 1878, a year after British annexation of the territory, and he made it a condition of his appointment that he would only serve in British territory. He was also somewhat over-attached to the institutions of his church, and retro-cession of the Transvaal to the ZAR in 1881 added despondency and a sense of betrayal to what was an autocratic and obstinate nature. He had little enthusiasm for missionary activity, although Sekhukhuneland was opened to missionaries again in the 1880s. Between 1893 and 1899, it was a missionary, Edwin Farmer, who brought to the diocese the energy which its bishop lacked, and, on one of his many expeditions, he visited Sekhukhuneland in 1897, finding communicants and catechists there, presumably migrants who had returned after a tour of duty in the sphere of an Anglican missionary.[16] The episcopate of William Marlborough Carter (1902-09) did not significantly advance the Anglican *status quo* in Sekhukhuneland, although it was clear that the bishop identified with Wolseley's aim of 1879, to wean the Pedi from 'the ways of savage life into complete submission to a civilized sovereignty'.[17] At the 1905 diocesan synod, he proudly quoted the views of the colonial Native Affairs Commission, on the positive impact of Christian missionaries in general:

> To the churches engaged in missionary work must be given the greatest measure of credit for placing before the Natives the higher standard of belief and conduct ... the weight of the evidence is in favour of the improved morality of the Christian section of the population.[18]

In 1908, in response to the appeals for missionaries which came from Pedi catechists in Pretoria, Latimer Fuller of the Community of the Resurrection visited Sekhukhuneland in a Cape cart drawn by four mules, preaching by moonlight to the courteous but cautious groups whom the local chiefs gathered to hear him.[19] The land was harsh and uninviting, and attracted no resident white Anglican missionary: the next priest passed through Sekhukhuneland on a bicycle in 1913.[20] But there were other missionaries at work in Sekhukhuneland, and although Christians were regarded as a divisive element in Pedi society and lived in separate areas of the villages, both Christians and those who practised traditional religion also shared a common life and a common experience of migrant labour.[21] Eventually, an African deacon was sent to work there, and in 1919 Father Augustine Moeka, called 'apostle of Sekhukhuneland',[22] settled at Marishane, where the chief had long opened his village to Christian missionaries of all denominations. An Anglican congregation developed here, a school was opened and St Peter's church was started.[23]

Marishane was not the only Anglican centre in Sekhukhuneland. About ten miles away, there was a mission hospital which bore the name of another South African-born child, who brought a quality of youthful ardour to her Christian faith, and who also died young, but whose circumstances in other respects differed greatly from those of Manche Masemola. In 1918, Jane Diana Furse, daughter of Michael Furse, Bishop of Pretoria, and his wife Frances, died two weeks short of her fourteenth birthday. She was a beloved only child, and the hearts of Christians, black and white, went out to her parents.[24] A memorial tablet in her memory was placed in Pretoria Cathedral: redolent with a spirit of loving service and the white man's burden, its attitude to African people captures the character of Anglican missionary work at this time:

> In great thankfulness to Almighty God for a most priceless gift and in memory of a dear child JANE DIANA FURSE.
> South African born and bred, she loved her country and her home: she loved all animals wild or tame, and with them had no fear: with the sure instinct for what was right and clean her childish indignation blazed forth at all that was less than just to the child races of her native land. In her short life of vigorous joy the purity of the love of God shone forth: and so she passed over to the fuller life beyond.[25]

Money was raised in her memory, both in South Africa and in England where her father became Bishop of the diocese of St Albans, and the hospital and mission centre named after Jane Furse opened in 1921.

By 1928, the work at Marishane was described as 'flourishing', and one visitor reported: 'It was delightful to go to this village and worship with this large congregation at an early Eucharist, to chat with the adults, to see the children in school.'[26] But the work at Marishane and Jane Furse were tiny outposts for the Church and Christianity, oases in a great desert, as another visitor remarked.[27] In the memory of the Pedi, missionaries were an integral part of their loss of freedom, and although by the 1930s the Pedi no longer realistically hoped to regain their independence, they also intended to preserve what autonomy they still retained.

Historical accounts of the Pedi are not plentiful, and early interpretations tend to reflect the views of missionaries, officials or settlers, while others contain narrative accounts of Pedi chiefs.[28] More recent accounts provide critical discussion of the economic and political context or examination of challenge and change within Pedi society itself. These shed light on the world of Manche Masemola. Of Manche Masemola herself, very little has been written. Most of the accounts we have were written by white clergy, although these are based on the oral evidence of those who knew her, particularly her cousin Lucia, daughter of Manche's mother's sister.[29] None of the writing attempts to understand Manche's life in the context of the history of Sekhukhuneland, or from the point of view of Pedi traditionalists or her parents. The events of her life are used to illustrate the Christian fortitude with which she faced persecution and death, rather than to depict her humanity, while the circumstances of her death and burial are presented in a way which further establishes her cause as a Christian martyr. We have no words written by Manche herself, only a few rather stereotypical sentences, in English translation from her native Sepedi, of her words to Father Augustine Moeka.[30]

Even the year of Manche Masemola's birth is uncertain.[31] Some sources give her age as 18 in 1928, but she was probably born in about 1913, in the village of Marishane. Manche had two older brothers and a younger sister named Mabule, while their cousin Lucia lived with the family because her mother had died.[32] In the Sekhukhuneland reserve, where shortage of land created a real danger that a landless class might emerge,[33] Manche's family were still able to obtain access to arable land. Her father was not a migrant worker, and the household was therefore dependent on the annual harvest for their subsistence. The fields allocated to Manche's father were far from Marishane, in the village of Mabuke, and the family moved here during the planting season, in order to tend their crops.[34] Although taboos with regard to women handling cattle were beginning to break down by the late 1920s,[35] ploughing was probably done by her father or older brothers, while Manche helped her mother with hoeing, weeding and reaping; she seems to have been a hard and willing worker. By the 1920s, a tiny minority of Pedi children, mostly from Christian families, attended the mission schools, and were being joined by *baditsaba* children, as the advantages of Western education became more apparent.[36] Manche did not attend the school at Marishane. Like other girls of her age, she worked at home, helping to fetch water and firewood and learning to gather wild plants and to cook; she was trained to grind corn, to gather reeds for fencing and baskets, and to maintain the mud walls and dung floors of the homestead.[37] This domestic routine was relieved by the repetitive songs, games and dances of children everywhere. Manche appeared mature for her age, and took on her fair share of caring for babies and small children in the village.

When she was about 13, perhaps during a visit to relatives in Marishane, she went with her cousin to hear Father Moeka preach at the church there. She seems to have been so drawn by what she heard that she asked her mother for permission to attend the twice-weekly hearers' classes in Marishane. This was the beginning of a long struggle between the Masemola parents and their daughter's desire to be a Christian. First, they attempted various delaying tactics. Manche was told to attend the traditional initiation school.[38] Initiation was the foundation of Pedi social organization, and it was compulsory for all youths. Initiation for young girls was supervised by the senior wife of the chief, older women and those who had already passed through the rites.[39] The process began with a symbolic circumcision ceremony, which was usually shrouded in secrecy but which has been described as follows:

> The girls are told that an operation is to be performed on them. A knife is sharpened in their presence and they are then taken, one by one, made to lie down, and covered with a blanket. The knife is then pressed between their legs. Although they are not injured at all, the girls cry out with fright when feeling the cold metal. As each girl is led away ... the women who perform the operation emerge from the blanket with their hands reddened with plant-juices. The girls still waiting their turn, thinking that the hands of the women are covered in blood, must obviously be terrorised. Although they do not undergo the pain that boys do when circumcised, the fright and bewilderment of the girls must be equal to that of the boys.[40]

The experience alone must have taught an impressive lesson in stoicism to those on the receiving end. The instruction which followed emphasized loyalty to chiefs and to parents, and especially the respect which women owed to men and to their elders, while the work and duties of women, as well as sexual matters, were explained. Missionaries, recognizing that initiation practices were intended to bolster Pedi values and traditions, forbade Christians to undergo initiation,[41] and Manche's mother may also have hoped that the Church would look with disfavour on her daughter if she had recently emerged from the initiation school. Neither the rite of passage, nor Manche's subsequent engagement, turned her heart from the longing for Christian teaching, and so her parents sent the two cousins away, to cook for youths herding cattle in distant pastures. But Manche continued to attend Christian classes at Marishane twice a week. At first, there was quarrelling and recrimination in the household; then she was told to await the return from a migrant labour contract of the young man to whom she was engaged, before making a decision. She rejected this stratagem, and refused to delay.[42]

The parents' next resort was to beat her. Christianity was closely associated with the conquest of the Pedi, with loss of their land, and with colonial demands for tax and labour. She might leave them: most of the women who left Sekhukhuneland to work in towns were Christians. Towns were regarded as centres of immorality, and, accordingly, Christianity was regarded as an example of 'truly delinquent behaviour'.[43] As a young girl, Manche did not enjoy high status in Pedi society: it was expected that she would respect and obey older women and all men. Communal solidarity was highly regarded, and Manche was placing her individual sense of vocation above the wishes and wisdom of her elders. Among the Pedi in Sekhukhuneland, there were also instances of violence and brutality against those who seemed to threaten stability and continuity within the society.[44] Other circumstances intervened. It was a time of sustained drought, and the Masemola parents may have been anxious about their ability to feed their family. Manche's mother seems to have been a hard and even unjust taskmaster, hiding tools so that her daughter could not work, and then berating Manche for laziness[45] and expressing resentment at the time the child spent attending church and praying. Manche herself told Lucia that 'her aim was to work hard and please her parents, so that they must not say that she left them when she went to church'.[46] Moreover, Augustine Moeka was trying to establish a religious community for women in Marishane,[47] and Manche's mother may have feared that Manche would ultimately join a celibate sisterhood. In Pedi society, failure to marry and bear children was a curse, to be avoided at all costs. From a material point of view, it also meant loss of the bride price to parents of their daughters. A determination to acquire cattle on Manche's marriage, and with them a more secure future, might well have been in the mother's mind.[48]

We know very little about the content of Manche's personal creed, for which she endured repeated beatings from October 1927. At first, it was the Christian call to repentance that seems to have drawn her, then the promise that those who died as Christians would go to God. Certainly the prospect of pain and death seems to have played a large part in her Christian commitment. In the 1920s, missionaries probably felt strong links between their own experience and that of the early Church. Because Sekhukhuneland was hostile to Christianity, the need to withstand persecution formed a large element in the preparation of catechumens. There was certainly no question of interference with parental authority, and the priest in Marishane advised children who were hard pressed not to defy their parents. In October 1927 Father Moeka recorded that Manche said 'If they cut off my head, I will never leave my faith' and she went on to predict that she would be baptized 'with a better baptism'. Her cousin Lucia remembered her saying 'I shall laugh the more they hurt me', and in January 1928, the last time he saw her, Father Moeka reported that she had told him: 'I shall be baptized with my own blood.'[49] The words are full of courage from a young girl, although they seem a little trite, but adolescents are sometimes given to portentous statements they do not fully understand. Apparently Moeka himself did not pay much attention to this at the time,[50] although we are told that Manche was a happy child, quiet and thoughtful, and not prone to self-dramatization. A small incident in January 1928 provides a revealing glimpse of her. The church tried to provide parallel rituals to replace Pedi institutions, for example equating confirmation with initiation. In January 1928, Augustine Moeka told the catechumens that they could continue to wear their traditional dress, which consisted of a short skirt, a piece of cloth draped across the breasts, and bracelets of grass and beads on their arms and legs. The young women turned down his suggestion, but Manche went back to him afterwards, and said she was sorry for this.[51] Did she do this to please the priest? Did she hope that a rejection of European clothing would lessen the causes of conflict with her mother and father? Perhaps she was also looking for ways to assert that it was possible to belong to the Pedi community and to be a Christian. Lucia recorded Manche's resolve on the way home from this meeting: 'Even if they kill me, I am ready.'[52]

Whatever social, economic, political and even historical forces were at work, and whatever the personal dynamic between mother and daughter, the focus on both sides rested on the question of Manche's Christian commitment. Her cousin Lucia was sent away, allegedly because she was a bad influence; this left Manche in a very isolated position. Pressure within the home was clearly building up, as the parents struggled with their child's stubborn resolve, alarmed at the forces of disease and destruction that her irresponsible behaviour and apparent disobedience could bring on them all. They were increasingly violent towards her. It was possibly an expression of her mother's own sense of helplessness, brought on by the lowly position she herself occupied in Pedi society. In a desperate search for an explanation of her conduct, the parents lit on the Anglican use of incense in worship, concluding that it had bewitched their daughter. A witch doctor was consulted, and, although Manche was forced to swallow his medicine, it did not produce the desired effect. Her mother then confiscated her clothes, to thwart her attendance at church meetings, but Manche continued to pray outdoors, morning and evening. Eventually, her father and mother took her away to a lonely place and, according to an eyewitness, Elesina Masemola, they beat her to death.[53] This took place on or about 4 February, which is kept as the feast day of Manche Masemola.[54] News of her death was brought to Marishane the next day by one of the Mabuke villagers. Augustine Moeka was away at the time, and the first to hear the news was a young woman who was later professed as Sister Julia of the Daughters of Mary. Manche's body had already been buried. Her body was sewn up in a blanket and taken to the community burial place, where the earth was usually soft and easy to dig, but tradition tells that wherever attempts were made to prepare a grave, huge rocks were found. This filled the people with fear, so that they acknowledged 'The ground will not receive her; she is not our child; she is the child of Moeka, the man of God, the teacher of the Christians'. Her parents, probably alarmed by this time at the prospect of an enquiry by the authorities, buried her on a distant hillside, at the base of a great granite rock. Within a fortnight, Manche's devoted younger sister Mabule, who had grieved at the treatment she received, was taken ill and died at Jane Furse hospital. She was buried at Manche's side. Their father planted euphorbia trees alongside their graves.[55]

From the first, it seems that Augustine Moeka regarded Manche's death as martyrdom. Certainly, no steps were taken to inform the government authorities of what had happened so that her parents' involvement could be investigated, although this silence can also be attributed to a realization that any government enquiry would meet with a wall of resistance in the Pedi community itself. The Church had no wish to provoke anger among Pedi traditionalists. But Father Moeka also went to considerable trouble to establish the site of Manche Masemola's grave, to ensure that his ecclesiastical superiors were informed of the circumstances of her death, and to encourage them to visit the site.[56]

Manche Masemola's death was not followed by a dramatic transformation in the impact of the Christian mission in Sekhukhuneland: resistance was too deeply rooted in past history and contemporary circumstances for that. The work of the missions continued to be hard and unrewarding, to demand 'patience, charity and understanding ... cheerfulness and perseverance in the face of all the difficulties'. Even then, Sekhukhuneland seemed 'a rather hopeless mission' to some of the priests who worked there.[57] What, then, were the fruits of her death? In some ways, they seem rather meagre. In 1929, the *Cowley Evangelist* published an appeal for funds to complete St Peter's in Marishane in Manche's memory, and by Easter 1930 the church was cleared of debt.[58] A small religious community, the Daughters of Mary, was established at Marishane: the five young women who were its first members also found themselves the focus of anger and fierce criticism, especially because their religious profession meant a rejection of traditional women's roles within their own society. For many years, the sisters, who wore very simple habits, supported themselves by doing laundry from Jane Furse. Their main apostolate was religious education of children and women, although they performed many chores in the small churches which were outstations of Marishane. Years later the ageing community eventually retired to Jane Furse, and the last of the Daughters of Mary died in 1986.[59] A children's ward at the hospital there is named after Manche Masemola.

For many years, Manche Masemola's mother continued to deny that she was responsible for her daughter's death, and vehemently warned others to avoid Christians who bewitched and killed people. For almost four decades, she struggled with her own sense of anger at the Church, but in 1969 she was baptized, taking the name Magdelene, was confirmed and made her first communion.[60] A photograph taken at the time shows a small wiry person, in sharp contrast with the comfortable figures and smiling faces of other Christian women in the picture; there is hardship etched on her face, with tension but resolve in her stance, qualities which were perhaps inherited by her elder daughter.

Manche's most obvious and lasting legacy lies in the annual pilgrimages to her grave. The first, in 1935, was a small one: the Bishop of Pretoria, Wilfrid Parker, celebrated a requiem mass there at Rogationtide, with the newly appointed Canon Moeka; Geoffrey Clayton, Bishop of Johannesburg, Stephen Carter CR, and a group of African Christians including the Daughters of Mary were also present. There was another visit to the grave in September 1941; then members of the Community of the Resurrection were accompanied by Agnes, a Daughter of Mary. In July 1949, Francis Blake CR led the pilgrimage, intending to hold a prayer meeting there, but the sense of the numinous on the hillside was so strong that the pilgrims knelt simply together in silence for thirty minutes, and then went quietly home. The pilgrimage was established as an annual event, held in August and not on Manche's February feast day, in order to avoid the rains. Today many hundreds attend, and the diocesan bishop presides at a joyful Eucharist celebrated in Sepedi at the altar built over Manche's grave.[61]

General histories of the Church of the Province of Southern Africa pay no attention to Manche Masemola,[62] nor is this particularly surprising. Ecclesiastical histories until recently tended to ignore the political and economic context of church life, and to analyse events from the point of view of episcopal activities and synod resolutions. Mission was seen as a one-way process introduced by white missionaries, and it was assumed that preaching the gospel entailed introduction of Western culture, especially Western education. The contribution of African Christians was acknowledged, but few were actually named, and the role of women in the Church was gratefully mentioned, but not systematically recorded and analysed.[63] Manche Masemola's life was not altogether ignored by the authorities of the Church. In 1937, the bishops suggested that her name be added to the Province's calendar of commemorations, 'at the first convenient opportunity'.[64] She was included in the calendar in 1975, in an age which had become increasingly conscious of the need for development of an indigenous Christianity.[65]

Manche Masemola is perhaps appropriately representative of the great masses of South Africa and even the numberless people of Africa itself because, like them, she has been hidden from history. It is difficult to imagine a more marginalized person. A member of an oppressed race, as a young woman within her own society, she owed respect and obedience to all except younger children. Living out her life in a poverty-stricken reserve, she knew only a rural existence and a domestic economy dependent on subsistence agriculture. Her labour was controlled by parents, and she could not read and write. To this day Sekhukhuneland falls into one of the most impoverished regions in South Africa, with low levels of literacy, income and life expectancy and where about three-quarters of the children live in poverty.[66] On some grounds, there may be questions about whether Manche is an appropriate figure to commemorate as a Christian martyr, particularly in her attitude to the standards imposed by mission Christianity with regard to Pedi custom and contemporary gender roles, but it is possible to argue that she pointed beyond the conventions of her own time in both areas. In entering the initiation school, in her attitude to the wearing of traditional dress, even in her desire to be a good daughter, Manche accepted the values and customs of the Pedi, but she was resolved to be a Christian. Her recorded words tend to universalize and stereotype her life and death, but in the very confined sphere in which she lived she submitted to both Christian and Pedi expectations that women's work should be confined to domestic duties and performed with unquestioning obedience. At the same time, to confess Christ in her own time and place was an act of rebellion, a serious challenge to constituted authority.

Manche Masemola lived her life in the context of the Pedi struggle to restrict the intrusion of colonial power, represented by white officials, farmers and missionaries, and enforced through the imposition of taxes, individual tenure and migrant labour. The effort to preserve their rural existence and autonomy meant the assertion of other power relations within Sekhukhuneland, including emphasis on chiefly rule, traditional family and gender relationships and maintenance of the initiation school. It is important to understand these social, political and economic processes. Manche Masemola's life was deeply rooted in Pedi society, yet the good news for which she is a witness is not only for Sekhukhuneland, nor is she simply a representative of an oppressed and needy people: she offers the world her hope, perseverance and fortitude. Perhaps we can hear her sing, like another obscure young woman who challenged conventions and responded to God with all her being:

> My soul proclaims the greatness of the Lord,
> my spirit rejoices in God my Saviour, ...
> You, the Almighty have done great things for me
> and holy is your name.[67]

Notes

1   There are no official birth registration records for Sekhukhuneland at this time. The notes which accompany the calendar of the Church of the Province of Southern Africa (*Liturgy 1975: Minister's Book* (Johannesburg, 1975) and *Saints and Seasons* (Johannesburg, 1993)) give Manche's age as 18. Other sources state quite clearly that she was born in 1914 and would thus have been about 14 at the time of her death (*CR Quarterly*, Christmas 1983). Canon John Tsebe, who served as Archdeacon in Sekhukhuneland and whose wife Nora belonged to the Masemola family, points out that if Manche had been 18, she would have been too old for the initiation school which she attended: he estimates that Manche was about 15 years old at the time of her death (interview, 7 August 1997).

2   Much of this account relies on Peter Delius's two works on the Pedi: *The Land Belongs to Us* (Johannesburg, 1983), and *A Lion Amongst the Cattle: Reconstruction and Resistance in the Northern Transvaal* (Johannesburg, 1996).

3   Delius, *A Lion Amongst the Cattle*, p. 10.

4   For a history of this republic see T. R. H. Davenport, *South Africa: A Modern History* (London, 1991), pp. 75-8.

5   P. Maylam, *A History of the African People of South Africa* (Cape Town, 1986), pp. 127-31.

6   Delius, *A Lion Amongst the Cattle*, pp. 12-13.

7   Ibid., pp. 15-21.
8   Rinderpest is a highly infectious disease which affects cattle; it had a devastating effect on cattle farming when it broke out in South Africa in 1896: Jean Branford (ed.), *Dictionary of South African English* (Cape Town, 1978), p. 202.
9   Delius, *A Lion Amongst the Cattle*, pp. 21-4.
10 Ibid., p. 25.
11 Delius, *The Land Belongs to Us*, p. 108.
12 L. M. Thompson, *Survival in Two Worlds: Moshoeshoe of Lesotho 1786-1870* (Oxford, 1975), p. 84.
13 On the missionary impact, see Delius, *The Land Belongs to Us*, pp. 108-25 and 158-80.
14 Ibid., p. 122.
15 C. Lewis and G. E. Edwards, *Historical Records of the Church of the Province of South Africa* (London, 1934), p. 576.
16 For Bousfield, see P. B. Hinchliff, *The Anglican Church in South Africa* (London, 1963), pp. 153-7; Lewis and Edwards, *Historical Records*, p. 590.
17 Quoted in Delius, *A Lion Amongst the Cattle*, p. 9.
18 Lewis and Edwards, *Historical Records*, pp. 599-600.
19 Alan Wilkinson, *The Community of the Resurrection: A Centenary History* (London, 1992), p. 230.
20 Lewis and Edwards, *Historical Records*, p. 639.
21 Delius, *A Lion Amongst the Cattle*, p. 25.
22 Lewis and Edwards, *Historical Records*, p. 640. Augustine Moeka, trained by CR, was ordained deacon in 1916 and priest in 1919. He served in Sekhukhuneland from 1919 to 1938.
23 Wilkinson, *The Community of the Resurrection*, p. 230; *CR Quarterly* (December 1983), p. 12.
24 Lewis and Edwards, *Historical Records*, p. 640.
25 University of the Witwatersrand Library, CPSA Archives, AB 775f, Jane Furse papers.
26 Lewis and Edwards, *Historical Records*, p. 640.
27 Ibid.
28 Delius, *The Land Belongs to Us*, pp. 2-3.
29 The main sources which are available are: an article by Mrs Moffat, wife of T. R. Moffat, priest-in-charge of Sekhukhuneland, published in *Cowley Evangelist* (November 1938); articles by Father Francis Blake CR in *CR Quarterly* (1950 and 1957); an article in *CR Quarterly* (Christmas 1983), which is based on a number of other oral and published sources; University of the Witwatersrand Library, CPSA Archives, f AB393, interview with Lucia Masemola, 3 May 1937.
30 Quoted in *CR Quarterly* (Christmas 1983), pp. 13-15.
31 See note 1.
32 CPSA Archives, f AB393, interview with Lucia Masemola, 1937.
33 Delius, *A Lion Amongst the Cattle*, p. 25.

34   Interview with Canon John Tsebe, 7 August 1997.
35   Delius, *A Lion Amongst the Cattle*, p. 28.
36   Ibid., p. 33.
37   Ibid., p. 28.
38   *CR Quarterly* (Christmas 1983), p. 30.
39   Delius, *A Lion Amongst the Cattle*, p. 30.
40   H. Mönnig, *The Pedi* (Pretoria, 1967), p. 126, quoted in Delius, *A Lion Amongst the Cattle*, p. 30.
41   Delius, *A Lion Amongst the Cattle*, p. 31.
42   CPSA Archives, f AB393, interview with Lucia Masemola, 1937.
43   Delius, *A Lion Amongst the Cattle*, p. 31.
44   See particularly Delius, *A Lion Amongst the Cattle*, pp. 172–211, a chapter entitled 'Cadres, comrades and witches'.
45   *CR Quarterly* (Christmas 1983), p. 14.
46   CPSA Archives, f AB393, interview with Lucia Masemola, 1937.
47   *CR Quarterly* (Christmas 1983), p. 16; interview with Canon John Tsebe, 7 August 1997.
48   Interview with Canon John Tsebe, 7 August 1997.
49   Quoted in *CR Quarterly* (Christmas 1983), pp. 12–17.
50   CPSA Archives, f AB393, interview with Lucia Masemola, 1937.
51   *CR Quarterly* (Christmas 1983), p. 15; CPSA Archives, f AB393, interview with Lucia Masemola, 1937.
52   *CR Quarterly* (Christmas 1983), p. 15.
53   Ibid.; CPSA Archives, f AB393, interview with Lucia Masemola, 1937.
54   There is some debate about the actual date of Manche Masemola's death, but this does not seem particularly significant.
55   Based on *CR Quarterly* (Christmas 1983), pp. 12–17 and CPSA Archives, f AB393, interview with Lucia Masemola, 1937.
56   CPSA Archives, f AB393, interview with Lucia Masemola, 1937.
57   Alan Wilkinson, *Community of the Resurrection*, p. 231.
58   *CR Quarterly* (Christmas 1983), p. 17.
59   Canon John Tsebe, 'African vanishing indigenous community', *CR Quarterly* (1987), pp. 18–20.
60   *Seek* (April 1969), p. 7; interview with Canon John Tsebe, 7 August 1997.
61   Since the division of the diocese of Pretoria, Sekhukhuneland lies within the diocese of St Mark the Evangelist. The story of the development of the pilgrimage is given in *CR Quarterly* (Christmas 1983), pp. 16–17. I am grateful to Bishop Michael Nuttall, Bishop of Natal and formerly Bishop of Pretoria, to Bishop Philip le Feuvre of the diocese of St Mark the Evangelist, and to Bishop Antony Mdletshe of Zululand for personal communications about their experience of the pilgrimage.
62   Lewis and Edwards, *Historical Records* and Hinchliff, *Anglican Church in South Africa* are the main general histories.
63   M. M. Goedhals, 'From paternalism to partnership: the CPSA and mission 1848–1988' in T. Paterson and F. England (eds), *Bounty in Bondage*

(Johannesburg, 1989). See J. Suggit and M. Goedhals (eds), *Change and Challenge: Essays Commemorating the 150th Anniversary of the Arrival of Robert Gray as First Bishop of Cape Town* (Johannesburg, forthcoming 1998), for a history of the role of women in the CPSA.

64 CPSA archives, f AB393, interview with Lucia Masemola, 1937.
65 *Liturgy 1975: Minister's Book*, p. 182; *Saints and Seasons*, p. 42.
66 Delius, *A Lion Amongst the Cattle*, p. 6.
67 David Stancliffe and Brother Tristam SSF (comps), *Celebrating Common Prayer: The Pocket Version* (London, 1994), p. 54.

Bibliography

Peter Delius, *The Land Belongs to Us* (Johannesburg, 1983).
P. B. Hinchliff, *The Anglican Church in South Africa* (London, 1963).
P. Maylam, *A History of the People of South Africa* (Cape Town, 1986).

Auschwitz:
Maximilian Kolbe of Poland

ROMAN KOMARYCZKO

THE LIFE and death of Maximilian Kolbe appeared to me to demand a distinctive response. How should I, a student of philosophy, represent the kerygmatic significance of his life; let him speak with his own words, bring to life his message and his deeds in a way that was direct, simple and characteristic? Here I wish above all to present his own doctrine, message and mentality, in a way that is true to the requirements of thoughtful scholarship and equally informed by my own sensitivities as a Polish Franciscan priest, trained in the spirituality that was Kolbe's own.

I, MAXIMILIAN KOLBE,

have been, through the authority of the Church, declared a saint and called 'the Martyr of charity'. Almighty God has thus accepted the homage that is due to him from all of us who are called to participate in his glory. Sanctity — which means completeness and fulfilment of love — is the greatest and the most permanent of all human monuments, because it is a gift 'coming down out of heaven from God' (Revelation 21:10). Love knows no limits because God is love, but 'no one has greater love than this, to lay down one's life for one's friends' (John 15:13).

While humbly accepting this place among my brethren in Christ here, I want therefore to reaffirm yet again the truth, which by the grace of God I was permitted to proclaim through the example of my life, that *only love can be creative*. Although 'for all these things you are staring at now' — as it is written (Luke 21:6) — 'the time will come when not a single stone will be left on another: everything will be destroyed', yet 'love no flood can quench, no torrents drown' (Song of Solomon 8:7). Love never ends.

* * *

The fact of my death and its circumstances are generally known from the accounts of witnesses. Later, fellow-inmates of mine in the concentration camp of Auschwitz gave evidence, under oath, during the legal proceedings which led to my beatification and, eventually, canonization. Their testimonies, though differing in matters of detail, conveyed the essence of the event, which took place on the last day of July 1941:

> A prisoner escaped from Cell Block 14 of the camp. The authorities ordered a search and threatened that if the escaped man was not found, ten other inmates would be sentenced to death by starvation. The man was not found, so one evening, during roll call, Commandant Fritzsch, Rapportführer Palitsch and other SS-men selected ten prisoners who would be taken to one of the bunkers to die there. I stood in the last row of Cell Block 8; behind me there were prisoners from Cell Block 14, from among whom the ten were to be chosen. I could clearly see what happened. At some stage a prisoner was selected; he stepped out of the rank and then burst into tears, saying that he had a wife and children, and now he was to die. Those already selected were standing together, on the right; he was made to join them. Then two or three more were picked, and the process was thus completed. The commandant of the camp and the SS-men were about to leave Cell Block 14, when suddenly Father Kolbe stepped out of the rank and told the kapo that he wanted to speak to the commandant. The kapo told him to go back to the ranks, but Father Maximilian did not obey him and insisted on speaking to the commandant. The SS-men accompanying the commandant told him about it. Then the commandant turned round to Father Kolbe and asked him: 'What do you want?' Father Kolbe answered that he wanted to die in lieu of the man who was despairing because he would be leaving a wife and children. The commandant asked him what he was. Father Kolbe said he was a priest. Then the commandant told him to join those selected to die. Father Maximilian quickly walked across, and the other prisoner returned to the ranks.

Everything happened very quickly in that camp yard. My stepping out of the rank was an instinctive reaction to a cry of despair, just the way a mother reacts instinctively when she hears her child cry. I did not consider any arguments for or against. I was aware, however, that if my offer was accepted, death was certain. I knew well what retaliatory measures were enforced in the camp following attempted escapes. All of us, I am sure, standing in the ranks all those long hours, kept thinking about the protracted agony of those who would be selected to die. The wild cries of those condemned always gave the shivers to those who were passing near Cell Block 11.

I know that later on, when my case was being examined by those who chose to beatify my name, my voluntary offer to die a certain death was discussed at some length. It was feared that it might have been a form of suicide. After all, in the early Church it was forbidden to volunteer, spontaneously, to die for Christ, for the reason that someone might break under the pressure of the suffering. But that did not even occur to me at the time. I just wanted to help that man, whom I had not met before. I did not think about myself. If anything, I just wondered whether they would listen to me at all, because we simply had no rights, not even the right to use our own names. I was a mere No. 16770, as tattooed on my arm.

Throughout my time in the camp I tried to serve, the best I could and as much as the conditions there permitted. I could not openly administer sacraments, but I noticed how great was the hunger for the Word of God, for what would keep up people's spirits, comfort them, prevent them from doubting whether Providence could exist at all if it permitted horrors such as those of Auschwitz. That hunger was even greater than hunger for ordinary bread; I shared my rations with others discreetly, in some cases sliding them into their pockets so that they would not feel embarrassed. What people lacked most dramatically was the hope that good would prevail. If people chose suicide, they did not so much reject life as fail to see the possibility of continuing to live. The conditions created by human pride, cynicism, elaborate brutality would prove stronger than inmates' psychological powers of resistance, so weakening their ability to survive. That is why during our secret meetings and improvised services I kept saying that the horror around us was not permanent, that it could not last because it was created by people acting against the will of God. I tried to awaken in my fellow-prisoners trust in the unshakeable permanence of Good, in the brotherhood of all people; I tried to show to them that we are created to love one another and to do good to one another. I encouraged them to forgive just as Jesus forgave when he said of his persecutors 'Father, forgive them' and not 'Father, punish them'. I explained that we give evidence of Christian love not so much when we love those who do good to us as when we patiently bear difficulties and sufferings, when we repay evil with good. I believed that was true love and the spirit of all Christianity, one which cannot be broken by the actions of hatred. Suicide, as an escape from evil or as a conscious decision to leave the human community which longs for direct examples, would be a refusal to serve — 'love of self that would be contempt of God'. But, as all who were there testified later, nothing did so much to rebuild in them their sense of humanity as that very act which affirmed the dignity of man and the sanctity of life itself. God himself wanted that in that centre of degradation, cruelty and extermination a moral victory over death could be achieved, that man could become, in a way, the master of his own destiny.

This kind of witness was needed in our camp of Auschwitz-Birkenau, but also in other concentration camps, which were designed not only to exploit cheap labour as efficiently as possible, but also to kill off the people who were no longer able to work. As a result, the conditions of living in the camp — the accommodation, the desperately small food rations, and the psychological terror — made it very difficult to survive there beyond a few months. To be sent to Auschwitz, where *Arbeit macht frei*, meant being sentenced to a certain death. It was similar to the ancient practice of *damnatio ad metalla*, whereby early Christians were sent to work in mines; the Roman emperors who sentenced them to labour in such conditions were convinced that the prisoners would soon die. Then the Church considered all Christians sentenced, because of their faith, to hard labour in mines or to long-term imprisonment, to be martyrs. It was said that they died *ex aerumnis carceris*. Similarly, the death of millions in modern labour camps can be seen as death suffered 'from the sufferings of imprisonment'.

The persecution in the camps was perpetrated not merely by the individual functionaries, but by the entire system of power based on the ideology of National Socialism. That system operated not only as a mechanism of political oppression; it was based, first of all, on the hatred of faith. The Nazi system never officially declared itself at war with the Church and religion, but the whole ideology and structure of power in Nazi Germany were essentially anti-religious. The philosophy of the system was based on the concept of racial purity, on the instrumentalization of the institution of the Church, on enmity towards church hierarchy, on total subordination of religion and of all social and educational institutions to the authority of the state. The Nazis attempted to disguise the actual motives of the persecutions: they talked of political reasons, of ideology, of the legitimacy of their power, of economic, social and cultural factors. It is for that reason that blame for Nazi atrocities can often hardly be ascribed to individuals; the whole system was responsible, from its doctrinal principles to the views of the officials who actually ran it.

Hatred of the Church and of religion was characteristic, too, of the functionaries of the camp. Not only I myself, but also many other clergy prisoners were treated particularly badly exactly because we were men of the cloth. This hatred manifested itself especially strongly in Karl

Fritzsch — the terror of the whole camp. On occasions, when a new transport of prisoners arrived at Auschwitz, he would pick out priests and put them in the charge of functionaries noted for their exceptional cruelty. Priests caught at prayer would be given a lashing, and the penalty for celebrating Mass was death. It is not surprising then that Fritzsch agreed to free Franciszek Gajowniczek and put me among those condemned to death when he heard that I was a Catholic priest. The whole system of power in the camp was based on people like him. Both the ordinary guards and the functionaries of the camp were chosen carefully — they served first of all because they wanted to kill and because of their hatred of religion.

It was not the first time I had come across people like those. Before I got to Auschwitz, I had spent three months at the Pawiak — the central Gestapo prison in Warsaw. One day a prison officer, with the rank of *Scharführer*, entered my cell. The sight of my habit infuriated him. He clutched at the cross of my Franciscan rosary and asked me if I believed in it; when I said I did, he gave me a slap on the face. Then he shook me a few times and repeated the question. He became more and more violent, hit me again and again, and then finally left the cell, slamming the door behind him. I tried to compose myself and not to show how nervous I felt, but when he left I began to walk up and down the cell and pray. Those poor people wanted to evoke hatred in us; they were afraid of the spirit of forgiveness. They expected slavish submission and they wanted those whom they persecuted to surrender all their rights, even the right to have their own identity. When they failed to obtain this, they tried to drive their victims to hatred. That is why 'do not hate, love' was the most frequent advice I gave when fellow-inmates asked me, in those hellish circumstances, to hear their confessions.

My canonization was unprecedented in the history of the Church, because I was the first person ever to have the legal categorization of the nature of his service to God changed: having been beatified as 'confessor' by Paul VI in 1970, I was canonized as 'martyr' by John Paul II in 1981. On the latter occasion, the whole procedure was based on the fact of my death, and not on the 'heroism of virtues'. It had to be proved that the true reason why I was sentenced to death was my faith, because 'they are not martyrs who die for any truth, only those who die for the truth of God' (St Thomas Aquinas). It was also when my case was heard that for the first time the notion of a 'corporate persecutor', governed by hatred of the faith, had been introduced. Since then, by way of analogy, this procedure has become a paradigm for considering other cases of martyrdom. However, the notion of persecutor as such

1. The Grand Duchess Elizabeth

2. Model for the statue of Manche Masemola

3. A village in rural Transvaal

4. The grave of Manche Masemola

5. Model for the statue of Maximilian Kolbe

6. Maximilian Kolbe

7. Sketch of
Lucian Tapiedi
by John Ewington

8. Memorial at the site of the martyrdom of Lucian Tapiedi

9. A crowd giving the Nazi salute

10. Dietrich Bonhoeffer, 1939

has not changed; all that has changed is the circumstances of place and time. Every epoch has its own specific kinds of martyrdom, because there are various kinds of tyranny, various scenarios of persecution, and, finally, various forms of the manifestation of love among martyrs. *Odium fidei* does not have to be understood literally, in the sense that it should have been declared by the persecutor directly. It is sufficient that it should transpire even from seemingly marginal aspects of the life of the persecutor and from the attitudes he demonstrates through his actions. The attitudes of the perpetrators of the crimes of Nazism were not motivated only by the hatred of humanity as such (*odium humanum*). After all, the truth of the faith is 'I believe in God, the Father almighty, creator of heaven and earth'. Therefore, an attack on human life is essentially a negation of the relationship between man and his Creator. To act against a person because he is 'sub-human' — something that is symbolized by Auschwitz — is not only to be inhuman, but to be anti-religious and anti-Christian. All those who plan such actions, organize them, and carry them out, participate in a way in *odium fidei*.

So far only five people[1] among all the victims of Nazism have been beatified as martyrs because they died as a result of hatred against priests and the priesthood, against the educational system of the Church, or against its pastoral mission. But there were hundreds of them. Among them there are also clergy and religious of other denominations, such as Archimandrite George Peradze, who helped Jews and the Polish underground, who died in 1942, or Mother Maria Skobtsova, who gave her life for one of her fellow-inmates in the women's camp of Ravensbrück in 1945. There was the Polish Jew Janusz Korczak, who was gassed in 1942 alongside the children he had under his care in the orphanage he ran because he wanted to protect them from fear and to be with them to the last. And is there no analogy between National Socialism in Germany and some Communist systems, particularly in Spain and Mexico, as well as in Eastern Europe? Does the description of 'persecutor acting out of hatred of the faith' not apply to terrorist groups such as Sendero Luminoso in Peru, responsible for the murder of two of my Franciscan confrères Zbyszek and Michał, and their Italian colleague Alessandro in 1992? It is indeed only from the heights of heaven that one can see the harvest of the Lord. Camps, prisons and other places where atrocities against humankind have been perpetrated, have been and will be places of great purification, from which the only way is to the feast of God's love. For love always pre-empts the wishes of the beloved.

* * *

When the door of the bunker was slammed and the echo of the derisive 'valediction' from one of the guards — 'you will come out like dried-up tulip bulbs' — died out, I could focus my thoughts on what had happened. My entire life appeared in my mind's eye.

I thought about my mother, who had lived for almost thirty years as a Tertiary and resident at the convent of the Felician nuns in Cracow. I owed a lot to her. It was only then that I had the time to realize how important in one's life is the influence of the family home. We inherit, after all, not only what comes biologically, but also ideas and values. As a superior, I had often been blamed for being too lenient on my younger brethren; the atmosphere in the community was too soft — too much benevolence, too little discipline that would strengthen the spirit. But I could not understand how the proverbial stick could be applied to human beings, capable of thinking and feeling. You can train people externally, as they do in the army, but what sort of life is that? Everybody has their own way, their own history of grace: different circumstances of birth and education, different talents, different state of health. 'One needs more' — I said — 'one needs love.' Yes, I did see the mistakes, but I also waited patiently. I tried sometimes to put in a discreet word or two, and only very rarely, when things were really taking a wrong turn, would I act more decisively. I believed in the power of free will, I loved them all and I cared mainly for the life in God that was growing in them, so that they desired sanctity, so that they trusted not so much themselves as the power of humble prayer. That is exactly what it had been like back at home: there had been winds and frosts, but most of the time it had been sunny and warm.

We first lived in the town of Zduńska Wola, where I was born on 8 January 1894 and baptized by the name of Rajmund. By trade my parents were both weavers, but it was mainly my father who worked to maintain the family; my mother looked after us children and after the household. But we soon had to move. There was a recession in the textile industry, and then the growth of the great industries gradually destroyed or took over the businesses of small independent workers. Thousands of them packed up their looms and sought employment in factories. My parents did likewise. They took a flat in the city of Łódź, called at the time 'the Manchester of the East', but that new environment did not agree with their feeling of independence, nor with the kind of work to which they had been accustomed — independent work in their own workshops. Also, the atmosphere of the city threatened the traditional values they cherished most: those of religion and morality. That is why I was brought up in Pabianice, a much smaller town near Łódź, but also an important industrial centre, and very mixed in ethnic and religious terms as well. Most of the people were Poles and Catholics, but there were also many Jews (20 per cent) and Germans, most of them Protestants (12 per cent). The smallest group were Russians, most of whom were Orthodox. I had four brothers, but two of them died young.

To earn a living, my parents opened a corner shop. But, as it turned out, they did not make very successful merchants. They often sold goods on credit, in the hope that the money would eventually be paid back; they were, however, too trusting and the shop eventually went bust. Closing it was a major trauma for all of us, but even that did not ruin the harmony of our family life or destroy in us the trust we had in people's goodness. My parents had so much energy, so much resilience, and such a strong faith in Providence, that they managed to cope with everything. They were even able to help those poorer than themselves and to give some of their earnings to charity.

But what I took from my family home first of all, for which I was now most thankful, was a living faith and a spirit of patriotism. My parents used to be much more devout than is common among Catholics. They attended Mass almost every morning, at 5 o'clock. At home, we would all pray in front of a small altar we had, with a picture of Our Lady of Częstochowa in it. We were often joined in those prayers by neighbours and friends, who were encouraged to do so by the friendly atmosphere of our home. We would organize more formal devotions too, at which my father sometimes played the violin. In this way, my parents' religious practices reflected the traditional Polish devotion to Our Lady – which they had acquired from their parents and grandparents before them.

At home there was always a great interest in Polish history and an ardent wish to see the country liberated from foreign rule. My father used to distribute an underground newspaper. Once he was even arrested for a few days. Soon after the First World War broke out he joined a Polish Legion. Then, when his unit was surrounded and taken captive by the Russians, he, as its commander, was summarily executed. We all wanted to fight for the freedom of the country and this kind of service – to God, to the country, and to other people – became for us a common moral duty. It took not only the form of armed struggle, but also that of an 'organic effort', broadly uniting people from all walks of life. Therefore, it was a matter not only of my youthful imagination and temperament, but also of that whole heritage of patriotism and of the desire to serve, that, when I was still in the minor seminary, I made a promise to the second Mother of mine, the heavenly one, that 'I would fight for her'. I did not at that stage know how, but I imagined I would use some kind of material, physical weapon ... I wanted to be a knight and to have my Lady.

Now I reflect. A knight fights on various battlefields, and finally finds the one on which he dies. I never thought mine would be so small – a concrete cellar of nine square metres, with very little daylight and in which there is nothing but a pail for faeces. We are all completely naked. Some of us curse out of sheer despair, but they know I am a priest. I have encouraged them to pray together with me – that is the only thing that is left to us. I cannot give them the Bread I had myself desired for so long, but I can put them all at one with God through confession. We have sung hymns, those we all knew from the liturgy of the Church; there were moments when we felt as if we were in a chapel. This must have been shared by prisoners from the other cells, because they would sometimes join in with us and their moanings would then subside.

I speak to them a lot about God, in words as simple as I can find. Well, I always try to speak and write very directly, without using elaborate language. I had completed two doctorates in Rome, but I am not a true scholar engaged in critical, systematic, methodical research. In my youth I was very eager to learn and I did indeed learn easily, particularly maths and the natural sciences. I remember that other boys at school would laugh at me when, not trusting our science teacher, I would myself try to work out all the calculations to confirm that a *perpetuum mobile* could indeed never be built. I would send designs of 'inventions' of mine to patent offices; I even produced a design of a rocket-propelled 'etherplane'. But all this God was later to use to a completely different end. I prayed a lot. I did not want to disturb the balance between getting to know the reality through the power of the mind and achieving a deeper and deeper understanding of the spiritual world through love. I was afraid of knowledge that would not be useful. I knew that nature never lets you go: your senses and your mind are always hungry for new experiences and can never be fully satisfied. Short, momentary pleasures become bitter, and knowledge ever so often leads to pride and self-love – which offers neither progress nor inner peace. Those come exactly from victory over nature. I wanted to overcome my own limitations and find access to the infinite Reason. I had my own method, which consisted in the belief that 'he who acts according to the will of God is indeed a superman, a supernatural being who rises infinitely higher than all geniuses and acts with infinite goodness and power. It is something that involves a share in the divinity of Jesus.' That is why I said 'Only that knowledge is valuable that grows from love'. In any case, when it comes to my theology, particularly Marian theology, I was not too interested in learned disputes or in achievements of biblical exegesis; I cared even less for all kinds of fashionable theological speculation. And perhaps it was all for the good, because I appreciated clear thinking, full of images and examples. I never lost touch with the working-class world in which I grew up. Later, too, most of my brothers 'given to me by the Lord' came from ordinary working-class families. In our work we appealed to ordinary people, whom we addressed in a manner appropriate for their needs, for their intellectual level, and for the type of religious experience typical of the common man and woman in the street.

My formal apostolic service began in the Eternal City, where I went, aged 18, to study philosophy and theology. I was first at the Gregorian University and then at our Franciscan *Seraficum*. On 16 October 1917, together with six other students, I founded an apostolic society called *Militia Immaculatae*. Its programme was very simple: to work for the conversion and sanctification of sinners through all possible means and through full submission to Mary Immaculate. The whole idea was born in prayer, spontaneously, but it was a response to specific events that were then taking place in public life. Around that time, a conflict had developed between the Holy See and the Italian government. The growth of anticlericalism and the corruption of moral standards were all attributed, in the ecclesiastical circles of Rome, to the influence of Freemasons. The Rector of our College, Fr Stefano Ignudi, who held an important office in the Roman Curia, maintained that 'Freemasonry is the tragedy of the country and it draws people away from God'. I fully trusted him, so I did not try to verify those views. Nor indeed did I find them surprising, particularly given that I had myself witnessed the events that took place in the streets of the capital on the occasion of the 200th anniversary of the founding of the Grand Lodge of England. On the day commemorating the death of Giordano Bruno a huge Masonic demonstration was organized. The participants may have voiced some progressive socio-political views, but they were also outspokenly anticlerical and the course of the demonstration was far from peaceful. I mentioned it some years afterwards in one of my articles:

> During the demonstration they went so far as to carry around a black
> banner with an image of Archangel Michael under the feet of Lucifer and
> to hang out Masonic signs opposite the windows of the Vatican. They did
> not even hesitate to write 'Satan will rule in the Vatican, and the Pope will

serve him as a Swiss guard'. Some souls had moved so far away from God
as to get into a state so deplorable as that.

All those souls I wanted to take back to God again.

We started with the simplest, spiritual methods of apostolic work. I
had always taken very seriously messages received in private appari-
tions. I was most impressed by the story of the conversion to
Catholicism of the Jewish lawyer, Alphonse Ratisbonne. Also, from that
time on I adopted as my favourite prayer words passed on through a
vision to the French nun Catherine Labouré in Paris, in 1830: 'O Mary,
conceived without sin, pray for us who have recourse to you', to which I
added 'and for all who do not have recourse to you, and especially the
Masons!' Furthermore, the order to have a small medal made after a
pattern, because 'all those who wear this medal will receive great graces',
encouraged me to give it to Jews, Buddhists, and pagans, 'on condition
that they agree to wear it'. This 'superstition' was symbolic of all our
further apostolic work: 'a maximum of instruction through a minimum
of words and symbols'.

But of the greatest importance for the theology of our society was the
answer heard by Bernadette Soubirous in Lourdes, when she asked the
Lady to give her her name: 'I am the Immaculate Conception' (1858). It
was around that mystery that I focused all my thoughts, plans and
actions. The ease with which I accepted as trustworthy instructions
coming from sources so subjective can certainly be accounted for in
terms of my particular intellectual character, but it resulted first of all
from a personal experience that I had in my childhood. One day, when
something I did angered my mother, and she said to me: 'Oh, what will
become of you?', I began to pray to Mary, asking her to tell me what
would indeed become of me. She appeared to me in the church, holding
in her hands two crowns: a white one and a red one. She asked me if I
wanted the crowns. The white one meant I would remain chaste, and
the red one that I would become a martyr. I answered that I did want
them. Except for my mother, I never told anybody about it, but since
then it never surprised me that people could have experienced
'visitations' by grace.

The time before I completed my studies and was ordained, in 1918, I
spent trying to develop both my knowledge and my spirituality. 'I have
to be as great a saint as I can become' was the first decision that opened
my Rule of Life; it was accompanied by the principle of 'first all of me for
myself, and then all of me for everyone'. I asked, through the
intercession of the *Immaculata*, that I could fulfil my *fiat* in the way
she had. She was my unattainable example, which is why I kept

contemplating her life and virtues, her ultimate openness to God and to his gifts. I understood that in herself she was nothing: a creature that had had a beginning in God's love and carried an image of him like every one of us. It was only out of consideration for his own dignity that God from the very beginning kept her free from sin. Not only was she immaculately conceived, but – as I tried to put it – 'she *is* the Immaculate Conception, just as something white differs from its whiteness, or something perfect from its perfection'. It was not in that, however, that I saw the greatest mystery of her life, but in her obedience. I admired the way she, in full consciousness and with all freedom of will, allowed God to lead her, accepted his will, desiring only what he wanted and acting by his will, never failing, never allowing her will to differ from his. It was in her that I saw clearly that 'will is the essence of love'.

I was criticized for my excessive devotion to Mary, I was called to moderation by 'defenders' of God's glory, but for all my concentration on her I could never fully imitate Jesus, who was obedient to her for thirty years in Nazareth, though he said himself, referring to his Father: 'I always do what pleases him' (John 8:29). She took, from the very beginning, an active part in his work of salvation, fully united with him, to the limits of suffering. Man fears suffering, but the will desires to suffer for love, to follow the path of the Cross, to atone, in part at least, for the love that has been rejected. I too wanted to burn at the altar of God's love, to do penance, to suffer illness, for love to leave love – but I felt God did not want that. Rather, he wants the soul to be healthy, to enjoy success, to sacrifice the idea of sacrifice and to submit to his will only. I could not live up to that in any other way but through the intercession of the Mother of Divine Grace. I addressed her because I considered her the real 'Mediatrix of all graces'. I prayed to her, and encouraged others to do likewise, that the truth on which the whole point of all our apostolic work was based might be declared a dogma of the faith. I had no doubt that it was only a matter of time, because a belief in the power of her intercession was commonly held among God's people. I explained everything by her inner, essential closeness to the Holy Spirit, whose Spouse she was. Their unity was so real that I did not hesitate to say that she was like 'the personification of the Holy Spirit', and he was like 'the *Immaculata* incarnate'.

It was because of her that I wanted to save the world from loss of the divine sources of development and progress. Since 'it is not against human enemies that we have to struggle ... but the ruling forces who are masters of the darkness of this world' (Ephesians 6:12), to whom

should I have sought recourse, if not to her? I was convinced that
understanding of historical events should be derived from an analysis of
the consequences of those events and of historical processes. What
created the confusion of my time was the ideologies that demonstrated
the weakness of man, his loss of freedom and direction – the
antireligious actions of Freemasonry, the anti-humanism of totalitarian-
ism, and the most radical trends of liberalism. That is why after I
returned to Poland and started lecturing at the Franciscan Seminary in
Cracow, I engaged very strongly in running the society founded to help
as many people as possible to serve, in all submission, her who 'all
heresies alone destroyed throughout the world'. I encouraged my
confrères and clerics to join the *Militia Immaculatae*, but not all of them
trusted my idea; some thought me a fantasist or a bore and called me
'the *Immaculata*'s fool'. But I was not distracted; I had the support of my
superior and of many lay people. Slowly, thanks to the 'endless
resources of Providence', we started publishing our own periodical: *The
Knight of the Immaculata*. I cared particularly for those who were not
Catholics, so in the manifesto I declared:

> The atmosphere of this magazine will be friendly to all, regardless of
> differences of faith and nationality. Its character will be shaped by the love
> which Christ taught. And it is out of that love for the souls which have
> gone astray, but which are nonetheless in search of happiness, that this
> magazine will condemn falsehoods, demonstrate the truth, and indicate
> the true path to happiness.

It is to this kind of universalism, based on the principle of personalism
which affirms man himself, that I tried to remain true to the end.

We developed our work quickly, though not without difficulties. Our
only capital was donations from our readers – more and more of them
as time went by. We found them not so much through the visual side of
the magazine, nor through the names of the writers, nor even through
the contents of the articles, which were often, admittedly, written at the
level of basic catechism; what attracted our readers was our
disinterested missionary zeal and the sense of direct contact we
maintained with our audience. The first issues I distributed myself – to
passers-by in the streets of Cracow. When, later on, we spent almost five
years (1922–27) organizing our own press in Grodno, we again wanted
to secure, in the first place, the support and trust of the local people.
Apart from editorial work, which often lasted until midnight, I founded
new branches of our society where possible. I encouraged those who
joined it to work together for the benefit of society, so that they could
discover, in the unity of common effort, the power of social love. As my

tactics I chose, alongside prayer, the love of one's neighbour. As I explained, 'It excludes nobody, it wishes everyone well, it extends a hand to everyone'. We did not focus on the evil sides of public life, and we avoided bad news — stories of fraud, theft, murder, rape — so as not to depress the weak and not to encourage them to commit evil.

Niepokalanów, the City of the *Immaculata*, was a priceless gift she gave us for this work. On 1 October 1927 we received from Prince Jan Drucki-Lubecki, rent-free, a permanent lease of a piece of land not far (some 26 miles) from Warsaw. Here we erected first a statue of Our Lady, and then a chapel and other buildings serving our community and publishing house. To retain the special character of the place, which was meant to challenge the modern model of affluent society and the tendency towards indifference to the needs of others, I published clear criteria according to which candidates wishing to enter our community were to be considered for admission:

> The decisive factor is neither education, theoretical (at secondary or university level) or practical (such as vocational qualifications), although both are desirable and useful, nor one's financial status and the amount of money brought to the community; the only thing that matters is the sacrifice of oneself, of one's will, so that all the strength, health, and life could be used for the work of winning all the world and every single soul for the *Immaculata* — beginning, of course, with oneself.

I tried to make sure that both my friars and our readers, as well as the authorities of the state, did not treat this place as an ordinary publishing house, let alone as a business venture aimed at generating financial profit. We wanted to serve everybody and to send issues of *The Knight* to all who wanted them, regardless of whether and how much they would be able to pay. To cover the costs we accepted small donations, and all the work on the magazine was performed within the community. We looked wherever we could to increase the efficiency of our work, we bought better and better equipment, we organized a system of professional training, and we tried to ensure that our community was as far as possible self-sufficient. In later years we even had our own fire-brigade and a small hospital.

I was in a hurry. I wanted to instil into Polish society, as fast and as deeply as possible, solid Catholic teaching and healthy moral attitudes. I dreamed of a Poland in which members of *Militia Immaculatae* were at the centre of things — but in a discreet, humble, non-aggressive manner. I wanted them to get, through their attitude of service, into the heart of all communities and all environments: from education, through learning and the arts, to business and industry, and perhaps even to government! I knew, after all, the Masonic practice of infiltrating various communities in order to gain influence in various countries. 'Having the press, we will have everything', they said openly. This is what prompted my call to study 'the first causes, the nerves that seem to give impetus to these tendencies and circumstances, pro and con, so as not – as often occurs in our good press – to fight only the "blind sword" instead of the "hand" that wields it … '.

That is why I wrote about the Truth that it was one, knowable and unchangeable. In this way I tried to oppose the notion of the 'multiplicity of truths', agnostic uncertainty and relativism. The difficulties we encountered in our work on account of these views of mine demonstrated that we were not too far from the truth. Aggressive criticisms and smear campaigns against us were mounted, and they intensified. Licences were withheld, purchases of paper and distribution of the magazine were restricted, even letters of thanks that arrived to us from our readers were ridiculed. In most cases I did not react at once, while whenever I dared to criticize Freemasonry, I would immediately be accused of every kind of obscurantism, dogmatism, and anti-semitism.

This was the most painful of charges. It is true that at the time the relationships between Polish and Jewish people were particularly strained. Both the authorities of the state and the Church perceived certain dangers in the attitudes of Jews. The Catholic press recommended to the faithful a programme of self-defence, avoiding contact with the Jewish world, boycotting services provided by Jews, guarding against the influence of the culture they created. *The Knight of the Immaculata* warned also against the negative impact of the popular press; it disseminated pornography, supported divorce, abortion, atheism, and attacked the Catholic Church directly. What was seen as particularly distasteful was conversions to Christianity not for religious reasons, but 'for the sake of the business'. I agreed with those who thought that this state of affairs was caused by the tragically bad economic condition of the country and its painful consequences, which is why I criticized some of my fellow-editors for certain inappropriate accents that found their way into articles published in *The Knight*. When I was in the Far East, I wrote to its editor that 'I would on the whole work for the development of Polish trade and industry rather more and criticize Jews rather less'. After all, our goal was to win them for the faith: 'One must approach others, but with great love and good will, and never growl in an angry or unfriendly manner.' We published *The Knight* in Hebrew and Yiddish, and we asked for critical opinions; we issued appeals and stimulated discussion. I have met a good many kind-hearted Jews; some of them I even visited in hospital, taught the Catechism, and lent books to. The only ones that irritated me were those who worked for the Freemasons — I could be rather sharp with them, and many a time I would lose my temper.

Later, during the Nazi occupation, our mission of love consisted not so much in spreading the Good News as in offering direct help. What mattered was an individual, and individual tragedy. Jews in hiding from the Gestapo were given birth certificates of people who had died, or blank but signed forms which were then filled in to produce identity documents. We had a wide network of contacts, and we knew people working for the local authorities in our area, as well as those who held office, such as the mayor. When in December 1939 several thousand people who had been forced to leave their homes in the west of Poland, 1,500 Jews among them, were brought over to Niepokalanów, many of them ill and all cold, tired and hungry, my brethren went begging for food around the neighbouring villages. Others pulled down some of the less needed sheds and fences for the fuel that was necessary to warm them.

At the time we did not have the theology that would stress the 'holy bond' between the Church and the Jewish people. In the atmosphere of prayer *pro perfidis Judaeis* no mention was made of the fact that Jews of the synagogue are naturally linked to the 'root' that supports the Church. We continued in the original state of suffering caused by the split between us, by the mutual alienation, even enmity; only a few of us saw in the other side brothers and children of one Father. Nor was I myself completely free from the faults of that 'familial sin': on many occasions I would argue *ad personam* and it was only sporadically that I would protest against actions and words that intensified the atmosphere of hatred. My *shalom* was only greater and greater love, which I learned exactly from Miriam/Mary, 'the great pride of Israel' (Judith 15:9).

The *Immaculata* called us to gather together God's scattered children. This truth caused me to go to the ends of the earth. Blessed by the General of the Order, but with no knowledge of the language, no money, and no letters of introduction, I set off, with four of my confrères, to Japan in 1930. I felt like Francis on his way to meet the Sultan. On the way I enquired about the possibility of establishing a new Niepokalanów in all big cities, but our destiny proved to be Nagasaki. The local bishop, who wanted to use my 'professorial' qualifications and to offer me a post in his seminary, gave us permission to publish a Japanese edition of *The Knight*. A month after our arrival, we published the first issue of *Seibo no Kishi*, winning a generous and sympathetic response from the local people. This we owed to our poverty and to our veneration of Mary. Then, when the Province approved our mission, we bought a piece of land at the foot of Mount Hikosan. It was difficult to manage and situated rather far from the city centre. For several centuries it had been used as a cemetery for untouchables. Nobody wanted to buy it and therefore it was very cheap. I believed that the *Immaculata* herself had chosen it for her *Mugenzai* (Garden), and I was not disappointed. Several years later, in 1945, when the city experienced its 'holocaust', our mission remained virtually untouched and it could begin its great work of charity straight away.

The life we lived there generated a lot of curiosity. We were visited not only by Catholics, Protestants and Buddhists, but first of all by unbelievers, both ordinary and educated, who volunteered to help us with the construction of our house and the publication of our monthly. In this way we carried out our ideal 'to radiate outside, to win souls for her so that also the hearts of our neighbours could open before her, so that she could become the Queen of all hearts, wherever they are in the world, regardless of the differences of race, nationality, language, and in the hearts of all who will live, to the end of the world'. I was becoming less and less militant in my efforts to encourage the Knighthood to fight against the enemies of the Church, and I was beginning to see its objective more and more often in terms of leading people towards the truth and to spiritual transformation of their lives. In conditions so different from those I had known in Poland, I stressed that her magazine 'taught people to listen to the voice of reason and to follow the path of virtue'. Mary brought me up in that way too, through widening my horizons and sending me out to meet all her children – and the more time I spent in her school, the more easily I began to discover that 'there is no love without sacrifice'.

I returned to Niepokalanów after six years, and found that it had risen from nothing, from the sheer desire to spread the gospel – and it had grown to become a real publishing empire. In all, we published nine periodicals, whose overall print run exceeded a million copies at a time – among them, most importantly, *The Knight of the Immaculata* (750,000) and *The Little Daily* (135,000). We also produced books and occasional publications. I was not against modern media: I dreamed that art, literature, theatre, cinema, writing, journalism, radio and television (at the time still at the experimental stage) would in the future serve divine purposes and the benefit of mankind. I thought that, as religious people who had taken the vow of poverty, we have the right to use all those modern media exactly for that purpose, and on condition that we do not keep anything for ourselves. 'In a patched habit, in patched shoes, in aircraft of the newest sort, as long as this is required for the sanctification of the greatest possible number of souls' I said to the lay people offering their donations. Our prices were the lowest in the country – indeed, many people received their copies free – and the conditions we lived in were truly difficult. We were over seven hundred in number, and always in debt, and yet nobody ever went hungry or without a place to sleep.

This religious community, the biggest of its kind in the world, may have been a publishing house, but first of all it was 'a modern workshop of the improvement of man'. 'The most important task to be performed in Niepokalanów is the sanctification of the brothers', I often repeated to myself and to them. I sometimes had to calm down their enthusiasm, just as much as mine was sometimes restrained by the Provincial when he sent me away for treatment for tuberculosis, or to have some rest in the mountain resort of Zakopane, 'so that the spirit of holy prayer and devotion would not be extinguished'. We were very particular about observing the rules of the constitution of the Order. The chapel constituted the heart of our city, but our duties extended beyond communal prayers, periods of silence, and days for reflection to include also recreation, fraternal conversations and caring for the sick – perhaps the most important aspect of our work. But the love of God increased in us first of all through obedience in faith. I was afraid of my own ideas. I had dozens of them, and my increasing practical experience multiplied them into hundreds. I prayed constantly for proper understanding of God's will, so that my own will could reflect his, so that my small 'w' could equal his capital 'W'. It was to him that I had made my vows.

About a fortnight or so after the war broke out, when the front was approaching Warsaw, our house was briefly left empty. Before I sent my brothers away, I told them they were going for a mission; they had to give witness, through their actions, that 'Niepokalanów was not just fences, buildings, or machines', but living people. Only a few dozen of us remained, but even so we were soon interned, and then moved from camp to camp. There we could share with others our peace of mind and awaken in them a faith in the victory of truth and goodness. For that reason, though requested to do so, I did not apply for release. That came on the very feast of the Immaculate Conception, on 8 December. We went back to our house, thanking her for the grace of 'dispersal' and of being able to preach love in all conditions and circumstances.

I felt that some final end of my earthly pilgrimage was approaching. Even a few days before the war broke out I had said to my confrères that, generally speaking, human life consisted of three stages: preparation for work, work itself, and suffering; in this way God draws us towards himself, in order to ultimately confirm us in love through suffering for love. I wished all of us then that we could, like true knights, shed our blood, to the very last drop, to bring forward the time when the world could be won for the *Immaculata*. Nothing else came to my mind at that time, and because I felt rather like the old St John the Divine, I repeated after him: 'Brethren, let us love one another' (1 John 4:7).

* * *

It is now the vigil of the feast of the Assumption of Our Lady, 14 August 1941. The guard will be coming in any minute now to give me an injection of phenol and thus to call, finally, 'Sister Death'. It is a sublime moment, so, for all the total exhaustion of my body, I am sitting upright, my back against the wall, and with my face serene, because lighted up by the expectation of that long-desired meeting. God has finally purified me through the fire of suffering, burning out even the most minute of my sins and falls, which have now become the fuel of love. I can say with him: '*Consummatum est*' – my sanctification and all that God has designed for me – 'is fulfilled' (John 19:30).

'The Rule and life of the friars minor is this: to observe the Holy Gospel of Our Lord Jesus Christ.' And the Lord, before a lance pierced his side, gave us, in the words of his testament, his mother. His beloved disciple, the Apostle John, fulfilled the last wish of his Master most faithfully: with love he took Mary into his most intimate self and became a man of faith in relation to Mary and to the Church, which she signified. That is why I want to be, in these last words of mine, *Alter Christus*, and – in order to remain true to my service as 'the Patron of this difficult century' – to leave behind me what has become the most profound inheritance I can offer:

> In a family, hope lies with the mother, and it is the same in the world of the spirit. Mary is a true Mother, and we are all her children, whom she wants to bring to the Heart of Jesus. Can a Mother leave her children, who, in suffering and tragedy, in pain and confusion, desire happiness and peace? Is it possible that she might not give special support to priests, whom she resembles so much that she has been called *Virgo-Sacerdos* and

whom she always comforts by her presence and encouragement to 'persevere to the last'? Mary Immaculate, Mother of Mercy, is our hope!

(Translated by Jan Jędrzejewski.)

Note

1   Titus Brandsma (1985), Teresa Benedicta of the Cross (1987), Michał Kozal (1987), Bernhard Lichtenberg and Karl Leisner (1996).

Bibliography

Bohdan Bejze (ed.), *Święty Maksymilian wśrod nas* (Łódź, 1994).
Diana Dewar, *Saint of Auschwitz: Maximilian Kolbe* (London, 1982).
L. Dyczewski, *Święty Maksymilian Maria Kolbe* (Warsaw, 1984).

Mission in a time of war:
Lucian Tapiedi of Papua New Guinea

ERROL HODGE

I N MAY 1945 the Bishop of New Guinea, Philip Strong, visited northern Papua. The Japanese forces that had occupied New Guinea three years before had been defeated and driven out. Now he offered a requiem mass for the victims of the occupation at the mission station of Sangara, in northern Papua. He proceeded to the graves of two Australian women, dedicated them, and then said the words of the burial office. After the service, as he disrobed, a small boy attached himself to the priest who was accompanying the bishop, Padre Arthur Bell. One word he repeated insistently; it was 'Lucian'. Bell later recounted:

> The little chappie was trying to convey something which to his mind was important, and then the name 'Lucian' came again. As in a sudden burst of inspiration it all came out, Lucian was buried here also ... Upon investigation, it was discovered that his body lay just outside the other graveyard, separated by a small railing and only a few feet away. (Bell, *Among the Ruins*, pp. 8–9)

Another service was held, and soon the railing was taken down, and extended to enclose all three graves.

Who was Lucian Tapiedi (pronounced TAH-pee-EDDy) Kaimogiei, to give him his full name? Some still remember him. Duncan Tiwekuri, a retired teacher aged 76, a cousin and close friend, who was with him at St Aidan's teacher training college, Dogura, where some of the future teachers and leaders of the church in Papua New Guinea were educated, recalls him as a short and powerfully built man, with a broad chest. He was bow-legged, but walked straight. His head was rounded, but his face long and pointed, and, unusual among Papuans, he had a pointed nose. His thick, fuzzy hair had the traditional 'mission cut', fairly close-cropped, and pointed towards the front. Canon Lancelot Sangetari, who as a young boy was a pupil at the school at Sangara where Lucian briefly taught, remembers him as a 'very good, strong sportsman'. He was a 'very humble, quiet friend', with a friendly, smiling face, one who would go with his students to their villages, to share their family life. To married men he was particularly helpful. But he was also a strong disciplinarian who sometimes rapped the knuckles of his pupils.[1] Elsie Manley, who worked as a secretary to Bishop Strong, speaks of memories in the mission that Lucian was 'a fairly outstanding young teacher'.[2]

Lucian Tapiedi was born the son of a sorcerer named Sidogei, of the village of Taupota, on the north coast of Papua, and his wife Wehuroai Joan, of Borovi village. Sorcerers were powerful men in traditional Papuan society, believed to have the power to effect vendettas, and even use their magic to carry out pay-back killings. When his father died, his mother took Lucian and his brother back to her own village of Borovi. It was then a local custom that on the death of a father the widow and orphans had to go empty-handed to the mother's village and remain there. She converted to Christianity and later, when a tropical ulcer on her leg threatened her health, she was admitted to a mission hospital. Here she dedicated her only two sons to the Church. She told the nursing sister and a missionary, Nita Inman, who was to become Lucian's first teacher, 'These two boys, Maclaren and Lucian, I am giving them to the mission as an offering to God, for what you have done for me, I leave my children in your care'.[3] The leg was amputated, but after many months in hospital at Samarai, she recovered.

Lucian Tapiedi began school in 1931, when he was almost ten. Free from the influence of his father, he was baptized in 1932 and confirmed a year later, together with his mother and his brother, Ono Maclaren. Tapiedi was taught by Nita Inman up to grade 4 at Taupota, and then by a priest, John Bodger, at Dogura for grades 5 and 6, which were not available at Taupota. When he showed his final certificate to Duncan Tiwekuri, his cousin held his hand very tightly and for a very long time in congratulation. Tapiedi then entered St Aidan's teacher training college in 1939. By training teachers for work beyond their home districts, the church hoped that St Aidan's would emancipate younger Papuans from narrow village loyalties. The first Bishop of New Guinea, Montagu Stone-Wigg (1898–1908), had declared that 'those who are called to be saints must be trained to become saints'. The education of Papuans was measured primarily in religious terms. It was the second bishop, Gerald Sharp (1910-21), who founded St Aidan's College. He chose as its patron saint the seventh-century missionary and teacher of Lindisfarne, off the coast of Northumbria, in England. St Aidan, it was said, had carefully educated a group of twelve English boys to be the future leaders of their people. Sharp had already chosen the name of the college when he announced that its students would 'devote their lives to the work of the Church'. Both of the first two teachers trained there were later ordained to the priesthood.[4]

The authorities of the church in Papua New Guinea recognized the dangers of their relationship with the political realities of Empire:

> Because the message of Christianity was proclaimed as available for all men, the racial problem associated with British colonialism could be resolved by raising up a native priesthood. Through it Papuans could share the prestige of the European to an extent unparalleled in any other profession. They could dispense the sacraments, wield discipline and mediate in disputes. They could hear confessions. They were, as Stone-Wigg reminded them from Sydney, princes of their people. They could, moreover, assist in the ordination of a white man to the priesthood, and several actually did so.[5]

However, there was a gulf fixed between the missionaries, who gave a Papuan priest the name 'Father', and the planters and townspeople, who gave him the name 'boy'.

Tiwekuri says Lucian was intelligent, enthusiastic, friendly, and quick to answer the questions of others and to help them or solve their problems. He was faithful and obedient, always the first to offer to do any work, enjoyable or arduous, when the teachers or prefects called for volunteers. Tiwekuri found him 'a very good adviser' when he broke the rules at St Aidan's College, or got into other kinds of trouble. He particularly enjoyed gardening, deep-sea and reef fishing, study, cricket and football. Some missionaries regarded sport as a morally elevating part of the missionary vocation, an acceptable substitute for the once-traditional Papuan pastime of fighting. But Lucian was also musical, and loved to play the organ.[6]

If Tapiedi was obedient, he was not compliant or lacking courage in the face of authority. Once when he was singing in the choir of St Aidan's College, the priest who was conducting from the organ lost his temper, threw the hymn book on the floor and left the chapel holding his head in his hands. Crying 'Oh terrible! Terrible!', he took to his bed. When the other choir members suggested leaving, Lucian dissuaded them, then went to the priest and said 'I'm sorry for the mistake we made. Would you please, Father, come and say sorry to the students, or you will miss them. What you are doing now is not good — a childish way, discouraging.' Then both of them returned to the chapel, where the priest apologized to the students. In Tiwekuri's memory, Tapiedi had done a brave thing; in the early days Papua New Guineans were not allowed to confront 'the big people like Father Jennings'.[7] After studying at St Aidan's for three years, Lucian was sent to Sangara on his first posting as a teacher and evangelist late in 1941. Working with Lilla Lashmar in the large school, he soon fitted happily into the life of the mission.

The Anglican missions of Papua New Guinea had existed for only half a century. Two priests, Albert Maclaren and Copland King, had landed there in 1891. But by then a version of the gospel had already been spread abroad at Taupota, Lucian's coastal home village, by a man called Abrieka Dipa. In, or near, the year 1883, Dipa had been recruited by a vessel collecting labourers for the sugar canefields of Queensland in Australia, and he had worked for several years near Townsville, north Queensland. When he returned to Papua he drew on what he had learned from a London Missionary Society (LMS) mission in Eastern New Guinea, and in Townsville, and 'initiated his hearers into some of the mysteries of the white man's religion'.[8] When Maclaren and King landed in Taupota they found that Dipa had prepared the people so well for the coming of a mission that they immediately sat down quietly on the sand expecting them to preach.

The religion of Tapiedi's ancestors, the Massim people, has been popularly referred to as animist. But the authority on Melanesian religion, G. W. Trompf, has argued that this is a mistake, as Papuan people did not believe all nature was endowed with a soul.[9] Virtually all Melanesian religions were 'deistic', dealing with gods of some kind. In this respect, he writes, traditional Melanesian religion provided fertile ground for a transition to Christianity. Differing classes and hierarchies of spirit-powers in Melanesia also presented 'a forest of complexity, with a special role for ancestors or the departed'.[10] Yet in 1891, Copland King found that he could never detect the slightest idea of a supreme being among the people he encountered. The anthropologist Octavius Stone had expressed a similar view a decade before, in 1880, writing that the Papuans were 'perfect infidels', believing in no god, but having 'a sort of belief' that after death their spirits would inhabit the space above the sea.[11]

In the spread of Christianity, Papua New Guinea was carved into a number of 'spheres of influence', with the commendable aim of minimizing competition between denominations. The Anglicans were allocated the north coast of Papua, the Methodists the islands to the east and a small part of the north-eastern tip of Papua, and the LMS the southern coastline, including the capital, Port Moresby. The Roman Catholic and Lutheran missions operated largely in what was once the mandated territory of New Guinea, including New Britain and New Ireland (before the First World War, German New Guinea). At the end of the nineteenth century, the Anglican Church supported its mission without enthusiasm. On the one hand, English bishops in Australia saw how badly the Australian Aborigines had fared at the hands of white settlers, and they feared that without a missionary presence the process might be repeated in New Guinea. But, at the same time, the Primate of Australia, Bishop Barry of Sydney, and Bishop Stanton of North Queensland tried privately to thrust responsibility for the mission onto each other throughout the 1880s. Other missionary societies seemed to hover in the background. A rumour that the evangelical Church Missionary Society was about to enter the field was quickly ended with a denial by representatives of that society in England. In New Guinea, Maclaren was told strictly to avoid trespassing on the domain of the Congregationalist London Missionary Society, which had also established a presence in New Guinea. Barry emphasized to him that if there were the slightest suggestion of Anglican interference with the work of the LMS, he would have nothing to do with the founding of a new Anglican mission. In 1896, the Governor of Papua threatened to write strongly to the Primate, remarking that if nothing more was done he would invite some other body in to bring the gospel to the area allocated to the Anglicans.[12]

Missionary attitudes to Melanesian culture in Papua ranged from views that held the people to be debased, or those that idealized them, and found them somewhat like Rousseau's noble savages. A Methodist missionary, W. E. Bromilow, said there was in Melanesian custom 'much deserving of admiration and encouragement'.[13] An Anglican priest wrote at Cape Vogel in 1904 'Every prospect pleases, and man is by no means vile'.[14] On the other hand, an LMS missionary, Charles Abel, wrote of the Papuans' 'unbridled passion' and 'animal propensity'. He put his beliefs into action by begging, borrowing or stealing as many babies as possible, and bringing them up away from their native villages.[15] A Methodist sister wrote 'These people are steeped in the blackest of sin'.[16] Missionaries set themselves the task of curbing lying, immorality, filthy conversation, cruelty to pigs and disobedience to parents. Warfare, murder and cannibalism were abhorred, and the burying of children alive with a dead mother was condemned as 'a horrible custom'.[17]

Mission reports of Tapiedi's own village were also contradictory. In 1905 the people of Taupota were described as 'simple and sincere' men and women who tried to fulfil their duties, and their village was portrayed as a place 'where nature is very beautiful, and everything breathes peace'. But in the same year, a government officer found the village 'in its usual dirty and ill-kept state'. The villagers, he complained, were 'a very lazy and immoral lot'.[18] Ten years later, another visiting officer wrote of Taupota as the dirtiest village he had seen on the coast. David Wetherell observes that since 1901 Taupota had been 'the scene of sturdy aloofness and on occasion mass apostasy from the mission'.[19] But a decade later, 300 people had become catechumens. Many of those baptized were old people who had remained indifferent to the claims of Christianity for up to 20 years.

New Guinea, the third largest island in the world, after Australia and Greenland, lies within eleven degrees of the equator, forming a barrier between two worlds. To the north and west are the animals and plants (and peoples) of Asia, and to the south and east are the animals and plants (and peoples) of Australia. There is little interpenetration. New Guinea has a spine of mountains nearly 1,800 kilometres long, at the eastern end soaring up to 4,700 metres. The island is drenched with flooding rains throughout the year, except in the scattered 'dry belts' of the east. Its soil is fertile, and even the mountain precipices sprout forest. In the lowlands, endemic diseases include malaria, typhus, leprosy, hookworm, yaws and skin diseases.

In 1942 this island became a scene of war. In December 1941 the air force of the Japanese government had attacked, and almost destroyed, the American navy at Pearl Harbor. In December troops invaded Malaya. The British army there retreated to Singapore and capitulated on 15 February 1942. The Americans were defeated in the Philippines on 9 April. By the end of that month the British had been driven from Burma. In 1942 Japanese forces thrust south and reached New Guinea. They decided to attack what is now the northern province, and try to cross the Owen Stanley ranges to the capital, Port Moresby. This strategy, in part the result of faulty intelligence, was a colossal military blunder. The great mountains are an almost impassable barrier between north and south. The Japanese believed that the Kokoda track that they found on their maps was a road, and they hoped to improve it to enable military vehicles to cross the Owen Stanleys. In reality, the route involved more than 150 kilometres of walking, or rather clambering and sliding up and down the muddy track. They landed on the coast at Gona and Buna, from where they intended to march to Kokoda, on the northern side of the range, then over the Kokoda track to the capital, Port Moresby.

At the onset of 1942 the question that presented itself to the missionaries of New Guinea was whether to escape to safety or remain. Few expected the Japanese to land in northern Papua. Bishop Strong had been bishop of the island for five years. Turning the matter over in his mind, he reached a moment of resolution, so striking that he found the experience of it religious. In January he broadcast to his staff:

> I have from the first felt that we must endeavour to carry on our work in all circumstances, no matter what the cost may be to us individually. God expects this of us. The church at home, which sent us out, will surely expect it of us. The Universal Church expects it. The tradition and history of missions requires it of us. Missionaries who have been faithful to the uttermost and are now at rest are surely expecting it of us. The people whom we serve expect it of us. We could never hold up our faces again, if, for our own safety, we all forsook Him and fled when the shadows of the Passion began to gather around Him in His Spiritual Body, the Church in Papua.
>
> No, my brothers and sisters, fellow workers in Christ, whatever others may do, we cannot leave. We shall not leave. We shall stand by our trust. We shall stand by our vocation.
>
> We do not know what it may mean to us. Many think us fools and mad. What does that matter? If we are fools, 'we are fools for Christ's sake'. I cannot foretell the future. I cannot guarantee that all will be well — that we shall all come through unscathed. One thing only I can guarantee is that if we do not forsake Christ here in Papua in His body, the Church, He will not forsake us.[20]

In January 1942 Rabaul in New Britain, to the north-west, fell to the Japanese. The parents of a nurse, Mavis Parkinson, who was 24 years old, sent Strong a radio message, saying they considered her return home imperative. The bishop immediately passed this message on to her and told her she must leave. Parkinson simply replied, by radio, 'Please let me stay'. Then she and May Hayman, a nurse who was engaged to be married to the British priest at the inland Sangara mission station, Vivian Redlich, set off on foot for Kokoda, to catch an aeroplane to Port Moresby. An officer of the Buna government accompanied them. With him he carried a radio set. According to one account, it was on this that they heard another message from Parkinson's parents to the bishop: 'Consent let Mavis decide. Thank you for your trouble.' Five days after leaving Gona, Hayman and Parkinson returned to the mission compound, 'with as much delightful self-possession as if they had been on a down-town shopping jaunt', as the Gona priest later remarked.[21] Later, Strong visited the mission at Gona and encouraged the two women to move to an inland station. They pleaded to be allowed to stay. When he said they did not know what might happen, they replied that they were in God's hands, and if he called them to suffer, they were ready to suffer. May Hayman asked what the sick people in the hospital would do if she went. Mavis Parkinson asked what the children would do if their teacher left. Strong exacted from them a promise that they would keep an emergency bag packed and at once escape to the inland stations if an invasion took place there.

On 21 July 1942, nothing appeared to stir the normal pattern of life at the Gona mission. Hayman put dinner in the oven and sat down with Parkinson to do some mending. But at about half past four that afternoon, Parkinson heard one of her pupil-teachers calling to her as he ran up from the beach. Less than two kilometres out to sea was a transport ship, escorted by two destroyers, with two other destroyers farther out. With the British priest of the station, James Benson, and a crowd of Papuans, the two women stood on the beach watching as the ships bombarded Buna, to the south-east, and as Australian planes attacked them. One of the women remarked 'Surely they won't come ashore here. They will go to Buna.' No sooner had she spoken than they saw boats being lowered from the transport vessel and hundreds of troops tumbling into them. Then the destroyers began to shell the mission itself. The three missionaries hurriedly packed a few necessities and fled into the bush.[22]

That night, alone in the jungle, they heard men moving along a road leading inland. They called out to them in English and Motu. It was only when they saw a torch flash and heard the clank of a bayonet that they realized they had been calling out to Japanese soldiers, marching unopposed towards Kokoda. Parkinson, who had pen and paper with her, wrote 'It gave us rather a horrible feeling having them so near, and we stood there expecting to see them come up our path every minute, and to get a bayonet or bullet in our ribs'.[23] For a fortnight they managed to steer clear of the Japanese forces. Parkinson began her last, uncompleted letter to her mother: 'Fr Benson, May and I are in a little hideout in the bush, and indeed, are doing what probably few white men have done before, living in the heart of the Papuan jungle.' She recounted their reception by a crowd of people from the village of Siai, some of them Christian:

> As long as I live I shall never forget the welcome they gave us. They
> hugged and patted us for ages, and actually cried over us – they thought
> maybe we were dead. They took us on to Siai station and there we had
> another demonstration, by the women this time. I was almost beginning
> to feel tearful myself. . . . The people decided the best thing to do would be

to build us a cottage in the bush, where we could be hidden until things cleared up a little – we could still hear the bombs falling on Gona.[24]

Benson decided that they should move on to avoid provoking trouble for the villagers if they were discovered hiding them. Now they had been joined by five Australian soldiers and five American airmen who had decided to try to cross the Owen Stanleys and reach Port Moresby. Soon Benson was separated from the others when they were attacked by a Japanese patrol, and after wandering lost in the jungle he gave himself up. The other twelve were then betrayed by a hostile Papuan; the bullets and bayonets of a Japanese patrol killed all of them except one of the Australian soldiers and the two women. The remaining three were handed over to the Japanese by the ringleader of the Papuan collaborators, a sorcerer named Embogi. He had resented the presence of missionaries, and one account suggests that his wife had been raped by an Australian soldier. Now he had been promised a position of authority by the new powers of the island.[25]

The soldier was taken to Buna, where he was beheaded. The two women were imprisoned for one night in a coffee hut at Popondetta. Their Japanese guards taunted them by proffering food and water, and then laughingly snatching it away as they reached out for it. Early in the morning, a Papuan approached the hut in an attempt to free them, but they made urgent signs to him to go away. He remembered later that they had been sitting on the floor of the hut, 'and it was very fearful: they were weeping'.[26] At about 8 o'clock, four Japanese soldiers passed his hiding place, two with rifles and two with shovels. They took the two women to a nearby plantation where there was a freshly dug grave. One of the soldiers tried to embrace Parkinson. When she fought him off, he plunged his bayonet into her side. Hayman screamed and covered her eyes with a cloth. Another soldier bayoneted her in the throat. The bodies of both were dropped into the grave.

Other mission workers were hiding in northern Papua. Henry Holland had been the first Anglican missionary in the region: he had arrived in Papua as a layman in 1910 to work with Copland King. In 1922, with the help of a Papuan teacher, he established the Sangara mission, learning the local language and translating the Scriptures and the services of the Church. Six years after arriving at Sangara, he established another mission station at Isivita, two hours' walk farther inland. Now he was priest-in-charge there. A ponderous, slow-spoken man from inland New South Wales, Holland was meticulous and thorough in everything that he did. He had supervised the construction of several roads and bridges in northern Papua. Some of his roads and bridges now facilitated the Japanese advance towards Kokoda. In 1942, Holland, too, had resolved not to leave his station. This resolution he broke because he realized that if the Japanese found him at Isivita the lives of his Papuan teachers and their families would be in danger as well as his own.

Holland had lately been joined at Isivita by John Duffill, a young lay missionary from Brisbane; Lucian Tapiedi; Margery Brenchley, a young nurse who ran the Sangara station; Lilla Lashmar, in whose school Tapiedi had recently begun to teach; and Vivian Redlich, from Sangara. Duffill had turned down an offer of leave earlier in the year. Brenchley and Lashmar had refused to be evacuated. Tapiedi had deterred other Papuans at Sangara from remaining at the mission if danger threatened: they had wives and children to care for, and they should withdraw into villages. For his part, he was determined to accompany the missionaries.[27] Redlich had seen the Japanese ships from his own boat at Buna and, rather than turning to safety and travelling across to Dogura, he had decided to go ashore and slip through the Japanese lines to Sangara. But invading forces reached the mission first. Redlich had then established a hideout in the jungle nearby, from which he wrote a letter to his father: 'I'm trying to stick whatever happens. If I don't come out of it just rest content that I've tried to do my job faithfully.' He also wrote to his bishop: 'Give me a thought sometimes but don't worry — I am prepared for whatever may happen.'[28] On the Sunday after the Japanese landing, he was told that a local man had gone to report him to the Japanese. He replied that it was the Lord's day, and he would celebrate mass for the people as planned. He completed the service before leaving for Isivita to join the other missionaries. On that same morning, Holland had been celebrating the sacrament in his church at Isivita, less than ten kilometres from the Japanese who were streaming along the road to Kokoda.

The six decided to try and cross the Owen Stanleys at a point far to the south-east of the Kokoda track, which had already become a battleground. On the first afternoon, they arrived at a village where local men announced to them that their day had passed, that the spirits of their ancestors had returned as Japanese soldiers, and that soon ships and aeroplanes would be bringing them valuable cargo. Holland replied dismissively and was knocked to the ground. They escaped from the village, and soon met another group of refugees: Louis Austen, a retired sea-captain who managed a government coffee plantation near Sangara, Tony Gors, his mixed-race assistant, Gors's six-year-old son, and a young mixed-race woman, Louise Artango, sometimes described as his wife. Some have suggested that Austen was disliked by the Papuans, possibly because of his treatment of some of their women.

There were now ten of them. They came to another village, inhabited by the Orokaiva people. The Orokaiva had been told the Japanese would punish them if they did not hand the Europeans over. A number of them offered to escort the group away from the village, and they set off together. Seeking to detach Tapiedi from the rest, they deliberately left Vivian Redlich's rucksack behind at a village near Jewaia Creek, where they had spent the previous night. When Redlich said he would retrieve it Tapiedi told him that they were in hostile company. Redlich they might kill; Tapiedi was himself a Papuan and, he judged, in less danger.[29]

But Lucian Tapiedi was of a different tribal group, and he spoke a different language from the Orokaiva. At the creek crossing, two of their escorts argued for and against killing him. One said that he was their friend, a mission teacher. The other, a man named Hivijapa, prevailed. He followed Tapiedi down to the stream near Kurumbo village and, with an axe, hacked him to death from behind. The two men then covered the body with a cairn of stones.

Accounts differ on the fate of the five missionaries, and the four fleeing with them. One man, Edric Wekina, later told Bishop Strong that Holland was not with the rest of the Sangara party, but was following them. He was pushed over a precipice on Mount Lamington by a village constable. The others in the party were handed over to the Japanese at Buna. Austen and Gors were shot, and the other six, including Brenchley, Lashmar, Redlich and Duffill, were beheaded on the grey sands of Buna beach. Transfixed with shock, the six-year-old boy was the last to die. 'I turned away, for the sight sickened me', a Japanese soldier wrote in his diary.[30] The bodies were apparently thrown into the sea, but in 1943 a box containing a head with long strands of dark hair, presumed to belong to one of the women missionaries, but perhaps that of Louise Artango, was found during excavations on Buna beach. Some Papuan informants believed the women were raped before being handed over to the Japanese, but an official enquiry found that this was not so.[31]

In June 1942, just two months before he was martyred, Lucian Tapiedi had written to Duncan Tiwekuri:

> My dear Cousin, I think this is the last letter I am writing to you. I am also sending to you my photo as your memory. The Japanese planes are flying over Higaturu and Sangara Stations every day. Look after yourself. Pray for me. If I'm lucky enough, you will see me again.[32]

The photograph was lost.

When he returned to the ruins of Holland's mission at Isivita, in 1943, Bishop Strong searched through some scraps of paper there to see if any of the missionary's translation work could be rescued. He found a letter written to Holland by his predecessor, Bishop Henry Newton, in 1934. Holland had wanted to spread his work of evangelism into a new area, but Newton had replied that the Australian Board of Missions had not increased its grant, and expenses would have to be cut. These were the years of economic depression. It was in this area that hostile Papuans had delivered him and the others into the hands of the Japanese eight years later.

Many Christians in Papua New Guinea lost their lives in the Second World War, by far the largest majority of them Roman Catholics and Methodists. *The Martyrs of Papua New Guinea*, an expansive work edited by Fr Theo Aerts in 1994, lists 333 martyrs, 198 of them Roman Catholics, 76 Methodists, 22 Salvationists, 16 Lutherans, 12 Anglicans, five members of the Evangelical Church of Manus, and four Seventh-day Adventists. Many died in the strafing and sinking of vessels and the strafing of survivors. Others died in prison, by sickness, old age or neglect. Aerts considers all of them to be martyrs, because they sacrificed or risked their lives in order to maintain the work of Christ in the face of the Japanese invasion.[33]

By a roadside at Ururu, near Popondetta, is now a shrine, with a concrete, open-air altar. A white, sheet-metal notice originally attached to an old tree, now gone, bears the words 'Under this tree Mavis Parkinson and May Hayman of Gona Mission Station glorified God by their death, August 1942'. The sorcerer Embogi, who turned the two missionaries and the Australian soldier over to the Japanese, was executed by the Australian authorities after the war. It was later that a Papuan police sergeant, Major Christian Arek, discovered the place of the martyrdom of May Hayman and Mavis Parkinson, exhumed their bodies and carried them to Sangara. They were buried side by side outside the church. In 1977, Arek, then living in retirement in Port Moresby, revealed that the bodies of the two women had been intact and largely, though not entirely, uncorrupted when he exhumed them from their shallow grave, even though the six months since their deaths had been the wet season. They were both fully clothed. At their new gravesite, two wooden crosses bearing their names were erected, and a small railing built around it. Several weeks afterwards, Arek exhumed the body of Lucian Tapiedi. He carried it to Sangara, where it was buried beside the other two martyrs, though outside the railing.

Father Benson survived three years as a prisoner of the Japanese and lived on. As an elderly man, Bishop Strong still ruminated on his decision to broadcast the radio message of January 1942. If, he reflected in 1977, he could have foreseen what was to follow, his decision might well have been different. But still he wrote:

> I have never had any doubt at all that my message was inspired by God and that the decision made was the right one, and the history of the Church in Papua New Guinea and its subsequent and present vitality is ample proof, for it would certainly not be as strong today or have had the devotion and wholehearted following of so many of the peoples of Papua New Guinea, if the missionaries in the hour of danger had left the people to whom they had been sent by God. What needs to be remembered however is that I was really only voicing what all at that time felt who were on my staff.[34]

The last letter of Vivian Redlich is now held at St Paul's Cathedral, in London.

The little cairn of stones that marks the place of Lucian Tapiedi's death, near Kurumbo, is still there. So too, on the other side of the stream, is a flat white stone, on which Tapiedi is said to have knelt in prayer before his death. His murderer, Hivijapa, escaped Australian investigations and retribution when the Japanese were driven back. Hivijapa was later converted to Christianity, in baptism taking the name Lucian. As a self-imposed act of penance, he built a church at Embi, not far from the site of the martyrdom, dedicated to St Lucian Tapiedi. Before his death a few years ago, Hivijapa Lucian served many years as a church councillor in St Lucian Tapiedi's church. On St Laurence's Day 1997, Bishop David Hand, former Archbishop of Papua New Guinea, preached in the Cathedral of the Resurrection at Popondetta. He proposed, with the approval of the Bishop of Popondota (the original Papuan name), that shrines be erected both at the place of Tapiedi's martyrdom and also in the cathedral. Fifty-five years after the death of Lucian Tapiedi, the Anglican Church of Papua New Guinea recognizes him almost as its patron saint. He, and other Melanesian martyrs, helped to break down the image of Christianity as a faith predominantly of white people and Europeans. Together, they laid the basis for greater indigenous involvement in church leadership. In death, too, Tapiedi has become a source of veneration among many tribal groups, and an inspiration for them to resolve conflicts which were, long before the coming of the missionaries, a source of hostility and violence between men.

Notes

1 Lancelot Sangetari, personal reminiscence, August 1997.
2 Letter to writer from Elsie Manley, 30 April 1997.
3 Account by Duncan Tiwekuri, 7 July 1997.
4 Wetherell, *Reluctant Mission*, p. 283.
5 Ibid., p. 302.
6 Account by Duncan Tiwekuri, 7 July 1997.
7 Ibid.
8 Wetherell, *Reluctant Mission*, p. 20.
9 Trompf, *Melanesian Religion*, p. 19.
10 Ibid., p. 14.
11 Wetherell, *Reluctant Mission*, p. 137.
12 Ibid., p. 134.
13 Ibid., p. 125.
14 Ibid., p. 127.
15 Ibid., pp. 123-7.
16 Ibid., p. 125.
17 Ibid., p. 130.
18 Ibid., p. 145.
19 Ibid., p. 197.
20 Tomkins and Hughes, *The Road from Gona*, pp. 27-8.
21 Benson, *Prisoner's Base and Home Again*, p. 16.
22 Ibid., p. 22.
23 Interview with the author, 1977, p. 10.
24 Ibid., p. 11.
25 Blanche Briggs, interview, 1 June 1977.
26 Ibid.
27 Account by Edric Wekina to Bishop David Hand, in a letter from the bishop to the author, July 1997.
28 Tomkins and Hughes, *The Road from Gona*, p. 146.
29 Account by a village man who helped to build St Lucian Tapiedi Church, Embi, in letter from Bishop David Hand to the author, July 1997.
30 Hodge, *The Seed of the Church*, p. 18.
31 Wetherell, *New Guinea Diaries*, p. 155.
32 Ibid.
33 Aerts, *Martyrs*, pp. 31-4.
34 Interview with Bishop Strong, 1977.

Bibliography

Theo Aerts (ed.), *The Martyrs of Papua New Guinea* (Port Moresby: University of Papua New Guinea Press, 1994).

Arthur Bell, *Among the Ruins: A New Guinea Epic* (Adelaide: Australian Board of Missions, 1943).

James Benson, *Prisoner's Base and Home Again: The Story of a Missionary P.O.W.* (London: Robert Hale Limited, 1957).

Errol Hodge, *The Seed of the Church: The Story of the Anglican Martyrs of Papua New Guinea* (Sydney: Australian Board of Missions, 1992).

E. C. Rowland, *Faithful Unto Death: The Story of the New Guinea Martyrs* (Sydney: Australian Board of Missions, 1964).

Dorothea Tomkins and Brian Hughes, *The Road from Gona* (Sydney: Angus & Robertson, 1969).

G. W. Trompf, *Melanesian Religion* (Cambridge: Cambridge University Press, 1991).

David Wetherell, *Reluctant Mission: The Anglican Church in Papua New Guinea, 1891-1941* (Brisbane: University of Queensland Press, 1977).

David Wetherell (ed.), *The New Guinea Diaries of Philip Strong 1936-1945* (South Melbourne: Macmillan, 1981).

Osmar White, *Green Armour* (Sydney: Angus & Robertson, 1945).

The writer would like to express his gratitude to Bishop (formerly Archbishop) Sir David Hand for his invaluable help in research for this chapter.

Totalitarianism and resistance in Germany: Dietrich Bonhoeffer

KLEMENS VON KLEMPERER

DIETRICH BONHOEFFER, German pastor and theologian, died for taking an active stand against Nazi tyranny. He was imprisoned in April 1943 and executed two years later, in the Flossenbürg concentration camp, for his work with the Resistance, one of the few German clergymen to suffer martyrdom for his faith. His posthumous writings, including the well-known *Letters and Papers from Prison*,[1] have influenced theological thought at all levels.

The word 'martyrdom' cannot be relegated to an 'antique lexicon'. As long as there is oppression there is also martyrdom, and in any lexicon covering the twentieth-century oppression, martyrdom must figure in capital letters. The ideologies that have swept across this century's stage – communism, fascism, National Socialism – and that have insisted upon rigid orthodoxies and their political implementation, have produced degrees and means of coercion, and indeed terror, unprecedented in a world that calls itself civilized. Symptoms of a spiritual and religious crisis in a secularized world – Dietrich Bonhoeffer called it the 'Western void'[2] – they were, each in its way, masquerading as light and social justice, offering the consolations and rewards of surrogate religions.

These were the circumstances in which Dietrich Bonhoeffer made his way as a pastor, theologian and finally as martyr. But let it be said here that, however extreme the challenge facing him from the militant ideology of German National Socialism, his response was also extreme. Bonhoeffer was no easy martyr, even for his friends; martyrs rarely are easy. His particular theology, which brought him to the point of a 'religionless' interpretation of Christianity, in itself constituted a challenge not only to his church but to all traditional understanding of the Christian faith. His friend and biographer Eberhard Bethge as much as conceded that he moved on 'the brink of heresy'.[3]

Moreover Bonhoeffer had come to the perception that 'there are no actions which are bad in themselves' and that 'even murder can be justified'.[4] Eventually he certainly acted on this premise. For a believing Christian, and a clergyman and theologian to boot, to take this position was a deeply perturbing proposition, to say the least. Until very recently the German Protestant Churches have found it hard to acknowledge that the saintliest of their martyrs suffered for his faith, preferring to identify his sacrifice with his political convictions. But this is a distinction that Bonhoeffer himself would have been loath to accept.

There was nothing particularly striking, not to say eccentric, about Bonhoeffer's personality. Fundamentally conservative in temperament, he was neither a rebel nor a zealot. He took his due place in the line of the Bonhoeffer generations and among his brothers and sisters. He was born on 4 February 1906 in Breslau. A robust fellow, he enjoyed going on hikes with family and friends. As a boy, he participated readily in the usual family games; he especially loved ball games. When playing tennis, he did so aggressively, and though invariably a good sport, he played to win. In the winter he took part in snowball fights.

'There must be certitudes in life', says one of the characters in the drama fragment he wrote in gaol in 1943. His extended patrician family gave him that sense of certitudes; it lent him a self-assurance and firmness of purpose that came to stand him in good stead later in particular, when his radical theological speculations, and his decision to go into active resistance against a murderous regime, led him down precipitous paths.

Bonhoeffer's decision to enter the ministry and become a theologian was not really a matter of 'conversion'. Quietly, undemonstratively, at the age of 13, he made up his mind to follow a calling which would guide him throughout his life. Naturally, the fact that forebears on both his father's and mother's sides had included theologians and preachers[5] may have facilitated his finding his vocation. To be sure, the Bonhoeffers, like many families of the upper bourgeoisie, had loosened their ties to the Church, and, except for mandatory attendance at confirmation classes, no one of them went or was sent to Sunday church services. Their mother, Paula von Hase Bonhoeffer, did take it upon herself to give the children some religious education: she saw to it that evening prayers were said, followed by the singing of hymns, and that the rituals of the Christian holidays were cheerfully observed. But all this took place within the household, and no need was felt for ecclesiastical guidance. Their father, Karl Bonhoeffer, after 1912 Professor of Psychiatry and Neurology at the University of Berlin and also Director of Psychiatry at the Charité hospital, was an agnostic, and merely lent a certain authority to the family observances. When Dietrich made his decision, then, it was met in the family with some scepticism. The father thought that his highly gifted son was 'too good' for a silent, remote pastor's existence, and when his siblings tried to confront Dietrich with the fact that he was about to devote his life to a defunct and boring 'bourgeois' institution, his response, at the time perhaps made in jest, was 'In that case, I shall reform it!'[6]

The tradition in Bonhoeffer's home was Lutheran, and his life as preacher and theologian revolved around the Lutheran faith. He began with Luther; he explored alternative channels of religious experience; he rediscovered Luther, albeit a Luther radically rethought and transformed.

From beginning to end Dietrich Bonhoeffer's religious life was a matter of steadfast witnessing, and of defining, redefining and confirming the premises of his faith in the face of extraordinarily difficult conditions. To begin with there was the problem of the reception of Luther's message on his own turf, in Germany, in the course of time. Siegfried Kracauer's observation that the history of ideas is often a story of the misunderstanding of ideas is astute, and certainly applicable to the reception of Luther in the nineteenth century, especially in Germany. Hajo Holborn has stated flatly that 'Luther's religion has been much misunderstood in modern times'.[7] He was referring to the so-called 'liberal theology' which sought to harmonize the modern forms of Christianity, above all the teachings of Martin Luther, with the historical process towards man's self-fulfilment. Such a theology reinterpreted Luther's Reformation as a religious parallel to the Renaissance, and as an agent of individualism and secularism. In fact, it had seemed 'preposterous and sacrilegious' to Luther to construct God in the image of man; as much as any Reformer, Luther insisted on the 'otherness' of God.

The University of Berlin, where Dietrich Bonhoeffer pursued his studies towards the doctorate in theology, was a fortress of liberal theology. His teachers, above all Adolf von Harnack, Karl Holl and his *'Doktorvater'* Reinhold Seeberg, were men of great distinction and reputation; but somehow their liberal understanding of theology, their correlation of the gospel with the modern spirit, left the novice theologian dissatisfied. He would reject such an approach. Bonhoeffer was anything but an establishmentarian clergyman; in fact the establishment, as he encountered it, left him deeply unpersuaded.

The nineteenth-century German reception of Luther was twofold.

First of all, the Germans adhered firmly to the thesis of the two realms (*Zwei-Reiche-Lehre*), which, while recognizing the kingdom of Christ as the realm of spiritual freedom, nevertheless assigned inordinate powers to the 'kingdom of the world'. The worldly state, while not part of the divine order, is appointed by God to maintain order in a world that is essentially imperfect and indeed sinful, and thus to secure space in which salvation can occur. The state, then, is the authoritarian state (*Obrigkeitsstaat*) and it is to be obeyed.

At the same time Germany had a way of making a national hero of Luther, the God-sent herald of German cultural and political unity.[8] This emphasis, it might be argued, constituted a particular German version of 'liberal theology' which relied on the interrelatedness of human progress and religious understanding. In this light Luther's religious understanding was made to appear as having been in tune with the national effort. No wonder, then, that since the events in the 1920s, 1930s and 1940s historians outside Germany have stressed the 'from Luther to Hitler' formula,[9] suggesting all too readily and wrongheadedly a connection between Luther and the extremist version of twentieth-century German nationalism. But without doubt acceptance of the *Obrigkeitsstaat* was consistent with the Germans' tendency towards political passivity and their disposition to submit unquestioningly to authority. The cult of Luther as national hero, however ill-founded, unfortunately fed into the cult of the twentieth-century *Führer*.

No one was so keenly aware as Dietrich Bonhoeffer of what has been called the 'incrustation' (*Verkrustung*) of Lutheranism during the past centuries, the habit of identifying Luther's position with the Christian believer's unquestioning obedience to worldly authority. The term goes back to Bishop Hermann Kunst who in a study of Luther's relations to the Counts of Mansfeld and the Electors of Saxony argued that the German Reformer, notwithstanding his basic commitment to 'suffering obedience', had come round to condoning 'suffering disobedience' in the face of princely injustice.[10] 'One wonders', Bonhoeffer wrote to his parents from Tegel gaol on Reformation Day, 31 October 1943, 'why Luther's action had to be followed by consequences that were the exact opposite from what he intended.'[11] Elsewhere, he argued accordingly that the 'outcome of the Reformation' was not in tune with its basic intention and that the 'followers of Luther' left out the essential ingredient of 'discipleship'.[12] The Germans' proverbial lack of 'civil courage' was, he maintained, due not to Luther, but to their having ignored the prescription of 'free and responsible action'.[13] The validity of this argument has since then been confirmed by Kunst's interpretation of Luther's stand, allowing for 'suffering disobedience'. Kunst was altogether in line with Bonhoeffer in his wistful conjecture that, had evangelical Christendom borne witness to Luther's message and acted accordingly as a body, it would have prevented much of what happened in German history.[14]

In view of the German misunderstandings, as they seemed to him, of Luther, it is no wonder that Dietrich Bonhoeffer was casting about for spiritual inspiration elsewhere. When he visited Rome at the age of 18, just before taking up his studies in Berlin, he was awed by the majesty of the Catholic Church and is said to have confessed to a close associate of his that while in one of Rome's churches he was sorely tempted to be converted.[15] But that is where the matter rested. More importantly, the visit confirmed his opinion that German Protestantism should never have become as closely tied to the state as in fact it had and that only once it loosened these ties could it be in a position to confront the truth.[16]

During his stay at Union Theological Seminary in New York City in 1930-31, Bonhoeffer's search for an authentic service to God took him regularly to the Abyssinian Baptist Church of Adam Clayton Powell, Sr,[17] where he hoped to find in Black Christianity a renewed expression of the Christian faith. He detected there the 'great religious power and originality'[18] that he found wanting in the Lutheran Church at home.

It was in New York City too that Bonhoeffer was first exposed to ecumenism. Back at home, 'international' activities were still frowned upon in Protestant circles. The perceived injustices stemming from the terms of the Treaty of Versailles would forbid any traffic even among churchmen across the borders with former enemies. Bonhoeffer, however, took the position that the Church of Christ could not stop at national and racial boundaries, that indeed it transcended boundaries and policies. The ecumenical Church was responsible to the commandments of God, and regardless of consequences it had to transmit these to the world. Not only did Bonhoeffer seize upon the ecumenical movement as a potent weapon in the 'Church Dispute' on behalf of the 'Confessing Church' against a nazified Protestant movement; he also declared the encounter between the two a confessional necessity and therefore he went so far as to call for an ecumenical theology. Ecumenical theology indeed was to rededicate itself to the premises of a confession of sin and therefore to the justification by faith alone and the grace of God and Jesus Christ.

Moreover the search for a deepened experience of faith made Bonhoeffer look to the East. Three times between the years 1928 and

1934 he considered visiting Mahatma Gandhi in India whence, he thought, the 'great solution'[19] might come. The third time, in 1934, he even managed to secure a personal invitation from Gandhi. A meeting with the great Indian advocate of passive resistance seemed particularly urgent, since by that time the National Socialists had seized power in Germany, and Bonhoeffer was exploring ways in which a Christian minister could reconcile the premises of his faith with political resistance. But this particular plan, like the earlier two, came to naught; he was needed in Germany to take his place in the 'Church Dispute'.

All these stations in Bonhoeffer's life were exploratory in nature: they certainly helped him towards settling on a theological vision of his own and at the same time relating it to the duties of the Christian at the time of the 'Western void' – and, even worse, at the time of the backlash against it represented by the surrogate religion, National Socialism.

But his great and decisive discovery in this connection came from his encounter with the Swiss theologian Karl Barth, twenty years his senior. The two first met immediately after Bonhoeffer's return from New York in July 1931 in Bonn, where Barth had been teaching since 1930. Bonhoeffer stayed for two weeks. On one occasion, while attending Barth's seminar, he suddenly interrupted to cite Luther's saying that the curses of the godless sometimes sound better in God's ear than the hallelujahs of the pious. This spontaneous interjection by a visiting student, so the story goes, delighted Barth.[20] It provides some insight into Bonhoeffer's evolving theology, which said 'No' to the sin and yet 'Yes' to the sinner,[21] and which indeed dignified the sinner by grace and salvation and by Christ's sacrifice. In any event, one thing led to another in the relationship between the two theologians. After Bonhoeffer's Bonn visit they met frequently and continued to communicate in agreement and disagreement, in perfect candour. Certainly the first encounter with Barth proved decisive for Bonhoeffer's thought.

Undoubtedly it was Karl Barth to whom, next to Luther, Bonhoeffer was most indebted. Barth had initiated a virtual revolution in Protestant theology by his rejection of liberal theology. His theology was not 'liberal' but 'dialectical'. The gap between reason and revelation was unbridgeable: God's will was not a corrected continuation of our own: it was the 'Wholly Other'. Bonhoeffer likewise came to postulate the 'deepest gap between Christianity and the world' and to emphasize the 'eschatological understanding of the kingdom which God alone can bring and which he brings in opposition to the world'.[22] And on 8 April 1936 he wrote to his brother-in-law, Rüdiger Schleicher:

We must not search for general eternal truths which correspond to our own 'eternal' values ... But we search for the will of God which is altogether alien and contrary to us, whose ways are *not* our ways and whose thoughts are *not* our thoughts, who is hidden from us behind the sign of the cross where all our ways and thoughts find an end.[23]

Following the footsteps of Barth's 'dialectical theology', then, Bonhoeffer returned to the original Lutheran insistence on the 'otherness of God'; God was the *deus absconditus* hidden from us behind the sign of the cross and accessible to us only through the gift of grace.

All along, Bonhoeffer's religious sensibilities made him struggle towards a wholly paradoxical perception of the distant, hidden God and the 'profound this-worldliness [*tiefe Diesseitigkeit*] of Christianity',[24] which related it to the very real suffering of man, his inadequacies and perplexities, and to the suffering of Christ on the cross. God's revelation after all was consummated in his incarnation, in his becoming fully human. This is also the way Bonhoeffer interpreted his position later when writing from gaol to Maria von Wedemeyer, his betrothed: 'I am afraid that the Christians who dare to stand with only one leg on earth, stand with only one leg in heaven.'[25] In any case, it was a difficult, very difficult paradox to envisage and he well knew that it was difficult to live with. But the sliding progression from this world to the transcendent God was a shallow and banal formula to him and fell short of true discipleship.

Bonhoeffer, then, brought the distant God back into the world by asking the basic question: 'What did Jesus mean to say to us? What is his will for us today? How can he help us to be good Christians in the modern world?' And he commented: 'The real trouble is that the pure Word of Jesus has been overlaid with so much human ballast ... that it has become extremely difficult to make a genuine decision for Christ.'[26] In Bonhoeffer's thinking, then, grace – that is the manifestation of God's 'otherness' through grace – assumes an all the more crucial place.

I am now impelled to wonder what Bonhoeffer's place in history would be, had there been no Hitler, no National Socialism to challenge his faith and his sense of decency. By the time Hitler came to power in January 1933, Bonhoeffer was well on his way to defining his theological position, to breaking the ice of the conventional German readings of the Lutheran message. On these grounds alone he would stand out for us today, just as Karl Barth does, as a conscience of the Christian faith leading back to its foundations, and, along with Willem A. Visser 't Hooft, then the Secretary General of the Provisional World Council of Churches, as a pioneer ecumenist.

However, the incidence of Hitler's dictatorship deeply affected Bonhoeffer's course. It was not that he changed direction – much to the contrary. Nor did it make him give priority to political activism. If anything, it confirmed him in his faith, and this meant that he had to break out of the confines of academic theology. He was no longer content with being the mere theologian. The challenge which came from without in fact amounted for him to a challenge from within, and the deepening of his faith in turn made him intensify his call to discipleship. Like Luther who left the cloister and went back to the world, Bonhoeffer left academic life behind in order to bear public witness to his faith.

An 'abstract Christology', namely a general religious knowledge, would, Bonhoeffer came to argue, amount to Christianity without the living Christ. Going back to the world was the Christian's duty, above all in times of need and distress, and not in glory but in suffering, in the discipleship of the suffering Christ. Then indeed, 'for the sake of Jesus', the law if necessary had to be broken.[27] When Bonhoeffer wrote these words,[28] he had come to the conclusion that resistance to tyranny was a necessary component of discipleship.

From the very beginning, of course, both Barth and Bonhoeffer were in fundamental disagreement with National Socialism which they opposed on religious as well as political and moral grounds: it was itself a religious movement, a counter-religion. As early as June 1932 the determined young pastor had given a sermon in Berlin in which, perhaps to the puzzlement of his congregation, he predicted: 'We must not be surprised if also for our Church there will be times again when the blood of martyrs will be called for ...'[29] The decisive moment, he knew, was bound to come.

Bonhoeffer fired the first salvo after the Nazis' so-called 'seizure of power' of 30 January 1933: two days later, at the time when Germany was virtually drowned in revolutionary hysteria, he gave a lecture over Radio Berlin on 'The Younger Generation's Changed View of the Concept of Führer', in which he warned his audience that, should the leader

> allow himself to succumb to the wishes of those he leads, who will always seek to turn him into their idol, then the image of the leader will gradually become the image of the 'misleader' ... This is the leader who makes an idol of himself and his office, and who thus mocks God.[30]

But before these decisive passages could be broadcast, the microphone was disconnected ...

A little later, in response to the anti-Jewish legislation of the German Reich in April 1933, Bonhoeffer lectured to an assembled group of pastors on 'The Church and the Jewish Question'. The lecture retained some of the traditional Lutheran views on the Jews: it spoke of the 'curse' they bore for having nailed the Redeemer to the cross and of the expectation of the 'homecoming' in the form of Israel's 'conversion' to Christianity. Indeed it conceded to the state the right to solve the Jewish question by law. However, Judaism was, Bonhoeffer insisted, not a matter of race, but of religious belief. He was concerned about the threatened exclusion of pastors of Jewish descent from office and of the flock of baptized Jews from Christian congregations. This, he argued vigorously, would put the Church *in statu confessionis*. Indeed, he envisioned the need 'not just to bandage the victims under the wheel, but to jam a spoke in the wheel itself'.[31] This was strong and indeed courageous language. Was this still Luther's language? In any case, some of the pastors present walked out of the gathering.[32]

Subsequently, both Barth and Bonhoeffer became embroiled in the so-called 'Church Dispute', unleashed by the nazified faction of Protestant clergy, the 'German Christians', who threatened to blend the Christian message with the racist doctrines of National Socialism. In reaction to the so-called 'Brown Synod' of September 1933, which, dominated by the German Christians, declared its loyalty to the new regime and furthermore adopted 'Aryan' descent as a requirement for ministry in the Church, Bonhoeffer together with Martin Niemoeller organized the Pastors' Emergency League (*Pfarrernotbund*), denouncing the Aryan clause as an infraction of the gospel. The Pastors' Emergency League was the nucleus of what came to be the Confessing Church (*Bekennende Kirche*), around which clergy and laymen rallied to stand up for the integrity of the confession.

Barth, who had taken the initiative by blasting the Nazi intrusions into the Christian preserve in a pamphlet, 'The Theological Situation of Today' (June 1933),[33] which he sent to Hitler, took the lead in the Barmen Synod of 29–31 May 1934. This set itself the task of affirming the premises of the Christian faith against its perverters. It was Barth who formulated the Six Points of the synod's Theological Declaration, unanimously agreed upon by 138 delegates, among them the most distinguished princes of the Protestant Churches of Germany. It became the constitution, so to speak, of the Confessing Church. The Barmen Confession, as it is generally called, in its first article affirmed the evangelical truth that 'Jesus Christ as he is attested for us in the Holy Scripture is the one word of God which we have to hear and which we

have to trust and obey in life and death', and went on to state: 'We reject
the false doctrine, as though the Church could or should recognize as
source of its message besides this one Word of God other events and
powers, figures and truths as God's revelation.' The Confession
amounted to a clear and firm statement of the prerogatives of the
Church. Indeed it reasserted the 'triple "*solus*"' of the Reformation:
'*solus Christus, sola scriptura, sola fides*'.[34]

The churchmen at Barmen thus had made their decision, a
theological one, to define the prerogatives of the Church as a sacred
institution, but had refrained from following it up with a political
statement. Could not everyone see that the Declaration amounted to a
clear-cut rejection of the totalitarian aspirations of National Socialism?
There is no doubt that its drafters thus avoided direct confrontation
with the regime, and they have accordingly been criticized for having
offered no more than 'limited disobedience'.[35] What about the question
of the Jews and the merciless campaign against other minorities and
political dissenters? Should their persecution not have stirred the
church to make it a matter of *status confessionis*?

Such were the questions which Dietrich Bonhoeffer, along with Karl
Barth, asked. He was not present at Barmen, and although at the time he
endorsed the Six Points, he harboured misgivings about the Synod's
restraint. The stand in church matters taken by the Confessing Church
in staving off the German Christians was not enough. The Church, he
concluded,

> has often been untrue to her office of guardianship and to her office of
> comfort. And through this she has often denied to the outcast and to the
> despised the compassion which she owes them. She was silent when she
> could have cried out because the blood of the innocent was crying aloud
> to heaven. She has failed to speak the right word in the right way and at
> the right time. She has not resisted to the uttermost the apostasy of faith,
> and she has brought upon herself the guilt of the godlessness of the
> masses.[36]

While the Barmen Synod was in session, Bonhoeffer was in England.
Earlier, in October 1933, he had accepted a pastorate in two German-
speaking parishes in the London area. As a matter of fact, Karl Barth by
no means approved of this step; he thought that the place of his
younger colleague was in Germany, since, as he put it, 'the house of
your church is afire'. But if Bonhoeffer expected to gain some time for
reflection, he was mistaken. During his sixteen months in England he
repeatedly intervened from a distance in the church dispute at home
and also was actively engaged in the ecumenical movement. In pursuing

his interests he met up with Bishop George Bell of Chichester, a distinguished statesman of the Church. The two soon developed a very close understanding of one another, and in the course of time the bishop became one of Bonhoeffer's most understanding and loyal supporters. He never lost sight of his German friend, and the more Bonhoeffer was hounded by the Nazis, the more he stood by him.

The circumstances of Bonhoeffer's life under Hitler's dictatorship put his act of witnessing to a test far more rigorous and troubling than any that his fatherly companion Barth ever had to face. When, after the death of Reichpresident Paul von Hindenburg in August 1934, all German civil servants including university professors were required to take an oath of loyalty to the Führer, Barth refused; he considered himself put into the *status confessionis*. Arguing valiantly before a disciplinary tribunal that he could obey the Führer only within the limits of his responsibilities as a Christian, he was nevertheless dismissed on grounds of being unfit as a teacher of German youth.[37] Almost immediately, however, Barth found a welcome in his native Basel, from where he continued his struggle against the pseudo-religious aspirations of Nazism. But his resistance remained first and foremost theological in nature and within the context of the church dispute, directed not against the political authority in Germany but against the 'German Christians', representing the newest and meanest version of liberal theology. When, in the later 1930s, Barth came round to advocate active resistance, and when, in the now famous letter to his fellow-theologian in Prague, Josef Hromádka, he argued that every Czech soldier fighting Nazi aggression was also 'doing it for the Church of Jesus', he did so from neutral Switzerland.

Bonhoeffer returned from England in the spring of 1935, strengthened in his resolve to stand fast and join battle with the regime. From London he had written to a Swiss friend that he had considered the church dispute after all only a 'way station' (*Durchgangsstation*) which was to lead to an 'altogether different opposition', namely 'opposition to the blood'.[38] He now was on his way to engage in just this kind of 'opposition'.

Immediately upon arriving in Germany he took over the direction of a seminary improvised by the Confessing Church. Designed to make up for the curtailment in preacher training imposed by the Nazi-appointed 'Reich Bishop', it was considered illegal. There, in Finkenwalde, near Stettin, he directed the so-called House of Brethren (*Bruderhaus*) in a veritably monastic way until it was closed by the Gestapo in October 1937. Nevertheless, he continued his work of training in a series of venues, until these too were closed by the Gestapo in March 1940. During those years Bonhoeffer composed two of his seminal contributions to theology, *The Cost of Discipleship* and *Life Together*.[39]

The year 1938 was a particularly difficult one for Bonhoeffer. The Third Reich was proceeding from triumph to triumph, sanctioned by the other powers and acclaimed at home. For Bonhoeffer, his family and a small number of like-minded people, this was dispiriting. They felt, and actually were, increasingly abandoned and isolated. After it was decreed that all German pastors must honour the Führer's fiftieth birthday by taking the oath of allegiance to him, the greater part of them, including those belonging to the Confessing Church, followed suit. Bonhoeffer himself faced the possibility of being called up for military service. Most discouraging was the Munich settlement of September 1938, in which Hitler was handed the Sudeten areas of Czechoslovakia with the sanction of Britain, France and Italy. These were largely responsible not only for the disastrous international repercussions of this surrender to German pressure and the betrayal of Czechoslovakia, but also for the collapse of plans in certain military circles for a coup against Hitler. In that abortive plot Bonhoeffer's brother-in-law Hans von Dohnanyi had played a central part. Then on 9 November came the dreadful Nazi pogrom against the Jews, the *Kristallnacht*. Bonhoeffer's twin sister Sabine, married to Gerhard Leibholz, a constitutional lawyer of Jewish descent, had packed up with her family just in time and fled to England. This, of course, was a blow to Dietrich.

From the burden of all this adversity Bonhoeffer sought relief by once again travelling to America.[40] His friends at Union Theological Seminary in New York had prepared the ground for him, and indeed Henry Smith Leiper, the Secretary General of the Federal Council of the Churches of Christ, had arranged to have him assume responsibilities as pastor for New York Christian refugees. Yet, almost as soon as he arrived in New York, Bonhoeffer was overtaken by remorse. Ever since his first stay at Union Theological Seminary he had harboured misgivings about the prevalence of social activism among American Protestants, and much as he respected their outgoing and public-spirited stance, he criticized their lack of theology. Now, however, came the realization that he had a responsibility to his struggling brethren at home. After much soul-searching he came to the conclusion that he must return 'to the trenches'. To his mentor and friend at the seminary, Reinhold Niebuhr, he explained himself most movingly:

> I have made a mistake in coming to America. I must live through this difficult period of our national history with the Christian people of

Germany. I will have no right to participate in the reconstruction of Christian life in Germany after the war if I do not share the trials of this time with my people ... Christians in Germany will face the terrible alternative of either willing the defeat of their nation in order that Christian civilization may survive, or willing the victory of their nation and thereby destroying our civilization. I know which of these alternatives I must choose; but I cannot make that choice in security.[41]

Dietrich Bonhoeffer had made what proved to be the gravest decision of his life. By deciding to return home Bonhoeffer had for all practical purposes set the course for his future. Since he was a man of steadfast determination, that course was bound to lead him into that 'altogether different opposition' the need for which he had foreseen some five years earlier. Already in February 1938 he had made the first contacts with the leaders of the Resistance (*Widerstand*); in the autumn of 1940 he signed up for service on the Munich staff of the Counterintelligence Section of the Armed Forces (*OKW/Amt Ausland/Abwehr*) where his friends, including his brother-in-law von Dohnanyi, formed a general staff of sorts for the *Widerstand*.

This step inevitably involved a test of Bonhoeffer's courage and ingenuity. He had known for some time that he would not have long to live; his whole life was in a way a preparation for martyrdom. Ultimately, moreover, this step meant a challenge to the set of innermost values by which he had lived all along. He now had to justify to himself the saying of Christ, 'I came not to send peace, but a sword', which was especially perplexing to him since he had all along considered himself a Christian pacifist. Then of course he had to come to terms with a proper reading of the Lutheran legacy.

Bonhoeffer's entanglement in the 'worldly sector', however, in no way meant a basic change of direction in his thought and action. All along he had maintained that keeping the peace was not an end in itself. Pacifist humanitarianism unrelated to God's commandment he viewed as a 'scandal'. 'There can only be a community of peace when it does not rest on *lies* and *injustice*', he had argued in July 1932 at a conference on peace in Czechoslovakia:

Where a community of peace endangers or chokes truth and justice, the community of peace must be broken and battle joined ... If the ordering of eternal peace is not timelessly valid ... simply because the complete oppression of truth and justice would threaten to make the hearing of the revelation of Christ impossible, then *struggle* is made comprehensible in principle as a possibility of action in the light of Christ.[42]

The distinction between Christian and humanitarian pacifism, and also between struggle and war, thus prepared Bonhoeffer for the justification of his commitment to conspiracy. He never identified himself with the faith of the Enlightenment and its dreams of an ultimately perfect world; nor would he make his peace with the symbiosis, shallow as he judged it, between the Berlin theologians and the worldly philosophers of progress. His theology was, like Barth's, dialectical, and therefore predicated upon the deep gap between Christianity and the world. 'The way of Jesus Christ', he insisted, 'and therefore the way of all Christian thinking, leads not from the world to God but from God to the world.'[43]

By returning to Germany Bonhoeffer moved from the scene of one form, however benign, of secularized religion, the social gospel of his American friends, to another, distinctly malignant one, back in Nazi Germany. 'The day will come', he had written late in 1936, 'when the animal, in front of which the idolaters bow, will display the blurred physiognomy of Luther.'[44] His return to Germany meant saving Luther from this ignominy. He made his decision deliberately, recognizing, as his friend Eberhard Bethge remarked, 'that he now was and would have to remain a German in full acceptance of guilt and responsibility'.[45] Conspiracy and resistance as necessary and responsible action became an imperative in the state to which he returned in July 1939, knowing what he had to do and what was ahead of him.

Bonhoeffer spent much of the time between his return from New York in September 1940, and his arrest on 5 April 1943, writing his *Ethics*, which was to become one of his major theological works. For him, ministry and conspiracy were not opposed. They became the two pillars of his theology, which in the most literal sense became a theology of crisis.

'The knowledge of good and evil seems to be the aim of all intellectual reflection', he wrote. 'The first task of Christian ethics is to invalidate this knowledge.'[46] Christianity and ethics thus were for him 'disparate and divergent entities'.[47] Ethics, he argued, are man-made and speak of righteousness. The Christian message is God-made and speaks of grace, proceeding from God to man. It ultimately demands that man deny himself and his ethical constructs, and that he accept the 'merciful love of God for unrighteous men and sinners'. Hence Bonhoeffer's insistence that the Christian message stands 'beyond good and evil',[48] and hence his tribute to Friedrich Nietzsche, whose thought he skilfully wove into the fabric of Luther's theology.[49]

Here, then, was Bonhoeffer's theological justification of resistance against constituted authority 'to the blood', that is, to the point of tyrannicide. No man-made constructs, not even ones as benign as natural law, or rationality, or universal human rights, can ultimately serve as guides for the Christian man, but only the gospel of Jesus Christ. And of all man-made constructs Bonhoeffer was up against the most absorbing, the most absolutist one, namely Nazi ideology. Ideology in itself was a chief manifestation of man's claim to self-sufficiency and omnipotence. 'All ideological action carries its own justification within itself from the outset in its guiding principle.' But to ideological action Bonhoeffer opposed 'responsible action' which 'does not lay claim to knowledge of its own ultimate righteousness', and he summarized this argument as follows: 'The man who acts ideologically sees himself justified in his idea; the responsible man commits his action into the hands of God and lives by God's grace.'[50]

It was not, then, irresponsibility, nor a violation of his duty as believing Christian, that made Bonhoeffer take part in the conspiracy; it was on the contrary his awareness of himself as a Christian who must act responsibly in the world. Indeed his action was prompted not by ideological motives, since this would have meant taking action out of God's hands, but by the awareness of responsible man acting in a world in which God has become man, and man abandons himself to God's grace and depends on it. In the last analysis, Bonhoeffer found his way into martyrdom as a sinner who as such stands before God. In the depth of despair he then evoked the majesty of God and validated the drama of sin and forgiveness.

Bonhoeffer's involvement in the world, then, meant for him anything but a denial of divine presence and a concession to the worldly order. Much to the contrary, it entailed facing up to the reality of a fallen and fragmentary human existence in the context of the divine dispensation. The paradox between the distant, hidden God and the prescription of responsible action was not lost sight of, but, if anything, reaffirmed.

In justifying this course of action Bonhoeffer was influenced by the thinking of Kierkegaard and Max Weber. Like Kierkegaard he was prepared to 'discover Christianity by himself' and to 'preach Christianity anew'. There was no way for the theologian Dietrich Bonhoeffer to remain without sin; there was no way for him to avoid involvement in political murder. Kierkegaard's radical theology had prepared the way for Bonhoeffer's decision, for his linkage of his grim resolve with the Christian message. This, then, was 'Christianity's paradox' that Bonhoeffer had chosen to live with and to die for. And to go back to Luther, was it not this kind of predicament that he had in mind when he issued his '*pecce fortiter: Esto peccator et pecca fortiter, sed fortius fide et gaude in Christo*'?[51]

Moreover, Bonhoeffer had occupied himself intensely with Weber's work and had emerged impressed by his 'extraordinary sense of realism'.[52] Might it not be argued that Bonhoeffer thus arrived at a Christian version of Weber's 'ethic of responsibility' that called for accountability for the hard and fast decisions and deeds as well as for their consequences? A 'trained relentlessness in viewing the realities of life' and 'the ability to face such realities and measure up to them inwardly', Weber said in his address on 'Politics as a Vocation' in January 1919 before the University of Munich,[53] would in the end induce the 'mature' man to say 'Here I stand; I can do no other'. 'Maturity' (Weber: *Reife*; Bonhoeffer: *Mündigkeit*), that is, facing up to the world of disenchantment and adversity, was a key concept in the thinking of both Max Weber and Bonhoeffer, and while with Weber it led to a prescription of a stoic 'trained relentlessness' in facing up to the 'polar night of icy darkness and hardness', in Bonhoeffer's case it meant a challenge to connect it after all with the Christian message.

Ultimately, to be sure, Bonhoeffer's 'Here I stand; I can do no other' was prompted by a 'time of storm' and by the agony of need (in German: *Not*) and suffering. It was *Not*, need, that catapulted him into a perception of a world that had irreparably become secularized. He did not often use the word 'secularization'; indeed he did not lament that development. It was a reality that had to be faced, the reality, as he preferred to call it, of the 'world come of age' (*mündige Welt*).[54] Nazism itself was a symptom of the modern loss of faith, the religious vacuum; it was a desperate effort to fill that 'Western void' with ideology which amounted to a new surrogate religion – and precisely in this lay for Barth and Bonhoeffer its chief menace.

The world come of age is the world without religion. 'We are moving towards a completely religionless time',[55] Bonhoeffer wrote, in which God, as he saw him, was not God almighty, but weak and powerless in this world. He is the suffering God, the God 'hidden in suffering' (Luther), the God on the cross. And man is called upon to suffer the grief together with God. It is not the religious act that makes the Christian, but participation in the suffering of God. This means, after all, the affirmation of a world come of age and compassion with the suffering God through acceptance of the drama of guilt and redemption. Bonhoeffer's decision to resist was not merely a political one: it had its justification in his *theologia crucis*. He was distinctly a Christian martyr despite the lingering disclaimers of the German Churches. Bonhoeffer's resistance was essentially an expression of his theology.

As a Christian living in a 'time of storm' Dietrich Bonhoeffer saw himself justified in translating Luther's 'suffering disobedience' into resistance. Indeed the 'time of storm' impelled him to define, more than Luther ever had occasion to, the relation between confession and resistance,[56] and the point at which confession without resistance denies itself and at which resistance alone validates confession.

Dietrich Bonhoeffer went to the scaffold on 9 April 1945 in the Flossenbürg concentration camp. He may after all not have 'reformed' the Church. But he had alerted his Christian brethren at home and abroad to the enormities of the Nazi menace and reminded the Protestant Churches of their obligations, and he had outlined a reading of the Christian faith that shook his own church. While he rejected the attribution of suffering and martyrdom,[57] he redefined martyrdom as a conscious assertion of the faith, not in opposition to a wicked world, but in 'mature solidarity' with it and in love.[58] His death, like all deaths, was lonely. But his memorial in the Flossenbürg church reads 'Dietrich Bonhoeffer — a witness of Jesus Christ among his brethren'.

Notes

1 *Letters and Papers from Prison*, enlarged edition, ed. Eberhard Bethge (New York, 1972).

2 '*Das Nichts*'; Dietrich Bonhoeffer (hereafter DB), *Ethik*, ed. Ilse Tödt *et al.* (Munich, 1992), pp. 119, 122.

3 Eberhard Bethge, *Dietrich Bonhoeffer. In Selbstzeugnissen und Bildokumenten dargestellt* (Hamburg, 1976), p. 109.

4 Dietrich Bonhoeffer, 'What is Christian ethic?' in *No Rusty Swords: Letters, Lectures and Notes 1928-1936* (London and New York, 1965), p. 41; it must be noticed that this passage was written during Bonhoeffer's tenure in 1928/29 as assistant pastor in Barcelona, long before Hitler's 'seizure of power' in Germany and of course before he could have aired these views with tyrannicide in mind.

5 His grandfather on his mother's side, Karl-Alfred von Hase, was court preacher under Wilhelm II in the Potsdam Garnisonskirche, but after he corrected the monarch for referring to the proletariat as *canaille* (rabble), the Kaiser ceased to attend his services, and he found himself forced to resign. Thereafter he moved to Breslau as Professor of Theology.

6 Eberhard Bethge, *Dietrich Bonhoeffer: Man of Vision, Man of Courage* (New York, 1970), p. 22.

7 Hajo Holborn, *A History of Modern Germany: The Reformation* (New York, 1959), p. 130.

8   Cf. in this connection Kaspar von Greyerz, Conference Report 'Martin Luther: influence and image in England and Germany', *Bulletin*, German Historical Institute, London, no. 16 (Summer 1984), pp. 5-9.

9   See especially William Montgomery McGovern, *From Luther to Hitler: The History of Fascist-Nazi Political Philosophy* (Cambridge, MA, 1941).

10 Hermann Kunst, *Evangelischer Glaube und politische Verantwortung. Martin Luther als politischer Berater seiner Landesherren und seine Teilnahme an den Fragen des öffentlichen Lebens* (Stuttgart, 1976), p. 400.

11 DB, *Letters and Papers*, p. 123.

12 DB, *The Cost of Discipleship*, revised and unabridged edition (New York, 1979), pp. 52f.

13 DB, *Letters and Papers*, p. 6.

14 Kunst, *Evangelischer Glaube*, pp. 400ff.

15 Julius Rieger, 'Contacts with London' in Wolf-Dieter Zimmermann and Ronald Gregor Smith (eds), *I Knew Dietrich Bonhoeffer* (London, 1973), p. 96.

16 Bethge, *Dietrich Bonhoeffer*, pp. 40f.

17 Ruth Zerner, 'Dietrich Bonhoeffer's American experiences: people, letters, and papers from Union Seminary', *Union Seminary Quarterly Review*, XXXI.4 (Summer 1976), pp. 266ff.

18 DB, *Gesammelte Schriften* (hereafter GS), ed. Eberhard Bethge, 6 vols (Munich, 1965-74), I, p. 77.

19 Letter, DB to Helmut Rössler, Berlin-Grunewald, 18 October 1931 in GS, I, p. 61.

20 This episode has been related in Bethge, *Dietrich Bonhoeffer*, p. 132.

21 See DB, *The Cost of Discipleship* (New York, 1979), p. 41.

22 DB, GS, III, p. 21.

23 Letter, DB to Rüdiger Schleicher, Friedrichsbrunn, 8 April 1936, ibid., III, p. 28.

24 DB, *Letters and Papers*, p. 369.

25 *Brautbriefe Zelle 92. Dietrich Bonhoeffer–Maria von Wedemeyer 1943-1945*, ed. Alice von Bismarck/Ulrich Kabitz (Munich, 1992), p. 38.

26 DB, *The Cost of Discipleship* (New York, 1979), pp. 37f.

27 Ibid., p. 65.

28 *Nachfolge*, the original German edition of *The Cost of Discipleship*, appeared in Munich in November 1937.

29 DB, sermon 19 June 1932 in GS, IV, p. 71.

30 DB, GS, II, 35, 37; see also Bethge, *Dietrich Bonhoeffer*, pp. 193-4.

31 DB, 'Die Kirche vor der Judenfrage', GS, II, p. 48.

32 Clearly, as Nazi discrimination and terror against the Jews intensified, Bonhoeffer overcame his ambiguities on the Jewish question and came to identify with the suffering of the Jews. After the 'Crystal Night' pogrom of 9 November 1938, in a discussion with friends, he 'utterly refused' to see in the destruction of the synagogues by the Nazis a fulfilment of the curse on the Jews, saying: 'If the synagogues burn today, the churches will be on fire

tomorrow' (Gottfried Maltusch, 'When the synagogues burnt' in *I Knew Dietrich Bonhoeffer*, p. 150). From the same time stems his saying: 'Only he who cries for the Jews may sing Gregorian chants' (Bethge, *Dietrich Bonhoeffer*, p. 512). In the autumn of 1940 he wrote in his *Ethics*: 'An expulsion of the Jews from the west must necessarily bring with it the expulsion of Christ. For Jesus Christ was a Jew' (DB, *Ethik*, p. 95).

33 Karl Barth, *Theologische Existenz heute!* (Munich, 1933).
34 See Klaus Scholder, *Die Kirchen im Dritten Reich*, vol. 2: *Das Jahr der Ernüchterung 1934, Barmen und Rom* (Berlin, 1985), pp. 191f.
35 Heinz Eduard Tödt, *Der Bonhoeffer-Dohnanyi-Kreis in der Opposition und im Widerstand gegen das Gewaltregime Hitlers*, typescript (Berlin, 1986), p. 25.
36 DB, *Ethik*, p. 129.
37 For this episode see Eberhard Busch, *Karl Barth: His Life from Letters and Autobiographical Texts* (Philadelphia, 1976), pp. 255-62.
38 '*Widerstehen bis aufs Blut*': letter, DB to Erwin Sutz, London, 28 April 1934 in DB, GS, I, p. 40.
39 DB, *Nachfolge* (Munich, 1937); *Gemeinsames Leben* (Munich, 1939).
40 For Bonhoeffer's second trip to America see Bethge, *Dietrich Bonhoeffer*, pp. 552-66; Zerner, 'Dietrich Bonhoeffer's American experiences ...', pp. 261-82.
41 DB, GS, I, p. 320; Bethge, *Dietrich Bonhoeffer*, p. 559.
42 Bonhoeffer at the World Alliance Youth Conference on peace in Čiernohorské Kúpele, formerly Bad Schwarzenberg, 20-30 July 1932: *No Rusty Swords* (London, 1974), pp. 164f., italics in the original.
43 DB, *Ethik*, p. 358.
44 Letter, DB to Erwin Sutz, Finkenwalde, 24 October 1936 in DB, GS, I, p. 47.
45 Bethge, *Dietrich Bonhoeffer*, p. 559.
46 DB, *Ethik*, p. 301.
47 DB, 'What is Christian ethic?' in DB, *No Rusty Swords*, p. 36.
48 Ibid., p. 37.
49 Ibid., pp. 37-40.
50 DB, *Ethik*, p. 268.
51 'Be a sinner and sin boldly, but more boldly yet have faith and rejoice in Christ': *Epistolae M. Lutheri* (Ienae, 1556), I, p. 345.
52 DB, 'Vorlesung "Die Geschichte der systematischen Theologie des 20. Jahrhunderts"', Wintersemester 1931/32 in Eberhard Bethge, *Dietrich Bonhoeffer: Theologe. Christ. Zeitgenosse* (Munich, 1967), p. 1,053.
53 Max Weber, 'Politics as a vocation' in H. H. Gerth and C. Wright Mills (eds), *From Max Weber: Essays in Sociology* (New York, 1949).
54 Cf. DB, *Letters and Papers*, pp. 327, 346, 361.
55 Letter, DB to Eberhard Bethge, 30 August 1944, DB, *Letters*, p. 279.
56 For this topic see especially Eberhard Bethge, 'Zwischen Bekenntnis und Widerstand: Erfahrungen in der Altpreußischen Union' in *Der Widerstand gegen den Nationalsozialismus. Die deutsche Gesellschaft und der Widerstand*

gegen Hitler, ed. Jürgen Schmädeke and Peter Steinbach (Munich, 1994), pp. 281-94.
57 See letter, DB to Eberhard Bethge, 9 March 1944, DB, *Letters*, pp. 231f.
58 For this thought see Eberhard Bethge, 'Turning points in Bonhoeffer's life and thought', *Union Seminary Quarterly Review*, XXIII.1 (Fall 1967), p. 20.

Bibliography

The new German Bonhoeffer edition:
Dietrich Bonhoeffer, *Werke*, ed. Eberhard Bethge (Munich), is scheduled to comprise 16 volumes. So far all but volumes 8 (*Widerstand und Ergebung*), 12 (*Berlin, 1933*) and 15 (*Illegale Theologieausbildung: Finkenwalde 1935-1937*) have appeared.
The English-language edition, scheduled to comprise 17 volumes (including a comprehensive index volume), is being prepared by Wayne Winston Floyd, Jr, Lutheran Theological Seminary, Philadelphia, PA 19119-1794, USA. Volumes 2 (*Act and Being*) and 5 (*Life Together and Prayerbook of the Bible*) have appeared in 1996 and 1995 respectively, and volume 3 (*Creation and Fall*) is scheduled to appear in October 1997.
A good anthology:
Dietrich Bonhoeffer, *A Testament of Freedom: The Essential Writings of Dietrich Bonhoeffer*, ed. Geffrey B. Kelly/E. Burton (New York: Nelson, 1995).
Many works by Bonhoeffer have appeared singly in Germany, England and the United States. One of the most widely read ones:
Dietrich Bonhoeffer, *Letters and Papers from Prison* (paper) (New York, 1972); (hardback) (London, 3rd edn 1967).

The standard biography of Bonhoeffer is
(German edition) Eberhard Bethge, *Dietrich Bonhoeffer. Theologe. Christ. Zeitgenosse* (Munich, 1986).
(American edition) Eberhard Bethge, *Dietrich Bonhoeffer: Man of Vision, Man of Courage* (paper) (New York, 1977); (British edition) *Dietrich Bonhoeffer: Theologian, Christian, Contemporary* (London, 1970).
A very handy small volume:
Dietrich Bonhoeffer in Selbstzeugnissen und Bilddokumenten, ed. Eberhard Bethge (paper) (Reinbek bei Hamburg, 1976).

Other books in English:
Sabine Leibholz-Bonhoeffer, *The Bonhoeffers: Portrait of a Family* (New York, 1971).

Mary Bosanquet, *The Life and Death of Dietrich Bonhoeffer* (paper) (New York, 1973).

Renate Wind, *Dietrich Bonhoeffer: A Spoke in the Wheel* (paper) (Grand Rapids, MI/London, 1991).

Mission and conversion in Pakistan: Esther John (Qamar Zia)

PATRICK SOOKHDEO

P AKISTAN WAS formed in 1947 when Qamar Zia was 17 years old. Like many Indian Muslims she and her family soon moved to the newly formed state which had been created specifically as a homeland for Muslims of the subcontinent. Pakistan's whole *raison d'être* was its Muslim character. In India, Muslims had often felt themselves to be oppressed, and Muhammad Ali Jinnah, the country's founder, now sought to found a state that was tolerant of all minorities. In his speech to the first session of the Constituent Assembly on 11 August 1947 he emphasized that all members of the newly formed nation had equal rights of citizenship. 'You are free; you are free to go to your temples; you are free to go to your mosques or to any other places of worship in this State of Pakistan. You may belong to any religion or caste or creed – that has nothing to do with the State.' As Keith Callard has observed, these words were spoken 'four days before independence at a time when Sind and Punjab depended heavily upon non-Muslims for commercial and technical services, and before pain and death had left their deepest scars'.[1] But they have remained important for many of Pakistan's citizens in the half-century that has followed. Jinnah died in 1948. Eight years later, in 1956, Pakistan was declared an Islamic republic and an Institute of Islamic Research was set up to research and interpret the Islamic inheritance in a modernist direction. It was later, in the 1980s, that the government of General Zia ul-Haq sought to create an Islamic state.

Today, non-Muslims make up 3-4 per cent of the Pakistani population. Government census figures are challenged by some of the minorities which claim they severely underestimate the size of the minority communities, so reliable statistics are not available. However, Christians probably constitute 2-3 per cent of the population (say, 3.5

million individuals) and Hindus a slightly lower percentage. Other minorities together make up 0.1 per cent. Of Pakistani Christians it is widely agreed that some 95 per cent are descendants of Hindus of the scheduled castes (labourers doing the most menial jobs) who converted to Christianity in mass movements from 1880 to 1930. The remaining 5 per cent are mainly descendants of individual converts from the Muslim and caste Hindu communities; many of these converted well before the mass movements began, while others converted in recent years. Some of the most famous church leaders in Pakistan have come from this kind of background. Since independence there have also been conversions to Christianity among the nomadic Hindu tribes on the Indian border in Sind and Punjab; mass movements are continuing among such groups today. In addition there are small numbers of Goans.

A belief that there existed a Christian church in what is now Pakistan by about AD 225, created by missionaries from the Church of the East, is often cherished by Christians there. But it was with the arrival of the Jesuits in the sixteenth century that clear evidence of a Christian presence in the area now known as Pakistan arose. In 1579 the Mughal emperor Akbar, who had a fascination with religions of all kinds, invited to his court Jesuit missionaries from the Portuguese enclave at Goa, whom he allowed to preach, make conversions and build churches. Akbar even donated funds for the construction of the first church in Lahore in 1600, though without ever embracing Christianity himself. Meanwhile Augustinians and Carmelites were active in Sind, particularly at Thatta, near Karachi. Akbar's son and successor, Jehangir, was initially very favourable and generous to the Jesuit work in Lahore, but reversed his policies when the Portuguese Goans seized a Mughal galleon in 1613. Good relations between Jehangir and the Portuguese were eventually restored, but the entire Christian community in Lahore had fled to Agra during the time of persecution and did not return. Jehangir's son succeeded to the imperial throne in 1626 under the title Shah Jehan. He had a grudge against the Portuguese Jesuits and immediately deprived them of their privileges at court. In 1632 he began to persecute the Jesuits in earnest, and had soon ordered the destruction of all Christian places of worship. He also issued a decree forbidding conversions from Islam, but this was not rigorously enforced. Shah Jehan later adopted a more lenient attitude towards Christians. There continued to be a Jesuit presence at Lahore and Carmelites at Thatta, but their work was very limited. Shah Jehan was succeeded in 1658 by his son Aurangzeb, who introduced a series of Islamic reforms and measures against Hindus and Christians. By

November 1672 the mission at Thatta was closed. The Jesuits continued in Lahore until 1760 when their order was suppressed in all Portuguese territories by Portugal's virtual ruler, the Marquis de Pombal.

Catholic work in Pakistan was then in abeyance until 1842 although nominal responsibility for the region was shared between the Carmelites (Sind and Baluchistan) and the Italian Capuchins in areas to the north. In 1842 the British conquered Sind and the Carmelites immediately sprang into action, setting up a centre in Hyderabad and a school in Karachi. Ten years later the Jesuits took over the work. In the succeeding decades Catholic work blossomed and flourished all over Pakistan, particularly in the Punjab, including Lahore, Sialkot and the canal colonies. Apart from the presence of British army chaplains, Anglican and Protestant Christianity in Pakistan began with the visit of John Lowrie, an American Presbyterian missionary, to Lahore in 1835. His successors established a college there. In 1850 British Anglican missionaries with the Church Missionary Society (CMS) settled in Karachi, and soon moved into all four provinces of what is now Pakistan. CMS missionaries were more widely spread over them than those of any other group. More Presbyterians from the United States and from Scotland arrived in Sialkot in the 1850s, the American work developing into the United Presbyterian (UP) Church of Pakistan, which became the largest Protestant denomination in the country. In 1873 American Methodists began work in Karachi, the Salvation Army arrived in 1883 and the Brethren in 1892. Danish Lutheran work began on the north-west frontier in 1903. Adventists, Baptists and Pentecostals also worked in Pakistan. The early decades of Protestant mission saw few converts. The work was aimed mainly at the educated and higher-caste city-dwellers, sometimes inadvertently, sometimes by design. As well as preaching, tract distribution and public disputations, schools, orphanages and medical work were established. Individuals who did become Christians were usually rejected by their families and thus became dependent on the missionaries, many of them living in the mission compound.

However, much changed with the emergence of the Chuhra Christian movement. The Chuhras were the largest of the scheduled castes of the Punjab. They were among society's lowest and most despised people, who performed the dirty and menial jobs. Their religion was a kind of Islamicized Hinduism, which included belief in a mediator and the need for sacrifices. In 1873 an elderly illiterate man called Ditt became the first Chuhra Christian. With some difficulty he persuaded the Presbyterian missionaries in Sialkot to baptize him.

Against the missionaries' wishes, he returned to his village, where he faced rejection and ostracism. Nevertheless he stayed in the village, and before long his wife, daughter and two neighbours had become Christians. The following year Ditt's uncle and three other men converted. Meanwhile Chuhras in Gujranwala and Gurdaspur also converted and were baptized. Missionaries began to turn their attention to rural people. The movement grew, and thousands of Chuhras joined denominations such as the Anglicans, Catholics, various Presbyterian groups and the Salvation Army. The Church of Scotland grew fortyfold in a decade to number 8,000 by 1892. By 1904 the UP Church had 10,000 communicant members, which increased to 32,000 in the following decade. Between 1902 and 1915 the Methodists increased from 1,200 to 15,000. By 1935 almost all the Chuhras had become Christians in a church which included many from other castes.[2] In his study of caste and Christianity, Duncan Forrester has observed 'Any religion which rejected caste and countenanced their aspirations had attractions for the Chuhras, and although the largest number became Christian, there were substantial movements into Sikhism, Islam and the Arya Samaj [a reform Hindu movement]'.[3] The majority of Pakistani Christians remain the descendants of the Chuhra movement. Many are doing dirty, dangerous and degrading jobs, such as sweeping the streets or cleaning the sewers. For some, this has added to the stigma of conversion from Islam to Christianity, despite the fact that there are Christians from other backgrounds in every area of business and professional life, particularly in teaching and nursing.

The creation of Pakistan in 1947 profoundly affected the Christians living there. As large numbers of Muslims arrived from India, their co-religionists felt obliged to provide them with work. Thus many Christians were displaced from their agricultural jobs and forced into the towns to take up work as sweepers (often displacing scheduled caste Hindus from these jobs). They settled in squalid *bastis*, and frequently had to move as their homes were demolished to make room for new buildings. This created particular problems for Protestants, whose missionaries had divided up the country into areas in the charge of different denominations. Thus a Protestant Christian might be forced to move into the area of a different denomination, where his or her former pastor would be unable to visit. Catholics, on the other hand, were welcomed by the local Catholic church wherever they went, and many Protestants converted to Catholicism at this time. A detailed study of the socio-economic status of Christians in Pakistan was conducted by the West Pakistan Christian Council between December 1954 and

December 1959 (a period which almost exactly coincides with Esther John's participation in the Pakistani Christian community). At this time the Christian community in (West) Pakistan numbered almost 433,000. The survey, which concentrated on Protestants, reported that low incomes, a low level of literacy and crippling debt were commonplace.

Many of those who converted to Christianity sought to escape the burden and indignities of caste Hinduism. Some became Muslim; before 1947 the British Punjab was only 56 per cent Muslim. The phenomenon of a Muslim-majority country where the vast majority of converts to Christianity had come from Hinduism rather than Islam was in no way surprising. In certain areas there existed powerful discouragements against conversion, and even the threat of physical danger. Many who adopted the Christian faith moved away from their community and locality. A further problem which many converts faced was suspicion and mistrust from the Christian communities they had joined. The genuineness of the convert could too easily be doubted by those who had been Christians all their lives. On occasion there was even good reason for this; some hoped for material gain by links with the Church and with Westerners at large in matters of schooling or health care. In some churches converts were described as 'Muslims', as if they had not embraced Christianity. In others, they were excluded from leadership by Christians who suspected that converts could never be as mature in their faith as those from a Christian background. A number of new churches, composed entirely of converts, were found developing alongside the historic churches of particular regions.

The problem of a convert not being fully accepted into the church often reached crisis-point when it came to the question of marriage. In the twentieth century, the majority of converts from Islam to Christianity were single young men. It was sometimes very hard for them to find wives from the Christian community, as there was a reluctance for the Christian parents to agree to their daughter marrying a convert. The obvious emotional stress caused by this kind of situation was exacerbated in a society where to be married is essential for social acceptability.

Certainly, not all converts from Islam faced physical danger, but almost all faced the emotional strain of rejection by their nearest and dearest. In most Pakistani communities, the convert's mother was a key figure, and maternal disapproval and tears, let alone estrangement, were almost unbearable. It was particularly hard for male converts to live with the knowledge that they were causing their mother distress, for the mother–son relationship was usually the closest in the family. Many Muslim men who converted to Christianity returned to Islam because of this factor, and it was something that could occur even after many years of Christian discipleship.

A study of the life of Esther John requires a consideration of the place of women in Islam. But then a question at once arises: how much of what Muslims generally believed and practised in the new Pakistan was derived from the explicit principles of their religion and how much from other distinct traditions and conventions? These are matters of intractable complexity, and the question itself may even be considered impossible and irrelevant. In most societies the religious inheritance informs a living culture and gives it a sense of form and identity. Equally, different cultures are found to emphasize different parts of that inheritance. But to challenge or question the habits and way of life of one's forefathers was, in many Muslim communities, shameful.

Most historic religions contain strains of ambivalence towards women. Women, however, featured prominently in the life of the Prophet, and he preached their equality and even their right to leadership. Women were allowed to hold property, and they were active in the lives of early Muslim communities. But many Muslim cultures in history granted to men authority over women in marriage. Husbands determined their wives' choice of religion. In some communities a respectable woman rarely left the home, and then only with her husband's consent. A man might have up to four wives simultaneously, but a woman could not have more than one husband. Though no small matter, it was easier for a man to divorce his wife than it was for a woman to divorce her husband. In Muslim communities it was held that the honour (*izzat*) of the family rested above all in the behaviour of its womenfolk. As one observes in most patriarchal societies, the disobedient son or roguish husband was often viewed with a greater tolerance than a daughter or a wife who had been guilty of the same things. Conversion from Islam was often seen to bring greater disgrace on a family if the convert was a woman. It is important to realize that the world of the 'family' reached beyond brothers, sisters, parents, grandparents and children, to uncles, aunts and cousins of all sorts. The extended family and other related families together formed the *biradri*, which could perhaps be translated as 'clan'. The *biradri* was a very significant unit within the Pakistani community. Most marriages would be arranged within the *biradri*, and issues of honour and shame would be felt throughout it.

Apostasy is a controversial theme in Islamic history. In the Qur'an the emphasis rests on God's punishment of apostates in the next life, not on human punishment in this life. There are a number of verses which are interpreted by certain commentators as calling for the execution of apostates, but in every case there is some ambiguity of language or context. Setting aside apparent commands to kill all pagans, it seems that the Qur'an itself, as opposed to Qur'anic commentaries, has no universally applicable command to kill apostates.

There is a tradition in Islam — some would argue that it is the dominant tradition — which sees moderation as a virtue and which eschews coercion and violence. How then was the apostasy law formulated and inserted into Islamic law? It is primarily from the examples of the *hadith* literature that the apostasy law was derived. Islamic law, *Shari'ah*, was worked out over the first two and a half centuries of Islam not only from the Qur'an but also from the *hadith* by two processes known as *ijma* (the unanimous agreement of learned Muslims representing the whole body of believers) and *qiyas* (analogical reasoning from the Qur'an, *a'hadith* and *ijma* in order to deduce further laws). The formulation of the *Shari'ah*, in its four schools, came to a close about AD 900 when scholars felt, firstly, that all essential questions had been settled and, secondly, that no contemporary or future scholars could equal the reasoning of the great minds of the past. This was called 'the closing of the door of *ijtihad*'.[4] The *Hedaya*, an authoritative textbook of Islamic law according to the Hanafi school, which is the dominant school followed in Pakistan, India, Bangladesh, Turkey and parts of Central Asia, affirms 'There are only two modes of repelling the sin of apostasy, namely, destruction or Islam'. This teaching is well known to all Muslims and would have been known to Qamar Zia. According to the *Hedaya* the apostate must be imprisoned for three days, after which, if he has not returned to Islam, he should be killed. It is desirable, but not obligatory, to explain the Islamic faith during this three-day period. A woman apostate should not be put to death, but imprisoned until she returns to Islam.[5] There are various other penalties for apostasy, including automatic dissolution of the apostate's marriage and the forfeiting of his or her property. Another aspect of Islamic law on apostasy, and one which has had very far-reaching consequences for many converts including Esther John, is that 'their blood if shed brings no vengeance'.[6] Indeed, to kill a convert is a meritorious act in the eyes of many Muslims. According to one *hadith* there is a special reward in heaven for the person who kills an apostate.[7]

In the 1920s and 1930s the laws of apostasy that existed in what is now Pakistan did more to encourage conversion from Islam than prohibit it. In British India, Muslim women chose apostasy as the only way to escape an intolerable marriage. Muslim leaders sought reform. In

1939 the Dissolution of Muslim Marriage Act was passed, and this defined other grounds on which a woman might divorce her husband, such as impotence, cruelty, or his failure to maintain his wife.

When the United Nations formulated its 1948 Universal Declaration of Human Rights, the freedom to change one's religion was specifically mentioned in Article 18. The previous year, when the draft was being discussed, some Muslim delegates expressed reservations about this part of Article 18. At the time of voting they abstained. Abul Ala Mawdudi, a significant figure in the Islamization of Pakistan, argued that Islam was a 'complete order of life':

> ... it is not a faith which a person may choose with only the concern of the individual in mind. It is that faith on the basis of which a society of people establishes a complete order of a civilization in a particular form and brings into existence a state to operate it. A faith and idea of this nature cannot be made into a game for the liberties of individuals ... When in this world was such a faith and membership in a society holding this faith made the toy of individual free wills?[8]

But Mawdudi's view was widely and persistently resisted in the new nation, by individuals, parties and legal movements. His critics often focused on the context of early examples of capital punishment for apostates, pointing out that these apostates not only rejected Islam but also rebelled against Muslim rule. The renowned Pakistani jurist S. A. Rahman wrote that apostasy which was not accompanied by rebellion against the Islamic state should not be punished.

But many Muslim families who had an apostate member felt an unspeakable shame, literally the shame of association with a traitor. This is why many converts from Islam could be thrown out of their homes and their jobs, and why some were even killed by their own family. If a Muslim converted to Christianity, as opposed to another non-Islamic religion, feelings of betrayal in the community were even exacerbated by the apprehension that Christianity was the religion of the oppressed, and much identified with low castes. Even members of historic churches, such as the Copts, could find themselves accused of being foreigners in their own country.

* * *

One of seven children, Qamar Zia was born on 14 October 1929. She attended a government school until her father's illness obliged her to leave at about the age of 17. After a while she was sent to a Christian school near her home. Later she recalled:

Just as soon as I set foot in this school I noticed a Christian teacher who
was different from anyone I had ever known. I saw her gentle way of
speaking, her kindness to all the students and her great faithfulness in her
work. Her life made so deep an impression upon me that I was really
puzzled. 'How could any human being be like that?' I wondered over and
over again. Later I realized that it was all because God's Spirit was in her.

In this school I began to study the Bible. Two days a week we studied
the Old Testament, and two days a week the New Testament. One day in
the week we did memory work, learning passages from the Bible and
many songs. At first I did not study with zeal, but rather indifferently. I
had heard the Christians called blasphemers, and I did not like even to
touch their book.

One day we were studying the 53rd chapter of Isaiah, memorizing
some parts of it, which was very hard for me. It was while studying this
chapter that God, by his grace, showed me that there was life and power
in this book. Then I began to realize that Jesus is alive for ever. Thus God
put faith in my heart and I believed in Jesus as my Saviour and the
forgiver of my sins. Only he could save me from everlasting death. Only
then did I begin to realize how great a sinner I was, whereas before I
thought that my good life could save me.[9]

After the partition of India in 1947, Qamar moved with her family to
the then capital of Pakistan, Karachi. She wrote to one of the teachers in
her school at Madras to tell her the news of her move, and this teacher
contacted a missionary in Karachi, Marian Laugesen. Laugesen
managed to find Qamar amidst the thousands of newly arrived Muslims
from India living in hastily erected barracks-like buildings on the
outskirts of the city. Qamar was obviously well aware of the serious
implications of her conversion, for she had concealed it from her family
and therefore could not speak freely to the missionary until her mother
and aunt left the room to make tea. She seized the opportunity to tell
Laugesen that she had had to leave her Bible in Madras and to ask her
to bring a New Testament.

This Laugesen managed to accomplish a fortnight later. Sensing that
the gift might provoke conflict in the family, Qamar fetched a pile of
school books and told Laugesen to teach her English from them. During
the course of the lesson the New Testament passed into her hands,
hidden in one of the textbooks. Marian Laugesen also gave Qamar her
address, but soon afterwards she was transferred away from Karachi.

For the next seven years, Qamar had no contact with any Christians,
but continued to read her New Testament secretly. Then her parents
began to take steps to arrange a marriage for her; naturally, the chosen
man would be a Muslim. On 18 June 1955 she ran away from home

and sought out Marian Laugesen, who had now returned to Karachi. It was arranged that Qamar would stay at the orphanage where Marian Laugesen was working. She helped care for the children and studied the Bible with one of the staff. It was apparently at this time that Laugesen gave her the name Esther John. Perhaps the name was chosen because of her great grace and beauty, like the Old Testament Esther. Later, missionaries remembered the words 'If I perish, I perish' (Esther 4:16).

After a few days Esther's youngest brother came, the one whom she felt to be the most kind and understanding. He did his best to persuade her to return home with him. When she refused, he agreed to return the next day with their mother. In fact, he did not come for several days, and when he did he was accompanied by another brother. This time the younger brother succeeded in persuading Esther to go home, telling her that their mother was ill. Esther was very anxious to see her mother, as she wanted to ask forgiveness for some hasty words on the day she left. She had intended to return to the orphanage the following day, but did not come until several days later. She told the staff how angry her family were, and how they were accelerating the marriage arrangements in order to marry her almost immediately.

A culture in which a wife submits absolutely to her husband, and normally lives with her parents-in-law to whom both she and her husband must submit, would have made it quite impossible for her to live as a Christian if she was married to a Muslim. Clearly both Esther and her family understood this, as evidenced by their intention of solving the problem by hastening the marriage and her desperation to avoid the marriage at all costs. The next day, 30 June 1955, she left to travel north several hundred miles to Sahiwal in the Punjab — a safe distance, it was hoped, from her family in Karachi. Here she lived in the nurses' home at the hospital of the Associate Reformed Presbyterian Mission. She played a full part in the life of the hospital and was delighted to be able to do the simplest service for others or to be able to share her faith. She also studied the Christian faith in preparation for baptism, and later that year was baptized in the nurses' prayer room.

After a few months Esther John went to stay in the home of Bishop Chandu Ray, the first Anglican bishop of Karachi. The bishop and his wife arranged for her to continue her education in a village school. Some months later she returned to the mission hospital and studied privately under the principal of the mission's girls' high school. She celebrated her first Christmas, but was rather troubled to receive gifts from all the nurses when she had nothing to give them in return. In the spring she returned to Karachi and visited Marian Laugesen, but did not see her own family.

She developed a great love for the Bible. Even before her baptism she told her friends 'I feel God wants me to be a teacher of the Bible. This book has great power. I want to see it do for others what it has done for me.' In September 1956 she entered the United Bible Training Centre in Gujranwala, returning in the holidays to the nurses' home at Sahiwal. She was known at Sahiwal for her love of singing and her sense of humour, telling many a hilarious tale about her own mishaps as she tried to learn to speak Punjabi or sleep-walked and sleep-talked. During one holiday at Sahiwal, in the summer of 1957, she had a period of serious illness. This was a time of great testing for her, as she questioned why God allowed the illness, feared that her friends would abandon her and sorely missed her family. An apt student with an enquiring mind, Esther John stood out from the other students, not least because her Madrasi features and her Indian sari contrasted with the Punjabi girls in their *shalwar-kamiz* (baggy trousers and long tunic). She spoke Urdu with a different accent and struggled when her turn came to cook, no doubt because Punjabi food is so different from Madrasi. Nevertheless she endeared herself to students and staff alike. During her time as a Bible student, Esther made two visits to her family in Karachi, where she was warmly received, and little pressure was put on her to return to Islam. She longed and prayed that they also would become Christians. The Christians in Sahiwal made three attempts to find a husband for her. It was essential that a respectable woman of her age should be married, but no respectable Pakistani woman would have looked for a husband herself. All three attempts failed, it was said, 'for perfectly good reasons'. They did not involve her own choice, however.

Esther John completed her studies at Gujranwala in April 1959 and went to live in Chichawatni, a small town about thirty miles from Sahiwal. She lived in the home of the Dale Whites, an elderly American couple working with the American Reformed Presbyterian Mission. Here Esther settled down very happily, rejoicing to have her own bedroom and kitchen and relishing the beauty of the flowering shrubs and trees, the birds, stars and sunsets. At this point in her life, she stopped wearing saris and began to wear the Punjabi *shalwar-kamiz*. Those who knew her were struck by how little interest she had in clothes, and none at all in jewellery. It was very different from the attitude of the young Qamar Zia, who, as a little girl, had been so proud of a pair of new shoes that she had sat waving her handkerchief over them to keep the flies off. Under the supervision of the Whites, she began to do evangelistic work in the villages around Chichawatni. She and Janet White would travel together from village to village, by foot or bicycle. Cycling was a rather rare accomplishment among Pakistani women at that time, but Esther John had learned it while at Gujranwala. Both women cycled barefoot, helping each other to lift their cycles over canals and sewage ditches. She would often have trouble with the ends of her *dupatta* (long scarf worn with *shalwar-kamiz*) catching in the chain or spokes. The Muslim women they visited mostly lived very secluded lives. Here it was a point of honour for women to stay at home and not be seen outside; they were immensely shocked to learn that she had renounced the faith of her forefathers to become a Christian. Many condemned her with scorn and bitterness for her great sin in leaving Islam. Others thought she must have been thrown out of her home by her family for some other great wickedness and then turned to Christianity because Muslims would no longer accept her. But Janet White believed that many of the women were nevertheless captivated by her radiant beauty and joy and even 'felt a racial pride in her, as if they themselves were responsible for her charms'. She met the hostility with equanimity, and told friends that she found consolation in recalling that Christ also was mocked and reviled.

During the cooler winter months, it was the Whites' practice to camp in the villages. They would spend five or six days in each village, teaching the Bible to the small community of Christians, who were very poor, mostly illiterate, and shared their pastor with perhaps a dozen other villages. Esther John was thrilled to experience tent life for the first time. The Whites were equally delighted to discover that she had a talent for playing the *dholki* (drum), which, accompanied by the *chimta* (long iron tongs) and singing, would draw people to the meetings. Though high-born, she was delighted to share the lives of the village Christians of low-caste origin; no mean achievement, as higher-caste women were normally extremely conscious of caste differences and reluctant to have contact with their social inferiors. (Indeed, Christians from a high-caste Hindu background sometimes refused to worship in the same building as Chuhra Christians.) This makes it all the more remarkable that Esther would happily join the cotton-pickers in their back-breaking work in the fields. She also put considerable effort into teaching a number of illiterate Christian women to read, hoping to break the vicious circle of poverty and ignorance.

Before Christmas the Whites and Esther returned to Chichawatni, and Esther John threw herself wholeheartedly into organizing a children's Christmas drama. But she was still troubled by thoughts of her family in Karachi. For several months they had been writing to her, urging her to come back home. The letters had grown more insistent, telling of the imminent marriage of her youngest brother, of whom she was particularly fond, which would leave her mother alone. She longed to see her mother again, but was afraid that her family would put pressure on her to renounce her Christian faith. She decided that she would go home after Christmas, and began to pack her trunk in preparation. The decision brought no sense of resolution. She remembered the pressure her brothers had put on her about marriage. They had made four arrangements for her, and she had refused each one. To refuse an arranged marriage, even once, was in those days extremely unusual, and required great courage. She wrote to her family by registered post, laying down two conditions for her return to them: firstly, that she should be allowed to live as a Christian, and, secondly, that she should not be forced into a marriage against her will. No answer came.

After Christmas she spent another month camping with the Whites, after which they all returned to Chichawatni for a few days, planning to camp again as soon as possible. On 1 February 1960, the monthly meeting of pastors and evangelists from the area was held at the Whites' home. After curry and rice, the men held their meeting and then went off with quilts and blankets into various rooms of the house to sleep. Esther spent the evening polishing her pots and pans, singing to herself, and went to bed early, having a slight cold. The next morning she did not appear. She was found dead in her bed, her skull smashed twice with a heavy, sharp instrument so forcefully that it probably killed her instantly. She was buried in the Christian cemetery at Sahiwal. Police officers took over the house, and laboriously searched for evidence. They suspected a disappointed lover had been involved. Having been through all her books and papers, they reported to Dale White 'Sir, we have found no clue. This girl was in love only with your Christ.' Esther John's murderer was never found or even identified, despite two police enquiries.

The death of Esther John remains mysterious. The story of Rahila Khanam, who was martyred on 16 July 1997, bears many resemblances to her story, but telescoped so as to bring the killing within a few weeks of running away from marriage. Rahila, a 22-year-old Muslim woman living in Lahore, had been attending Bible studies with a Christian friend at the home of a pastor. When her family discovered what she was doing, they promptly arranged for her to marry a Muslim. She fled into hiding at a women's refuge called Dar-ul-Aman, but was found by her family some weeks later. She was immediately shot by her brother,

11. Esther John

12. The March on Washington, 1963

13. Martin Luther King

14. Model for the statue of Wang Zhiming

15. The grave of Wang Zhiming

16. Idi Amin in a crowd in Kampala, 1971

17. Archbishop Janani Luwum

18. Archbishop Oscar Romero

who readily admitted his act, saying that he had done his religious duty by killing an apostate from Islam.

In both cases, the choice of an individual to abandon one faith and follow another challenged a complex web of religious, cultural and social norms. For Rahila Khanan, the family and *biradri* had been brought into disrepute by the apostate, whose action combined treachery, disobedience to elders, and the breaking of hallowed customs in a culture which looked primarily to the past for guidance, with a move to join another community generally considered to be lowly, immoral and unclean. When her brother declared that he was fulfilling his religious duty by killing his apostate sister, he was only giving half the story. He was also fulfilling his family duty by taking action to remedy the dishonour and shame which she had brought on them.

It would be encouraging to think that the appalling death of Esther John had borne fruit in, say, making the lives of future converts from Islam less insecure or making it more acceptable for Christians to share their faith with Muslims. But there is no indication of this. Indeed, it has perhaps had the opposite effect. Years later, the story of Esther John was analysed in a book by Maulana Kausar Niazi, Communications Minister of State in the Pakistan People's Party government of Z. A. Bhutto. His study used her life and death as the basis for an anti-Christian apologetic and a strong condemnation of Christian missionaries.[10] But if her death seems to human reckoning pointless and useless, her life certainly bore fruit in the example of her courage, commitment, self-sacrifice, faith, gentleness and love, and the joy which she brought to so many who knew her.

Notes

1 Keith Callard, *Pakistan: A Political Study* (London: George Allen and Unwin Ltd, 1957), p. 233.
2 David B. Barrett (ed.), *World Christian Encyclopedia* (Oxford: Oxford University Press, 1982), pp. 542-5; Donald Hoke (ed.), *The Church in Asia* (Chicago: Moody Press, 1975), pp. 475-99; Frederick and Margaret Stock, *People Movements in the Punjab: With Special Reference to the United Presbyterian Church* (Bombay: Gospel Literature Service, 1975; copyright by the William Carey Library), pp. 17-32, 57-139, 280-1, 309-26.
3 Duncan Forrester, *Caste and Christianity: Attitudes and Policies on Caste of Anglo-Saxon Protestant Missions in India* (London, 1980), p. 87.
4 *Ijtihad* (independent reasoning) had come by this time to be restricted to *qiyas*.

5   The other schools of Sunni law vary in the treatment of female apostates, some requiring death as for male apostates. In Shi'ite law the woman is to be imprisoned and 'beaten with rods' five times a day at the Muslim prayer hours.
6   Mohammed Al Abduri Ibn Hadj, *Al Madkhal* (Cairo edition), vol. 2, p. 181.
7   *Hadith* of Ali ibn Abu Talib, recorded by Bukhari and Muslim.
8   Abul Ala Mawdudi, *The Punishment of the Apostate According to Islamic Law*, translated and annotated by Syed Silas Husain and Ernest Hahn (1994), pp. 46-8.
9   Esther John, *My True Story* (translated from the Urdu).
10 Translated into English as *The Mirror of Trinity*.

Bibliography

Ann Elizabeth Mayer, *Islam and Human Rights: Tradition and Politics* (London: Pinter Publishers, 1991).

Fr John Rooney MHM (general ed.), *Pakistan Christian History Monograph Series* (Rawalpindi: Christian Study Centre, 1984-86).

Seppo Syrjänen, *In Search of Meaning and Identity: Conversion to Christianity in Pakistani Muslim Culture* (Helsinki: Missiologian ja Ekumeniikan Seura, 1984).

Janet Ballantyne White, *Esther: A Pakistani Girl* (Ambassador Series no. 6; Bible and Medical Missionary Fellowship, 2nd edition 1962).

Canon R. W. F. Wootton (ed.), *Jesus – More Than a Prophet: Fifteen Muslims Find Forgiveness, Release and New Life* (Leicester: Inter-Varsity Press, 1982).

Christianity, racism and protest in the United States: Martin Luther King

SEHON GOODRIDGE

T HE NAME Martin Luther King conjures up images of non-violent protest, of the Christian power of love, and of messianic personal sacrifice. In hindsight, he is held up as a martyr of the civil rights movement, and of the age in which he lived. At the same time, his life remains an inspiration, encapsulating a struggle for justice which is timeless. In his own words, Martin Luther King recognized that the nature and the challenge of his struggle might culminate in the ultimate human sacrifice. On 5 June 1964 at St Augustine, Florida, he said 'If physical death is the price I must pay to free my brothers and sisters from the permanent death of the spirit, then nothing could be more redemptive'.

King's ideas were continually evolving, and he came to be seen in many different ways throughout his stages of development. He was primarily fighting against racial injustice out of concern for the welfare of society and, in this respect, his particular concern for the African-Americans of the United States became increasingly indivisible from his determination to confront injustices in other forms. For much of his life he was prepared to accept verbal and physical abuse, a fact that testifies to the sincerity of his Christian faith and the totality of his commitment to the condition of his fellow man. According to John Ansbro, he would not let himself be confined: 'He raised his prophetic voice against the evils of racism, economic exploitation, militarism, violence and materialism.'[1]

Martin Luther King was born on 15 January 1929 to a prominent Black Baptist family in Atlanta, Georgia. At the Ebenezer Baptist Church in Atlanta, he drank from the wells of the Black tradition under the inspired and educational leadership of 'Daddy', Martin Luther King senior. Here he found what he later described as a 'second home'. He was therefore a product of a distinctive Christian culture which gave the Black middle class a sense of self-worth and belief. He experienced a community at worship, praying, praising, preaching and testifying. This reality was decisive in shaping his faith and forming his qualities of leadership. James Evans has observed:

> Most intellectual treatments of King's thought focus on the influence which white thinkers had on him, but neglect the important, the impact of the most important formative factor in his life, the Afro-American Baptist Church. Liberal theology failed him. Gandhi's non-violent methods had been confined to personal relations and was incapable without modification of addressing the structural misuse of power. Thoreau's civil disobedience only worked in a situation of moral and political equality which did not exist between white Americans and Afro-Americans. The bedrock of King's theology was not laid at Crozier Theology Seminary or at Boston University, but in the Afro-American Baptist Church of his youth and at Moorhouse College. King's dream grew out of the spirituality of the Afro-American tradition. People turned to the Black Church for spiritual sustenance and for social and political support. Black Churches played major roles in mobilizing meetings and demonstrations. The Black Church culture was pervasive in the movement from oratory to music, from rituals and symbols of protest to the ethic of non-violence.[2]

The literal interpretation of the gospel ensured a strength of practical evangelical faith that constantly comforted and strengthened. Humanity was accountable to itself and to one another in a faithfulness which was owed to a faith in God's kingdom. The liberation motive and theme of the civil rights movement were largely fashioned by the Black church tradition, and developed a deep religious significance among Black people. Liberation meant freedom from all forms of oppression. As a public figure King was later able both to symbolize and to articulate this total freedom.

The civil rights movement with which Martin Luther King's name became synonymous had its genesis in action against a culture of legal discrimination and segregation, particularly in the southern States of America. Growing up in the South during the 1930s and 1940s left an indelible impression on him. In later years he recalled 'Certainly a Negro child in Atlanta could not go to any public park. I could not go to the so-called white schools ... in many of the stores down town ... I could not go to a lunch counter to buy a hamburger or a cup of coffee ... I could not attend any of the theatres.'

He also remembered scenes of violence, of the police and the Ku Klux Klan 'beating Negroes on some of the streets in Atlanta'.[3] At the age of 15, he entered Moorhouse College in Atlanta. Later, he chose Crozier Theological College. Set in the North, Crozier was an integrated seminary, where he was able to build relationships with whites which would have been unheard of in the southern states. He lacked confidence but soon found himself embracing these new freedoms and new ideas. He began also to question the literal biblical interpretations of his southern Black church upbringing. Increasingly, however, he was aware of his need to return to the South and there to use his newly acquired powers of language to fulfil his calling; a calling which he described as 'not a miraculous or supernatural thing', but 'an inner urge calling me to serve humanity'.[4] He married Coretta Scott, a music graduate from the North, and duly returned to Alabama.

After the Second World War American society was experiencing a new awakening. The repressive and violent measures to sustain the laws of a racially segregated society were increasingly contested by vocal groups in a number of states. The civil rights movement was a new socio-political animal in American life and although it has become heavily associated with certain prominent personalities, from the first it comprised a diverse array of organizations and groups. King's contribution to the civil rights movement was not only entirely to transform its method of protest, but also to add a new moral authority to the task at hand. He formed the Southern Christian Leadership Conference (SCLC), and took part in sit-ins and demonstrations throughout the South as a means of challenging social injustice. As a pastor in Montgomery, Alabama, he too was confronted with blatant segregation. This was particularly evident in the transportation system of the city. The bus service was segregated, and such discrimination was buttressed by legislation which required white taxi operators to serve white passengers exclusively, while stipulating that Black people should have their own means. Black people were subjected to abuse by white bus drivers who openly called them 'niggers', 'black cows' and 'black apes'. They could command Blacks to surrender their seats to whites, even though they were not in seats reserved for them. When King was at Montgomery, a 15-year-old student was dragged off a bus, handcuffed and taken to gaol because she refused to give her seat to a white passenger. The incident led to the establishment of a 'citizens' committee ... to talk with the manager of the bus company and the citizens' committee'.[5] Martin Luther King served on this committee and provided leadership for the Montgomery bus boycott. It was this campaign, in 1956, that signalled his rise to prominence as a Black leader. His placement on his return to Alabama to the Dexter Avenue

Baptist Church in Montgomery had produced all-inspiring reactions from the local community. Rarely had it witnessed such a powerful and articulate preacher. Having shown a natural sympathy for the boycott movement, Martin Luther King attended a protest meeting calling for a Black boycott of all buses in defence of the unjust arrest of Rosa Parks. Parks, a Black seamstress, had refused to obey the laws of segregation by sitting at the rear of a bus, and she had been arrested. It was not so much that Martin Luther King took up the cross by leading the protest, but rather a matter of finding the cross laid upon him. But he now made his mark.

King's maturing contribution to the civil rights movement represented a marked departure from previous leaders and thinkers, such as Marcus Garvey and W. E. B. Du Bois. He was an inclusivist. He did not believe in the philosophy of separatism which readily lent itself to social division and alienation. His vision for humanity went beyond the significance of race and of class, but cut to the very foundations of Christian brotherhood and the basic rights of man. To the public he presented a powerful combination of Christianity, Americanism, democracy and non-violent protest. He told a gathering at Montgomery on 5 December 1955:

> I want it to be known throughout Montgomery and throughout this nation that we are Christian people, we believe in the Christian religion, we believe in the teachings of Jesus. The only weapon that we have in our hands this evening is the weapon of protest. This is the glory of democracy.

But he also knew how to relate and develop those themes:

> We must keep God in the forefront. Let us be Christian in all of our actions and I want to tell you this evening that it is not enough for us to talk about love. Love is one of the pinnacle parts of the Christian faith. There is another side called justice and justice is really love in calculation.[6]

The source of King's idea of integration was to seek out our common humanity. The white race as a whole was not the enemy, for 'it is not the race *per se* that we fight but the policies and ideology that leaders of that race have formulated to perpetuate oppression'.[7] Social change would only be realized if a disciplined measure of suffering and self-sacrifice was engendered by those wanting that change. The strength to call for lasting non-violent change drew upon the deepest reserves of love in the protester. Such love called for the transcendence of hate, embracing the true meaning of *agapē*; it was the conscious freedom to love one's subjugator as a fellow human being, to draw upon the power of faith and of human kindness, and to erode the unjust conscious thinking of the segregator. King was also convinced that as a result of their historical experience Black people had a peculiar capacity to love their enemies, to endure hardship and suffering and thereby, as he put it, 'teach the white man how to love', or 'to cure the white man of his sickness'. In King's prophetic imagination God was using Black people to bring about the blessed community:

> I am sure that the entire world now looks to the Negro in America for leadership in the whole task of building a world without want, without hate and where all men live together in shared opportunity and brotherhood.[8]

He argued that forgiveness of those who inflict evil and injury is evidence of the power of love at work. Love brought reconciliation. His depiction of a moral universe of tangible, recognizable reality was eloquent:

> Returning hate for hate multiplies hate, adding deeper darkness to a night devoid of stars. Darkness cannot drive out darkness. Only light can do that. Hate multiplies hate; violence multiplies violence and toughness multiplies toughness in a descending spiral of destruction.[9]

Hatred harms the person who hates, corroding his personality, destroying his sense of values and confusing truth with falsehood. King was not prepared to concede or to fall victim to the violence which enslaved racial oppressors. He declared 'We shall match your capacity to inflict suffering by our capacity to endure suffering. We shall meet your physical force with soul force.'[10]

The moral and intellectual thought of Martin Luther King drew explicitly on the inheritance of the great Indian teacher, Mohandas K. Gandhi. In Gandhi he found the power of a non-violent doctrine of love and goodness towards God's creation. Like Gandhi, too, he took particular delight in the verses of the Sermon on the Mount: 'But I say unto you that ye resist not evil, but whosoever shall smite thee on thy right cheek, turn to him the other also.'[11] He absorbed the power of Gandhi's weapon of love and exclaimed 'We will return good for evil; we will love our enemies. Christ showed us the way and Gandhi showed us it could work.'[12] His admiration for Gandhi's adherence to *satyagraha*, meaning 'holding onto truth', led him to adopt this as a primary principle of protest. Gandhi's second contribution to King's practical philosophy was his adherence to *ahimsa*, or 'non-violence'. This was to become the method of expounding *satyagraha*: the truth.

King's adherence to following the truth often led him into the realm of politics. It was here again that he gained comfort and strength from Gandhi's example. Like Gandhi before him, Martin Luther King shared this common experience of spiritual calls for justice which demanded that the powers within society be faced in a way that was highly political. It was impossible to retain religious neutrality and be silent in the face of blatant violations of human rights. Silence, King observed, is betrayal.

It was the moral obligation to protest which Martin Luther King utilized within American society. He believed that the structural reality of racism denied him his vision of humanity, of the freedom of self and equality of rights. Throughout his theological training both at Moorhouse and at Crozier Theological Seminary King had also been confronted by new intellectual forces. This path of theological enlightenment gradually helped to form the foundation of thought which would set him apart from many other leading lights of his generation. His introduction to Nietzsche's *Genealogy of Morals* provoked a crisis over his belief in the power of the Christian faith. To Nietzsche, Christian ethics were a personification of weakness in either an individual or a society. They produced a 'slave ethic' which entrapped the individual in a depressing position of ineffective pity. This represented a fundamental challenge to King's belief in an all-powerful God whose power would overcome every obstacle in life. Nietzsche's belief that Christian value systems were alien to natural humanistic instinct he finally overcame by recourse to the faith to love exemplified by the life and works of Gandhi. King's personal conflict with the writings of Nietzsche also led him to seek solace in Paul Tillich's reassuring defence of a God of love. Tillich strengthened King's belief in his weapon of love as a powerful force of social justice. He believed that 'power at its best is love implementing the demands of justice. Justice at its best is love correcting everything that stands against love.'[13] King now drew attention to the powers of different kinds of love as a means of expressing the power of love in struggles of a societal nature. He chose the Greek word *agapē* as expressive of the form of love possessing the power to effect social change: *agapē* refers to 'an understanding creative, redemptive goodwill toward all men', which 'enables us to love every man not because we like him or because his ways appeal to us but because God loves him'.[14]

In the America of his own day, Martin Luther King found that 'racism is a philosophy based on a contempt for life. It is the arrogant assertion that one race is the centre of value and object of devotion before which other races must kneel in submission.'[15] The realities of community, justice and struggle were inherent aspects of the moulding of his dream. For, as Cone argues, King made history but was also made by history.[16] He now sought to organize Blacks in America, to help them recognize their power as a unified force, and he offered a non-violent framework from which justice could be achieved. The Montgomery bus boycott led to the employment of Black people as bus operators and to the policy of 'first come first served'. Despite arrests, bombings, economic disabilities and deprivations, and the militant racist harassment by the Ku Klux Klan, King's way of non-violent resistance was seen to be effective. But its dangers were all too evident. During this time he said 'Once more it might well turn out that the blood of the martyr will be the seed of the tabernacle of freedom'.[17]

In Washington, the Federal Governments of Kennedy and Lyndon Johnson introduced measures in support of equity and justice. Oppressors no longer had a pretext for greater acts of injustice and violence. King and his non-violent followers gained dignity and respect not only in the United States but also abroad, where the civil rights movement embarrassed a nation that proclaimed to the world a belief in freedom and democracy. It was this sense of dignity and worth that he sought to bring to Black people themselves. On 5 August 1962 he announced 'We feel that we are the conscience of America. We are its troubled soul. We will continue to insist that right be done because both God's will and the heritage of our nation speak through our echoing demands.' Throughout the students' sit-ins, the demonstrations and the freedom rides, culminating with the triumphant 'March on Washington for Jobs and Freedom' on 28 August 1963, Martin Luther King's impact on America and the world beyond continued to grow. In Congress, the actions of the civil rights movement were beginning to bear fruit. The Civil Rights Act, which prohibited segregation in public places, and in almost all hotels, became law on 2 July 1964. The determination of authorities in southern states to discriminate as they wished now faced a far more powerful threat of intervention by the national government. Schools across the country were encouraged to desegregate. In the following months, demonstrations positively influenced the realization of the Voting Rights Act in 1965. By the end of the year almost 250,000 Black voters had registered. In the same year, the Elementary and Secondary Education Act accelerated desegregation in the schools.

King saw his message as appealing to the very tenets of democracy both in a political and a social sense. Challenging the founding principles of American political culture, he added a new universalism to concepts of equality and justice. This sense of fairness challenged the very foundations of judicial process as a blatant perpetrator of institutional racism. In April 1968 his growing concern for issues of social welfare took him to Memphis where he helped to bring attention to the plight of the local sanitation workers. King concerned himself increasingly with the divisive forces of income disparity and class which were effectively leaving Black and white citizens of America unable to participate in broader society, but left eking out a living at the fringes. As Ansbro observes, Black people were readily 'expected to live in cities suffering from financial crises, polluted air and water, obsolete and inadequate public facilities and slums so squalid that they were unparalleled in any other industrial nation'.[18] Discrimination exacerbated this position for the economically margin-alized and depressed Black underclass. King's challenge to America emerged from the grass roots of society. It spoke of the basic human freedoms and the sanctity of all human life under the law, irrespective of colour and class. This defence of social and economic rights was to add a further dimension to the timelessness of his vision. As he moved his campaign northwards into the big cities, he was increasingly struck by the condition of those who were socially disadvantaged. How, he asked, could such divisions be acceptable to a society which prided itself upon democratic principles?

King simultaneously challenged the Christian Church actively to live out Christ's gospel within society, to act as representatives of the downtrodden and to side with the powerless. He believed that the Church had a responsibility to speak out against racism and any other social injustice. It, too, must be an example of equality, tolerance, love, and a firm reflection of God's word. This dream was not widely accepted in many of the churches. By contrast they showed reluctance in involving themselves in the affairs of secular society. King confessed his disappointment: 'The laxity of the white church collectively has caused me to weep tears of love.'[19] On other occasions he spoke more firmly: 'As the Negro struggles against grave injustice most white church men offer pious irrelevancies and sanctimonious trivialities ... too much of the white church is timid and ineffectual.'[20] His struggle for justice on a national and now also on an international stage had far-reaching repercussions on issues pertaining to militarism, class, democracy, the role of women and the importance of youth. He placed great emphasis on family life and the importance of women and children within any context of social change. Coretta's loyalty and respect for her husband offered a strong model for women. True hope for an integrated society lay in the future of American youth. This faith showed forth in the great emphasis he placed upon the role of youth in the non-violent struggle. Similarly, young people were attracted to him both for his caring nature and for his courageous strength. King increasingly became concerned with America's foreign policy and causes of injustice abroad. During the late 1960s he saw America's war in Vietnam as immoral and hypocritical, considering the injustices prevalent on home soil. American defence of the Saigon government was also democratically untenable. This was not to mention the participation of Black American forces in Vietnam who, he observed, 'were recognized as heroes in the war', but 'still had to return home to the same lack of recognition in the form of second class citizenship'.[21] For such words he was heavily criticized but he continued to mature in his commitment to fighting injustice, whether at home or abroad, and facing up to the challenges of true leadership.

In 1967 Martin Luther King was awarded the Nobel Peace Prize. It represented for him an international recognition of the accomplishments of the civil rights struggle. He was only too aware that the personal publicity given to his leadership could easily be used to centralize all the achievements of the movement. He was therefore quick to emphasize that 'he accepted such applause and honours only as a trustee on behalf of the thousands of unsung people whose contributions and aspirations he sought to represent'.[22] Then, on 4 April 1968, he was assassinated in Memphis. He had often remarked to friends that he would not live into his fortieth year. That January he had celebrated his thirty-ninth birthday.

Taking forward his dream is still an ongoing struggle in a myriad of contexts and amongst a spectrum of peoples and struggles. The prevalence of institutional racism in the Western world continues to perpetuate itself in schools and workplaces, where the mixing of ethnicities has led to host nations having to grapple with fundamental meanings of equality. King's struggle has also been moved out of its racial context to be viewed as a determined struggle for justice, peace and love amongst all peoples. His voice still cries out in love against every outrage on the human person, whatever their colour or creed. It will still lead the choir and congregation, indeed the human family in the Black Diaspora, who sing 'We shall overcome, some day'. This was King's vision, inspired by prophetic conscience and the gospel of Jesus. For him the Bible was not just text but Scripture which challenged as well as comforted. He was convinced that the biblical drama could be told in terms of the relationship between God and a poor oppressed people. The God of Moses and the God of Amos was the God of Jesus. By retelling the story, King sought to let the oppressors hear again the sound of freedom and cause the oppressed to experience hope, and the power to pursue their freedom. Sorrow would give way to joy; justice would, in God's eternity, be realized. With imagination and discernment, with a theological perspective born out of an interaction between Scripture, tradition, reason and the Black experience, and with a distinctive homiletic style and rhythm, King offered his vision to his Black 'brothers and sisters' everywhere. His conviction that every human being lived in the love of God helped him to challenge laws of convention with such confidence that it literally told America to wake up – for now was the time to ring in a new era of justice and equality for its citizens. He set a new standard for African-American leadership, and it is for his courage, self-respect and love for humanity that he will be remembered. The night before he met his death he voiced his hope to those who followed him: 'I may not get there with you, but I want you to know that we as a people will get to the promised land. Love shall overcome.'

Notes

1   John J. Ansbro, *Martin Luther King Jr.: The Making of a Mind* (Maryknoll, NY: Orbis Books, 1992), p. xiii.
2   James H. Evans, 'Keepers of the dream: the Black Church and Martin Luther King, Jr.', *American Baptist Quarterly* (5 March 1986), p. 82.
3   Martin Luther King, *Stride Toward Freedom* (New York, 1958), p. 37.
4   James H. Cone, *Martin and Malcolm and America* (New York: HarperCollins Fount, 1993), p. 25.
5   Martin Luther King, *Stride Toward Freedom*, p. 41.
6   Martin Luther King, 5 December 1955, Montgomery, Alabama.
7   King's last words, quoted in Ansbro, *Martin Luther King Jr.*
8   Martin Luther King, 'A mighty army of love', *SCLC Newsletter* (1964), p. 51.
9   Ibid.
10 Martin Luther King, *The Strength to Love* (New York: Harper and Row, 1963), p. 54.
11 Ibid., p. 129.
12 Catherine Johnson *et al.* (eds), *The Wisdom of Martin Luther King in His Own Words* (New York: Lancer Books, 1968), p. 61.
13 Paul Tillich, quoted in Ansbro, *Martin Luther King Jr.*, p. 8.
14 Ibid.
15 King, quoted in Ansbro, *Martin Luther King Jr.*, p. 107.
16 Cone, *Martin and Malcolm and America*, p. 20.
17 Address to the First Annual Institute of Nonviolence and Social Change, 3 December 1956, *Martin Luther King Collection*, I, no. 11, p. 18.

18 Ansbro, *Martin Luther King Jr.*, p. 236.
19 *Playboy* interview: Martin Luther King Jr, January 1965.
20 Ibid.
21 Ansbro, *Martin Luther King Jr.*, p. 236.
22 David J. Garrow, 'Martin's legacy' in *Encyclopedia of African-American Culture and History* (New York, 1995), p. 1545.

Bibliography

John J. Ansbro, *Martin Luther King Jr.: The Making of a Mind* (Maryknoll, NY: Orbis Books, 1992).

James H. Cone, *Martin and Malcolm and America* (New York: HarperCollins Fount, 1993).

Coretta Scott King, *My Life with Martin Luther King, Jr.* (New York, 1969).

Martin Luther King, Jr, *The Strength to Love* (New York: Harper and Row, 1963).

The abolition of religion in Yunnan: Wang Zhiming

T HE QUESTION of martyrdom in the Christian history of Asia poses special problems of interpretation for the international Church. This is particularly so in the case of China, where the introduction of the gospel was inextricably linked with Western colonialism and expansionism. The conflict between the missionary message and Chinese society and culture more often reflected the encounter between imperialism and a growing nationalism than it did the scandal of the gospel in an unbelieving world. One thinks, for example, of the Chinese 'Rites' controversy, the 'unequal' treaties, the missionary cases involving property claims, or the Boxer Rebellion. That the lives of foreign missionaries and new converts were often lost in such incidents in no way implies that they were all martyrs for their faith. Some were actively seeking to expand their secular influence, while many more were victims of violence whose causes were much broader and deeper than they could understand. How is martyrdom understood in light of such inter-civilizational conflicts?

The question should not be glanced over lightly. Shortly after the founding of the People's Republic of China, David Paton, himself a former China missionary, argued that communism was exercising God's judgement upon the Church for its too easy alliance with Western expansionism. In failing to speak or act against the evils of incursions in the developing world, and in its tacit alliance with those very same forces, the churches had become 'tools of the capitalist and imperialist West', and were therefore no longer able to proclaim the gospel effectively.[1] If this indeed were the case, could those who lost their lives in this encounter really be termed Christian martyrs?

Because of the link between colonialism and Christianity, churches in many parts of Asia have not chosen to dwell on the issue of suffering or martyrdom in their own history. While acknowledging that part of the price they have paid for rooting the gospel in their own soil has been the suffering and even death of those who have gone before, they have chosen to focus on what they have to share with their own peoples and cultures. This is part of the task of inculturation and contextualization. It may be difficult for Christians in the West to understand why they should deprecate the experience of Christian suffering, but this may be one of the insights which churches in Asia have to offer to the international Church. Christians are taught to rejoice and be glad when others revile and persecute them (Matt 5:11-12), and Christians in China interpret this literally in the sense that we should not dwell on our own suffering, lest we become self-centred and self-indulgent. That Christians in difficult situations still speak of the joy of this kind of suffering represents a recovery of a biblical insight which churches in many parts of the world have lost.

In China, therefore, theologians and church leaders have cautioned against speaking of martyrdom in the contemporary period too easily and too often.[2] The upheavals of the past 150 years, from the forcible entry of foreign gunboats to the warlord period, to Civil War, and from 'Liberation' in 1949 to the chaos of the Cultural Revolution era between 1966 and 1976, affected Christian and non-Christian alike. Why, remark Chinese church people, should the suffering of Christians receive particular emphasis? They go on to argue that any focus on Christian suffering, as somehow separate from the suffering of the Chinese people, would in some way detract from the broader witness of the Church, the effort to root the Church in Chinese soil, and the greater glory of God's promise made known in Jesus Christ.

All of this is true, and yet it does not finally resolve the question. For just as many Christians at the end of the twentieth century judge that they must speak forcefully against the ways in which the Church has been used in colonial expansion and inter-civilizational conflict, so they continue to reflect upon the importance of those who died bearing witness to their faith. This is not to separate Christian suffering from the broader suffering of a people, but to understand all human suffering in light of the communion of saints, which includes martyrs not only from the Christian tradition, but from other traditions as well.

A purpose of this book is not to glorify martyrs but simply to remember them justly. Christians in history affirmed that martyrdom was a gift of God to the whole Church, a gift which strengthened its witness in each age. In the twentieth century, the confrontation between

Christianity and power has taken place under capitalist, fascist, communist and feudal societies, in the 'Christian' countries of the West, as well as in Asia, Africa and Latin America. The legacy of Christians who paid the ultimate price for their faith in these contexts is not now bequeathed to an individual church, a particular country or a given confessional tradition. We may say that they are lifted up in the unity of God's grace and love and they are an inheritance of the whole Church. It is for this reason that in 1978 the Faith and Order Commission of the World Council of Churches declared:

> In the martyr, the Church discerns Christ himself, the very heart of its faith, beyond all interpretations and divisions. That is why the martyrs of the early Church and some great witnesses in the later history of the Church are the common property of all Christians.[3]

The statement continues:

> This makes it possible, too, to recognize with joy and appreciation the ultimate witness of non-Christians whose love was great enough to lay down their lives for their friends.

* * *

In the seventeenth century there broke out in China a sporadic persecution of Catholics. The imperial proscription of Christianity at that time led to the martyrdom of both foreign missionaries and Chinese converts.[4] The first Protestant martyr is said to be Chea Kam-Kwong, who died in 1861. His efforts in spreading the gospel in and around his hometown in Guangdong provoked local officials, and he was murdered when he refused to renounce his faith.[5] Although we know a great deal about Chea, there is relatively little biographical information about most Catholic and Protestant martyrs in China. This also reflects what is probably the general situation of many 'ordinary' Christians who have died for their faith in other Asian countries. In the second half of the twentieth century, religion of any description was an obvious target of attack in the Cultural Revolution, a repository of 'old ideas' which had to be eliminated in order to make way for a revolutionary society. During this time, all churches and Christian institutions were closed, Bibles were burned and pastors and church leaders were transferred to other jobs, imprisoned or sent to labour camps. There were also some, like Wang Zhiming, an ethnic minority pastor from the south-western province of Yunnan, who lost their lives. Chinese Christians recall that they walked through the valley of the shadow of death during the Cultural Revolution. For the most part, they kept their faith in private, and if they were able to meet for worship and prayer at all, they did so in secrecy and in small home groups.

If the church in China, for very sound reasons, prefers not to dwell on the sufferings of its adherents during this time, the government also discourages undue attention to the period. Because of this, a full account of the experience of the church during this period cannot, at this time, be written. But although the Cultural Revolution era has been inadequately documented, a number of accounts have appeared which provide a general picture of religious life in China during these difficult years.[6] These have been supplemented by stories told to Chinese and overseas visitors in the years since 1978, when religious freedom was restored, churches were reopened and the injustices committed over the past decade were addressed.

The experience of Christianity in China's minority areas during the Cultural Revolution is even less well known than that for China as a whole. Fortunately, in recent years there have also been several excellent studies published in both China and the West calling attention to this neglected history.[7] We are concerned with Christians of the Miao nationality in Yunnan province, and particularly with the experience of the church in Wuding county, which lies a day's bus ride north of Kunming, the provincial capital. Christianity is a major religious force among a number of minorities in south-west China – the Miao, Yi, Lisu and Nosu, for example – and it has played a formative role in their recent history. Although the encounter between Christianity and Chinese (Han) culture is centuries old, the church has been present in the ethnic and tribal cultures of China for less than 100 years. It became important for the religious, cultural and socio-economic life of the people among whom the early missionaries worked. But it also provoked conflict.

The Miao are a mountain people found in several provinces of south-west China, as well as in Vietnam, Laos and Cambodia, where they are known as the Hmong. They speak a Sino-Tibetan dialect, and are divided into several distinct linguistic and tribal groups. The Miao are named according to their distinctive dress, with the Flowery Miao, the Blue Miao, and the Black Miao among the most prominent. Today, they are the fourth largest national minority group in China, numbering almost 7.4 million in 1990. Ancestors of the Miao lived in Hunan and Guizhou provinces 2,000 years ago, and they first settled in Yunnan in the ninth century. The Miao are a settled agricultural people with a simple social system dominated by landlords and village chiefs. Historically, there was intense rivalry between the Miao people and the Han Chinese. The Miao were fiercely independent and resisted both incorporation into the Empire and 'civilizing' initiatives on the part of the Chinese. Historical accounts as far back as the Tang dynasty (618–907) record the periodic Miao rebellions and subsequent attempts at pacification. Mutual hostility and suspicion extended into the modern period, and the Miao led or took part in major rebellions in the eighteenth and nineteenth centuries.[8] The last of these was not put down until 1874, shortly before the arrival of the first Protestant missionaries in south-west China. The rebellions and conflicts arose from a combination of ethnic, economic and political factors, and contributed to the history of exploitation and oppression of the Miao people. As a result of this history, the Miao became dispersed all over China and South-East Asia. Forced into inaccessible border regions and mountainous areas, they eked out an existence on the land as best they could, but remained largely impoverished and isolated from the broader society. In addition, they had to contend with other minorities who were in similar situations. Although they generally coexisted amicably, patterns of settlement depended upon when a particular group arrived in the area, with those who came later going higher into the mountains, where life was more difficult. In Wuding county, where Wang Zhiming was born, the Miao were the last group to arrive and, as such, they settled in the highest, poorest and most remote areas.[9]

Forced migration, isolation and impoverishment took a devastating toll on Miao culture. By the late nineteenth century, it began to undermine the Miao sense of identity. Their situation was often so desperate that one Chinese observer commented 'Hopelessness became a way of life for them'.[10] Like oppressed minority groups in other countries, the Miao became known to be 'backward' and 'wild', a people with low moral standards and little education. This reflected the prejudice against them, but it also became a self-fulfilling prophecy, the effect of an overall situation of exclusion and oppression. The establishment of the People's Republic of China in 1949 brought important changes to Han Chinese treatment of the Miao and other ethnic minorities. The 1954 Constitution declared that China was a 'unitary and multinational state', and in principle, minorities were guaranteed equality and the right to autonomy. Both ethnic separatism and 'Han chauvinism' were to be avoided, and the new government established policies which sought to respect minority cultures, promote integration and contribute to the social and economic development of minority areas. Thus, for example, the political campaigns of the early 1950s were conducted differently in Yunnan than in other parts of the country, and they were designed to express favourable treatment of the customs and cultures of the minority nationalities. If this appeared a promising beginning, however, radical policies introduced after 1957 resulted in a wholesale rejection of reformist and integrative policies. 'Class struggle' became the touchstone of the period, even though the minorities had not yet developed what Marxists could properly call class societies. Respect for the distinctive culture and experience of the ethnic minorities was rejected by the radicals who were in power as evidence of weakness or 'reformism'. The era of the Cultural Revolution intensified this trend, and new coercive policies intensified Miao–Han antagonism, eventually resulting in a total rejection of the principle of co-operation and integration with minority people.[11] During this period there was active struggle against religious belief in many parts of China, and it was this which led to the martyrdom of Wang Zhiming in Yunnan.

The first Christian missionaries went to Yunnan at the end of the nineteenth century, but they concentrated their early efforts not on the minorities but on the (Han) Chinese. A Protestant presence among the Miao was established in neighbouring Guizhou province with the arrival of J. R. Adam of the China Inland Mission (CIM). His colleague Samuel Clarke went to work among the Black Miao in 1896, but he was murdered by bandits together with Pan Sheoshan, the first Miao Christian, shortly thereafter. In 1903, Adam established a CIM headquarters in Kunming, by which time other missionaries were already working with the Miao in Yunnan. In the northern part of the province, the English Methodist Sam Pollard, who became an almost legendary 'apostle to the Miao', began working in the city of Zhaotong. He later moved to Shimenkan in Guizhou, from which base he and other Methodist missionaries worked tirelessly to foster evangelism, education and social development.[12] Over the next twenty years, other Protestant groups became active in Yunnan, and in their work they also came into contact with the Miao. But in Yunnan, it was the CIM who became most extensively involved with evangelistic efforts among the Miao, and Miao Christianity came to reflect the mission's own particular brand of piety and evangelical fervour.

Christianity entered Wuding county in 1906, when two Miao lepers who had travelled first to Guizhou and then to Zhaotong told others about the message of Jesus Christ which they had heard. Pollard visited Wuding, but because he was unable to work there himself, he asked for help from the CIM, and they sent another minister, Arthur Nicholls. Nicholls moved to Sapushan, 150 km north of the Wuding county seat,

which became the base of CIM operations. He soon established five
small churches in the county. Within a few years, Miao preachers were
also spreading the gospel, not only among their own people in
Wuding, but also to other minorities in neighbouring counties and
villages, particularly the Yi, the Lisu and the Gobu. The CIM also set up
Christian primary schools for the Miao in Wuding. They trained
teachers for the schools in the New Testament which had been
translated into Miao, using the script which was developed by Pollard
and his colleagues.[13] These were among the first schools established
specifically for the Miao. Christianity grew rapidly among the ethnic
groups in Yunnan, and especially among the Miao. In 1907, 1,412 Miao
from 71 villages were baptized. By the 1930s, 20,000 Miao had become
Christians, and by 1950, there were reportedly 131,191 believers
among all Yunnan minorities.[14] Since there were only 700,000
Protestants in China at that time, minority people from Yunnan
represented a sizeable percentage of the Christian population, even
though Yunnan itself had a fraction of the population for the country as
a whole. The CIM estimated that there were 2,000 Christians in
Wuding county in 1932. By 1950, the number had grown to 2,419, and
they were meeting in 41 places of worship.[15] As in any account of
Christian conversion, there were a variety of personal, religious, and
social factors at work in these figures, and no single interpretation of
conversion can do justice to the complex process of transformation
which was evident, both in the individuals and in the communities.[16]
However, one important aspect of the conversion process among the
Miao was that Christianity helped to transform and strengthen the
people's sense of identity and selfhood, which in the early twentieth
century was in danger of being undermined. Conversion meant a sense
of personal acceptance, by God and by the community. Miao churches
helped to strengthen community organization as they established
relationships among brothers and sisters in Christ which functioned
almost like an extended family. Christian discipline fostered moral
renewal and the eradication of social practices that were deemed
unhealthy. The creation of a written language for translating the New
Testament also helped to preserve Miao culture and tradition, and
reinforce minority identity vis-à-vis the larger community.[17] And Miao
Christian music — for which their churches are justifiably famous even
today — further reinforced the sense of identity and acceptance which
came with Christian faith.

    By 1949, Christianity was well established among the Miao, and was
in a very real sense an aspect of Miao culture. However, although Miao

Christians were eager evangelists and generous in their practice of self-support, little had been done in the way of promoting an independent Miao church. The Christian presence remained largely under the authority of foreign missionaries. The Miao themselves felt warmly for the missionaries who went to work among them, something that is still evident today. They resisted new government policies which attempted to distance the church from the missionaries. In this sense, the Chinese government was in part correct to draw the conclusion that the missionaries had sown the seeds of ethnic and religious separatism among minority Christians. For if Christianity helped to reinforce a Miao identity, then the corollary was that it helped the Miao to desist from assimilation into the broader society. According to T'ien Ju-kang, conversion to Christianity meant that the Miao avoided sinicization. Foreign missionaries succeeded in 'the uniting of the widely dispersed minorities into social entities, entrusted with political power, [and] established with ecclesiastical as well as civil orders'. T'ien adds that the most pronounced case of this was in Wuding county.[18]

When the missionaries left Yunnan in the early 1950s, and the policies of the new Communist state began to take effect, the Miao Christians found themselves on their own. A land reform movement was followed by the 'Accusation Movement'. After the outbreak of the Korean War, Christians were forced to denounce landlords and their missionary colleagues. But there were few Miao landlords in Wuding, and most Christians refused to denounce the missionaries. The government persisted in efforts to win over the Miao Christians. It set up a United Front Work Department in Sapushan to help implement religious and minority policy. Furthermore, Miao Christian leaders were sent on visits to Beijing and were invited to join local political bodies in order to encourage patriotism and integration. Although Christian activity declined somewhat during the political movements of the 1950s, the church continued to function. The government approved the sending of Christians to other provinces for seminary study and ordination. Christian Three-Self Patriotic Movement committees (TSPMs) were organized in many areas, although a provincial TSPM was not established in Yunnan until 1963. Some Christians in border areas emigrated to South-East Asia in the 1950s and 1960s, but most minority churches continued as before. By 1954, almost one-third of the churches in Yunnan were concentrated in the prefecture which included Wuding, and this area had almost half of the Christians in the province.[19] On the eve of the Cultural Revolution, there were 2,795 Christians in Wuding, more than there had been in

1950. A government report published in 1990 declared that 'basically all of them supported Party policy and the socialist road'.[20] This was a judgement made in hindsight, and it testifies to the tremendous changes which have taken place in China over the last twenty years. For the statement certainly did not reflect the official attitudes towards Miao Christians in the 1960s.

We know little about the life of Wang Zhiming. He was a prominent Miao Christian leader, but he was not very well known outside of the church in his own province, let alone overseas. He did not leave behind a body of writings. But he is remembered and celebrated still in the church and community he sought to serve. He grew up in Wuding where he attended Christian schools, later becoming first a teacher and then an evangelist. In 1944, he was elected chairman of the Sapushan Church Council. He was apparently widely respected in the church, for, after 1949, he became the general superintendent of all Miao churches in Wuding and Lequan counties. In 1951 or shortly thereafter, he was also ordained as a pastor.[21]

The new government needed and wanted the support of Miao leaders such as Wang because of their standing in their own communities. His was one of six names, representing 30,000 Christians from northern Yunnan, which appeared on a statement in 1951 promoting the Christian Three-Self Patriotic Movement, criticizing the linkage between Christianity and imperialism, and endorsing government policies and programmes.[22] Such statements were common at the time, and many signatures were extracted under pressure. Still, the fact that he signed such a statement is significant. By all accounts, he was a man with a deep sense of integrity, and so it seems likely that he accepted the general sense of the statement. Wang Zhiming was not a dissident, nor was he someone out to oppose the government. In 1956, he was part of a delegation which went to Beijing and was received by Chairman Mao. And in 1958, prior to the outbreak of the 'Anti-Rightist Movement' he was named a model worker.

Although not opposed to the government, Wang Zhiming was also not prepared to reject the things in which he believed. Between 1951 and 1953, accusation meetings were held in Wuding county to denounce landlords and American imperialists. Miao Christians were required to attend the meetings, and Wang told them 'We Christians stress forbearance. Now is the time to stick to it.' When he himself was asked to write something which would be used to denounce a landlord on behalf of a Han villager, he replied 'My hands have baptized many converts, and should not be used for sinfulness'.[23] There was thus already some conflict in his words and actions, between his acceptance of the new order and the demands of his Christian faith.

Religion came under attack in Yunnan during the Anti-Rightist Movement in 1958, and, according to government records, all religious activity ceased or went underground shortly thereafter.[24] Beginning at this time, minority Christians began to escape across the border into Burma and Thailand in large numbers, but this was not a possibility for Miao Christians who lived in the mountains further to the north. By the time of the Cultural Revolution, even the TSPM committees were disbanded, and all churches were closed and put to other uses. Because of the vitality of its Christian community, Wuding was singled out as an area in which 'to do battle against religion' and Christians themselves became 'objects of dictatorship'.[25] Wang Zhiming was declared to be a counter-revolutionary and came under criticism in the early 1960s, and perhaps as early as 1958. He was arrested on 11 May 1969, and charged with 'carrying out anti-Party and anti-socialist activities under the cloak of religion'.[26] The exact circumstances of his arrest and imprisonment are unclear, and the vague charges against him were similar to those made against many who were being victimized. But it is certain that by this time it was no longer possible for Wang Zhiming to maintain his Christian faith without coming into conflict with radical political forces.

Professor T'ien Ju-kang, who consulted the archives of the Yunnan Academy of Social Sciences, and who visited Wuding in 1988, suggests that local rivalry may have been involved in Wang's arrest and imprisonment. Two brothers in Wuding, surnamed Long, had once been Christians but had left the church in the 1950s. The younger brother eventually became a local official and had little contact thereafter with Miao Christians. The older brother actively propagated atheism and was disliked by the Christian community. Although he was never allowed to join the Communist Party, he became involved in efforts to oppose Christianity by setting up a cultural centre and troupe to counter Christian singing. Evidently, it had little effect. In 1966, the elder Long joined a rebel group of Red Guards, and they began to persecute Miao church leaders. Wang Zhiming had worked assiduously to combat Long's campaign, and he had proved an influential opponent. But in December 1973, Long secured his arrest and that of a number of other Christians, including several members of his family. Wang Zhiming was sentenced to death. Before his execution, he is reported to have said three final sentences to his family:

You should not follow my example. This was taken in a paradoxical sense to

mean that Wang wanted his family members to hold fast to their faith in
Christ.

You should follow the words from above and repent once again. The word
'above' was taken to mean God, not the authorities.

In all of your work, you should pay attention to cleanliness. This meant that
they should maintain standards of purity and holiness in their lives.

These words became part of the tradition in Wuding which grew up
around his martyrdom. They represented a last will and testament.
According to Professor T'ien:

> The execution took place at a mass rally with an attendance of more than
> 10,000, most of them Christians who were compelled to attend to
> frighten them into submission. Yet the result was opposite of the
> intended. The converts did not manifest the slightest fear of ruthless
> suppression. Right after the barbarous murder was committed, a group of
> Miao church women, disregarding the consequences, rushed to the stand
> where Elder Long was sitting together with the public security officers
> and where he uttered his speech of denunciation, crying indignantly
> against the odious backslider, 'Dire Satan, you previously preached the
> Gospel, now you are committing a heinous crime in opposition to it. Dare
> you come down!' This courageous protest, the report goes, suddenly
> threw the whole stadium into turmoil. Even in 1988, when the author
> was visiting Wuding, everyone who had attended the rally without
> exception talked about the execution with scornful disdain.[27]

Wang's wife was sentenced to three years in prison, but she was later
released, and she died an elderly woman in 1995. Two of his sons were
sentenced to nine-year prison terms. A third reportedly took his own life
while under detention.

Between 1969 and 1973, at least 21 Christian leaders in Wuding
were imprisoned, three others were sent to do penal labour under
surveillance and many more were criticized, denounced and/or beaten.
Houses were repeatedly searched. Some Christians were persuaded to
reject their faith and denounce their leaders. Such actions were directed
not only against Christians, but also against the Hui minority Muslims
in Wuding. In this way the region became the scene of some of the
worst excesses against Christians in China during the period. The most
notorious example took place at Narrow Stone Bridge village
(Xiaoshiqiao). A Miao village, it had been declared an 'advanced work
unit' in the 1950s because of the people's willingness to respond to
government calls to raise production. Every family in the village was
Christian. When in 1969 they had been asked to renounce their faith
and give their allegiance to Chairman Mao, the villagers refused. Their

leaders were beaten and imprisoned, but the Christians kept to their faith. When told that even their land belonged to Chairman Mao, not to God, they responded that they would therefore not farm, and so their fields were confiscated. Neighbouring villagers brought food to them under the cover of darkness, and they were also punished. The villagers eventually formed themselves into a separatist Christian group called the 'Little Flock', in defiance of the authorities. Their leader Yang Guangrong was sentenced to a seven-year prison term but the Christian villagers continued in their faith as before.[28]

The attempt to eliminate religion in Wuding was a total failure. The witness of Wang Zhiming and others only strengthened the faith of the church, and it continued to grow. In 1978, after the radical policies of the Cultural Revolution were overturned, the government counted 3,682 Christians in Wuding. Two years later that number was estimated at 10,000. These figures do not include the 'Little Flock', which between 1975 and 1980 had increased from ten to 1,800.

The death of Mao and the fall of his leading collaborators, the so-called 'Gang of Four', in 1976 served as a prelude to Deng Xiaoping's return to power and the rejection of the radical politics of the Cultural Revolution. Beginning in the late 1970s, the state became more accommodating towards religion and minority nationalities, and churches began to reopen all over China. This ushered in a new era of restoration and reconciliation in both government attitudes and religious practice. The cases of those killed, persecuted, gaoled and wrongly accused during the Cultural Revolution were taken up by the government in the late 1970s. They were found to include people from all walks of life — workers and intellectuals, Christians and members of other religious groups, high-ranking Communist Party officials. In places like Wuding county, a great deal had to be done to make amends for the past. At the end of 1978, high-ranking officials were sent to look into each case. All of those who had been arrested with Wang Zhiming or in subsequent years were released and given compensation. In October 1980 the name of Wang Zhiming was completely rehabilitated and his family was given a payment of RMB 1,300 as 'comfort and compensation' for his unlawful execution. Nineteen people who were arrested with him were rehabilitated at the same time, including all his family members. The Sapushan church, which had been destroyed during the Cultural Revolution, was also rebuilt at government expense and returned to the Christians. Yang Guangrong, the leader of the 'Little Flock', was released from prison in 1978 and was declared to have been wrongly charged. The Narrow Stone Bridge villagers were given back their land, and apologies were made. But deep feelings of resentment endured there. In 1988, government leaders visited 70 families who had been victimized in Narrow Stone Bridge and in neighbouring villages in order to show their good faith. An investigation committee was set up to look into the cases of those who had been arrested, beaten or charged, and 213 people were rehabilitated and given compensation totalling RMB 56,000. The 'Little Flock' is now more or less tolerated, and by 1990, an official Wuding county report declared that religious life in Narrow Stone Bridge village 'had returned to normal'.[29]

The TSPM was reorganized all over Yunnan province, and a Yunnan Christian Council was also formed. In 1981, more than 100 church leaders attended the first Christian Conference in Wuding. Some of these were also appointed to church committees at the provincial level, and Wang Xisheng, Wang Zhiming's son, became a member of the national committee of the TSPM. Later he was asked to join its Commission for Minority Church Affairs. There are now said to be more than 100 places of worship in Wuding for its estimated 30,000 Christians. Church leaders from many other parts of China have visited Wuding in order to promote reconciliation, to encourage the church and to learn from the example of Christians there. Miao Christians have chosen not to bring any charges against those who persecuted them. In the same year a memorial to Wang Zhiming was erected not far from his home. It remains the only known monument to a Christian who died in the Cultural Revolution. On the tablet these words are inscribed:

> Wang Zhiming was educated in Christian schools from childhood, and had deep feelings for the faith, and a love to serve the Lord. He was on the staff of a Christian school for more than ten years and also served as an evangelist for five years. In 1944, he was elected chairman of the Sapushan Church Council, Wuding County, Yunnan Province. In 1951 ... [unclear], he was ordained a pastor. In peace and with a clear sense of calling, Pastor Wang gave of himself throughout his life. Learning from the shining example of Jesus Christ, glorifying God and bringing benefit to people was his life's work. He loved his country and was dedicated to the church although he endured many storms. In spite of all kinds of setbacks he kept on fighting. Calmly and courageously, he learned to contribute everything to the church. Unfortunately the Gang of Four emerged in China and brought cruelty, evil and inhumanity to the country. Wang Zhiming was unjustly arrested on 11 May 1969. Fabricated evidence led to Wang's conviction and he was martyred in Wuding on 29 December 1973. He died at the age of 66. As Scripture says of the Saints, 'They will rest from their labours for their deeds follow them' (Rev 14:13).

Notes

1 See David Paton, *Christian Missions and the Judgment of* God (Grand Rapids: Eerdmans, 2nd edn 1996); Paton's short book was first published in 1953.
2 See K. H. Ting, 'A Chinese Christian selfhood' in *Christian Witness in China Today* (Kyoto: Doshisha University Press, 1985), pp. 47–8; also 'Prophetic challenges' in *No Longer Strangers: Selected Writings of K. H. Ting* (Maryknoll, NY: Orbis, 1989), p. 109.
3 'Witness unto death' in *Sharing in One Hope: Bangalore, 1978* (Geneva: Commission on Faith and Order, 1978), p. 200.
4 Kenneth S. Latourette, *A History of Christian Missions in China* (London: SPCK, 1929), pp. 103, 269 and *passim*; also Bob Whyte, *Unfinished Encounter: China and Christianity* (London: Collins, 1988), pp. 79–83.
5 Lauren Pfister, 'From the golden light within: reconsideration of James Legge's account of Chea Kam-Kwong, the Chinese Protestant proto-martyr', paper presented at the International Conference on James Legge (April 1997); also Ma Jingquan, 'Chea Kam Kwong China's first martyr', *Hui Xun* (Hong Kong Council of the Church of Christ in China), nos 242–43 (July 1977), p. 6.
6 For example, Whyte, *Unfinished Encounter*, pp. 282–337; Tony Lambert, *The Resurrection of the Chinese Church* (Wheaton, IL: Harold Shaw, 1994), pp. 9–26; and my own *Seeking the Common Ground: Protestant Christianity, the Three-Self Movement and China's United Front* (Maryknoll, NY: Orbis, 1988), pp. 179–84.
7 See especially T'ien Ju-kang, *Peaks of Faith: Protestant Mission in Revolutionary China* (Leiden, New York and Cologne: E. J. Brill, 1993) and (in Chinese) Zhang Tan, *The Stone Threshold in Front of the 'Narrow Door': Christian Culture and Miao People's Society on the Border Regions of Sichuan, Yunnan and Guizhou Provinces* (Kunming: Yunnan People's Publishing House, 1992).
8 See Ralph Covell, *The Liberating Gospel in China: The Christian Faith Among China's Minority Peoples* (Grand Rapids: Baker), pp. 84–5; and Colin Mackerras, *China's Minorities: Integration and Modernization in the Twentieth Century* (Hong Kong: Oxford University Press), p. 28.
9 T'ien, *Peaks of Faith*, p. 10.
10 Zhang, *The Stone Threshold in Front of the 'Narrow Door'*, as quoted in Covell, *The Liberating Gospel*, p. 86.
11 This discussion is based on Mackerras, *China's Minorities*, pp. 139–59.
12 See R. Elliott Kendall, *Beyond the Clouds: The Story of Samuel Pollard of South-West China* (London: Cargate Press, 1954).
13 T'ien, *Peaks of Faith*, p. 23. For early Protestant work among the Miao see Covell, *The Liberating Gospel*, pp. 83ff.
14 T'ien, *Peaks of Faith*, pp. 22, 26.
15 The 1932 figure is quoted in Covell, *The Liberating Gospel*, p. 92. Other

142   *Philip L. Wickeri*

figures here and in the pages which follow are from *The Wuding County Gazetteer (Series of Local Gazetteers of the People's Republic of China)*, ed. Compilation Committee of the Wuding County Gazetteer (Tianjin: Tianjin People's Publishing House, 1990), pp. 354-5. This latter source contains an open and objective criticism of the injustices committed in Wuding county during the years of the Cultural Revolution.

16 Lewis Rambo, *Understanding Religious Conversion* (New Haven: Yale University Press, 1993).

17 See Norma Diamond, 'Christianity and the Hua Miao: writing and power', unpublished manuscript, 34pp.

18 T'ien, *Peaks of Faith*, p. 40.

19 *Yunnan Province Gazetteer*, vol. 66: *Religion* (Series of Local Gazetteers of the People's Republic of China), ed. Compilation Committee of Yunnan Province Gazetteer (Kunming: Yunnan People's Publishing, 1995), pp. 254, 256. The exact figures cited are 294 out of 901 churches and 50,000 out of 12,886 Protestant Christians.

20 *Wuding County Gazetteer*, p. 354.

21 Basic information on the life of Wang Zhiming is found on the tablet erected in his memory and cited in full on p. 140. See 'Grave of Christian martyr of Cultural Revolution erected in Yunnan', *Amity News Service* (2 May 1996). Other information in the pages which follow is from interviews conducted by independent researchers, not this author, in Wuding county. These have been cross-checked where possible.

22 *Wuding County Gazetteer*, p. 356. The statement is dated 17 February 1951 and the other signatories are Christian leaders from other minority churches.

23 T'ien, *Peaks of Faith*, p. 76.

24 *Yunnan Province Gazetteer*, p. 230.

25 T'ien, *Peaks of Faith*, p. 111.

26 *Wuding County Gazetteer*, p. 354.

27 T'ien, *Peaks of Faith*, pp. 95-6. The author cites the *Yunnan Academy of Social Sciences Archives*, vol. 413, Section 35 for the record of Wang Zhiming's activities in Yunnan. These archives are not open to foreign scholars. T'ien's account of Wang's execution is given without footnote, and is apparently drawn from oral accounts during his 1988 visit to Wuding.

28 *Wuding County Gazetteer*, p. 354; T'ien, *Peaks of Faith*, pp. 111ff.; Huang Jianru, 'Returning from a visit to Yunnan', *Zongjiao*, 1 (1979), pp. 20-4; Tony Lambert, 'The Church among the hill tribes' in *The Phoenix Rises*, ed. Leslie Lyall (Singapore: Overseas Missionary Fellowship, 1992), pp. 80-1. The 'Little Flock' (*xiaozhongjiao*) mentioned here should not be confused with Watchman Nee's 'Little Flock' (*xiaoqun*) in East China.

29 *Wuding County Gazetteer*, p. 354.

Bibliography

Tony Lambert, *The Resurrection of the Chinese Church* (Wheaton, IL: Harold Shaw, 1994).

Bob Whyte, *Unfinished Encounter: China and Christianity* (London: Collins, 1988).

Tribalism, religion and despotism in Uganda: Archbishop Janani Luwum

JOHN SENTAMU

> Daily daily sing the praises
> Of the city God hath made;
> In the beauteous Field of Eden
> Its foundation-stones are laid.
>
> *Hymn of the first Ugandan martyrs*

THE STORY of Uganda presents a striking picture of religious and political currents, all of them interweaving in the midst of different tribal cultures and powerful external pressures. In the nineteenth century it was the missionaries of the Western churches, and not the political powers or the economic migrants of Europe, who first came to East Africa. They built their stations on the mainland there from the middle years of the century, several decades before the establishment of colonial administration. Protestant and Roman Catholic missionaries sought to spread Christian civilization, promote agriculture and encourage commerce. They were also firm in their commitment to abolish the slave trade that was the currency of Arab and Swahili merchants. They provided schools, in which many of the region's future leaders were educated.

Uganda in the late nineteenth century was a country of Protestants, Catholics, Muslims and pagans. By the 1880s, these faiths had become an integral part of the language of political power, and also vehicles for violent rule. The Kabaka Mwanga, who claimed the paramountcy of Buganda in 1884, was a Muslim. In 1885 he executed a number of Christians in his court and ordered the murder of an Anglican bishop, James Hannington. During 1886 some 200 Christians, the first martyrs of Uganda, died. Later, Mwanga renounced the Muslim faith and united with pagans to drive out the missionary religions. This provoked a coalition against him, and he was defeated. This deep relationship between religion and politics would endure long after. Over half a century later, as Ugandans sought independence from British colonial authority, religious identity would still do much to define political expressions. The Democratic Party which contested the 1961 elections with the Uganda People's Congress owed its origins to the Roman Catholic Church.

The state of Uganda was a creation of colonialism; it did not answer to the realities of tribal life. Within its borders were gathered several kingdoms, many different customs and identities, and many rivalries. Dominant among them was the kingdom of the Buganda, governed by its Kabaka. In the twentieth century there were only 10,000 white settlers living in Uganda, and 70,000 Asian settlers, many of whom had been brought there by the British. In a new age of African nationalism, this did not represent a force to obstruct the demands of Ugandans who sought independence. But nationalism as a movement struggled to generate momentum in a country where tribalism remained the dominant social fact. The colonial rule had done little to diminish its strength. On the one hand the British had encouraged participation in national life: in the 1950s the Legislative Council had a growing number of Africans. But, equally, the arrangements that they had created over half a century had confirmed and even deepened tribal identities. Now, it was the Buganda, more than any other group, who were not easily reconciled to a place in a greater, independent state.

Even so, when nationalists sought to present British rule with a united front that could govern the country once it was given its liberty, the British were persuaded. In October 1962 Uganda became an independent state. Its president was the Kabaka of Buganda, but real power lay with the chief minister, the Roman Catholic Benedicto Kiwanuka. If this appeared to frame a stable equation of power, and one that acknowledged the privileged status of the Buganda, it did not last long. In 1963 Kiwanuka was succeeded by Milton Obote. Obote sought to create a united nation by the suppression of inherited practices and a certain amount of coercion. In 1966 he removed the special rights previously conceded to the Buganda. The Kabaka went to England to live as an exile.

In September 1973 I was posted as a magistrate to Gulu, northern Uganda, by the Chief Justice of the High Court of Uganda.[1] It was an area that had by then suffered greatly from political and military oppression: Gulu itself had more widows and orphans at that time than elsewhere in Uganda. A number of townships had been deserted. Janani Luwum, the Bishop of Northern Uganda, based in Gulu, had heard that I had arrived in Gulu and he came to meet me. This tall, imposing figure gave me a huge hug – I almost disappeared in his bosom. 'Praise the Lord and thank you for coming to this strong and yet currently sad part of Uganda. God has answered our prayers!'[2]

Back at his bishop's residence, a fairly humble homestead, a feast had been prepared. Luwum lost no opportunity in telling me that he wanted to build up this *muganda* from the South into a strong judge, like the Acoli tribal warriors. He asked me to become the Chancellor of his diocese and to assist him in alleviating the plight of many refugees from the Sudan. 'We must be Christ to these people: be our advocate and take up their cases. The local prison is filled to capacity with innocent people suspected of opposing the government. Even wearing a mini-skirt is a crime.'

Luwum struck me then as a man intimately aware of the realities of a world of power. His way of working in his diocese clearly revealed a Christian whose method was specifically geared to building the confidence of the people and the Church in northern Uganda. He was not afraid of talking about power, and was impatient with those who tried to keep a lid on it. Luwum himself strongly believed that it was the abdication of power which had resulted in yielding to other forces in the country that were too ready to flex their muscles: from the World Bank and tribalism to the president of Uganda, Idi Amin. The Church, as he saw it, had legitimate and urgent roles to play on the world stage. 'We have the power of Christ to participate and thereby discipline the powers and institutions to be more responsive to human need', he often said, with a twinkle in his eye. The Church had the urgent task of developing the disciplines of exercising power because such things could not grow automatically. He saw many Christians conspicuously avoiding the abuses of power. But abdication of the exercise of responsibility was not a moral option. Luwum took the view that abdication was as much an abuse as was the oppression of others. What was required of the Church was to be holy. For power without purity to guide is a terror to others. Since the earth is full of God's glory, of the glory of his power and purity, the Christian is called to be like God – 'Just in all his ways, and kind in all his doings' (Psalm 145:17), 'holy as God is holy' (Matthew 5:48). Spending time with Janani Luwum in the flat savannah plains, rolling hills and rugged mountain peaks of northern Uganda made me realize that at the heart of the story of creation what we see is the gift of power by the Creator to all his creatures. Pentecost was God the Father giving power away in Jesus' name. Creation and Pentecost were not instances of succumbing, or bowing down, to power, but of the gaining of it. 'You will receive power

when the Holy Spirit has come upon you; and you will be my witnesses
... ' (Acts 1:8). For Luwum this meant that his ministry as a bishop was
primarily one of building relationships, and giving power to people, and
particularly to the church community in northern Uganda, and later on
in the whole Province. It was the best way of witnessing for Christ.

In her book *Janani, the Making of a Modern Martyr*,[3] Margaret Ford
drew on the reminiscences of men and women who knew Luwum well,
from the time of his childhood to his brief years of leadership in the
church. Ford found that the seeds of his later ideas were sown early in
life, in his country of birth, his childhood and early life, and in the
church to which he belonged. All inculcated a distinctive sense of
responsibility. He was raised in a generous and hard-working family.
His tough, tireless and persistent mother made sure that the earthen-
ware cooking pot, perched on the traditional fire between three large
stones, was seldom empty, and there was always chicken for the visitor.
His father, Elijah, an early convert to Christianity, was a dedicated
Christian who had committed his life to serving the Lord as a teacher.
Janani was a skilled marksman, dancer and musician, and a leader at an
early age. He roamed the savannah plains, stalked wild animals, climbed
trees and walked to and from Gulu High School, a distance of 80 miles,
at the beginning and end of each term.

Later in life, Luwum often spoke of how he was influenced by
reading the story of Henry Morton Stanley, the foreign correspondent of
the *New York Herald*, who for eight months searched for the explorer
David Livingstone, and then discovered him in a state of exhaustion on
10 November 1871 in Central Africa. After spending some time with
him, Stanley had said 'If I had been with him any longer I would have
been compelled to be a Christian and yet he never spoke to me about it
at all'. For Luwum, it was not words but deeds that made such a life
irresistible. Accordingly, he kept the story of his own conversion to
Christianity to himself for 28 years. It was even said in revivalist
churches that his faith was unmoved by dramatic, charismatic
experience. But in December 1976 he told me about it.

His conversion to a witnessing and a confessing Christianity, known
as the East African Revival, or the company of the saved ones, the
abalokol, was dramatic. He testified to giving his life to Christ on 6
January 1948, at half past noon, in his own village during the preaching
of Yusto Otunno, a member of the 'saved ones'. During Yusto's
preaching the young Luwum felt convicted; twice he broke out in a
heavy sweat. When this happened a third time he confessed Jesus Christ
as his Lord and in tears repented of his sins, crying aloud before God

and men, so that the villagers came running to see what was happening. After the preacher and his wife Josephine had prayed for him, he stood up and said 'Today I have become a leader in Christ's army. I am prepared to die in the army of Jesus. As Jesus shed his blood for the people, if it is God's will, I will do the same.' Such were the words of a primary-school teacher in his own village where he was well known and where his family and village had wanted him to be a chief. He told me:

> When I was converted, after realising that my sins were forgiven and the implications of Jesus' death and resurrection, I was overwhelmed by a sense of joy and peace. I suddenly found myself climbing a tree to tell those in the school compound to repent and turn to Jesus Christ. From time to time I spoke in tongues. I stayed up that tree for a long time. Later on I discovered that some boys were converted due to a sermon I preached up that tree. The reality of Jesus overwhelmed me – and it still does. But I would be wrong to demand that those who are converted should climb a tree and speak in tongues.

At an open-air rally, he called his hearers to turn away from the excessive drinking and smoking which was ruining many lives, and to follow Christ. He challenged the Church's catechists for turning a blind eye to the evil in the community. Within a month of his conversion he was arrested with eight others, at the instigation of church leaders, brought before the sub-chief of his village and charged with disturbing the peace. The following day they were taken to Kitgum, the administrative centre of East Acoli and gaoled for two days. The warders manhandled them and promised to give them food if they undertook not to denounce excessive drinking and smoking.[4] Luwum told them 'We have not disturbed any peace. Our Saviour is the Prince of Peace and he wants you to know that he loves you.' He then deplored smoking and drinking once more. Tired of being exhorted to turn to Christ, the warders released them a few days later.

Luwum's new-found courage and confidence was to be put to the test three months later when his brother Aloni Okecho, and Yusto Otunno, the man who converted him, were arrested, badly beaten up and made to appear before the local magistrate. He went to the court to demand: had the accused had been assaulted because they had been preaching the good news of Jesus Christ? If that was the case, the court should order him to be beaten up as he too was one of the saved ones. The magistrate charged Luwum with contempt of court and sentenced him to one month's imprisonment or a fine of 20 shillings. Yusto and Aloni were sent down; Janani Luwum opted for imprisonment, but he was persuaded to find the money to pay the fine. The gospel needed to be preached both on the outside and the inside of prison. Eleven months after his conversion, on one Sunday afternoon, Luwum was moved to address an open-air meeting at All Saints Church in Kitgum:

> The Holy Spirit has been showing me how many educated men are deserting the Church. When the Church dies out of existence they won't be there to take the blame. I feel deeply convicted that if the Church faces extinction in this my native land, I will be around to die first before the Church falls, collapses or dies. It will have to fall on me. I totally surrender myself to the Church.

Then he fell on the ground and wept bitterly amid loud shouts of praise, thanksgiving and tears of joy and repentance. Yusto Otunno responded by saying that Luwum, as one of the educated brethren, should join the full-time ministry of the church. God was calling him to sacrifice his teaching career, and the real possibility of being a local chief, and to offer himself for ordination.

In January 1949 Luwum left his wife Mary and their three-year-old daughter at home in Acoli, and travelled to a theological college at Buwalasi near Mount Elgon, in the east of Uganda. He completed his course a year later and returned to Gulu as a catechist. In 1953 he returned to Buwalasi to train for ordination, and he was ordained deacon on St Thomas's Day, 21 December 1955. He was priested a year later. In 1958 Luwum went to England to spend a year at St Augustine's College, Canterbury, and he returned to Buwalasi Theological College as Vice-Principal. In 1963 he spent two years at the London College of Divinity, where he obtained the College Diploma. Now he returned to Buwalasi as College Principal.

Janani Luwum was appointed Provincial Secretary of the Church of Uganda, Rwanda, Burundi and Boga-Zaire in September 1966. When he arrived at the Provincial headquarters he found himself at the tail end of a furious row over the appointment of a successor to Archbishop Leslie Brown.[5] As far as the Bagandan Anglicans were concerned, it was a foregone conclusion that their own Dunstan Nsubuga, only recently consecrated as a bishop, would be elected as the new archbishop. Instead, Erica Sabiti, a bishop from Ankole, south-west Uganda, was elected and duly installed as archbishop at St Paul's Cathedral, Namirembe. It was a sign of future difficulties. Luwum found it hard to work with the Baganda, who now refused to accept Archbishop Sabiti's appointment and threw up other obstructions for the new Provincial Secretary. Nsubuga had occupied the archbishop's official residence, and he refused to leave. Since there was no other house available on Namirembe Hill, nor even an office there, Archbishop Sabiti continued to live at Fort Portal, the headquarters of his own diocese of Ruwenzori. Taxed by the long and frequent journeys to Kampala, which lay 200 kilometres away on a rough non-tarmac road, his health began to decline.

But Luwum made himself busy, and his gift of leadership was soon evident. He organized the building of a new archbishop's house and Provincial offices on Namirembe Hill. He also proposed the creation of a diocese of Kampala for all future archbishops, carved out of Namirembe, something that came into effect only later when he became Bishop of Northern Uganda. He wholeheartedly endorsed the Bikangaga Report. This ten-year plan embodied the vision of the first Anglican bishop to take up residence in Uganda in 1890, Alfred Tucker. It spelled out a vision of a self-governing, expanding and self-financing church. Luwum's enthusiasm for the plan won support amongst other members of the Provincial Assembly of the church, but did not heal the hurt felt by the Baganda. The Bikangaga Report had proposed the establishment of Church Commissioners to hold all church land on behalf of the Province. But the diocese of Namirembe owned more land than all other dioceses put together, and the Baganda quickly saw the idea as a conspiracy by both church and state to appropriate their assets. The foundation of the plan, however, lay not with these matters. Its advocates sought to prepare the church for its centenary in 1977 by putting in place an efficient administrative machinery, the training of the laity, and clear programmes of discipleship, stewardship and evangelism.

Luwum travelled extensively throughout the Anglican Province, seeking support for the Bikangaga proposals. At Jinja, Busoga, in October 1968, he told a large crowd that had gathered to hear him:

There was once a middle-aged man whose wife died in childbirth, leaving him with a baby boy. He took good care of the child. He never forgot to bring him food from the garden. But one day, he decided to put the boy to the test, to find out whether he would look after him in his old age. He gave the child some potatoes as usual but on this occasion asked the boy to share them with him. The child refused and hid the potatoes from his father. Yet the old man continued to care for the boy, until he grew into a man and married. Tragically, this is how we are with God. He gives us gifts, and when he asks us to give him back a little of what he gave us, so that he can use it to enlarge his kingdom and help the needy, we refuse. Yet still he continues to look after us, hoping that we will change and become good children.

Janani Luwum was consecrated Bishop of Northern Uganda on 25 January 1969. The service took place in a large field, known as Pece Stadium, in Gulu. Margaret Ford found it almost as much a political rally as a religious ceremony. Amongst the congregation could be seen the president of Uganda, Milton Obote, a leading politician, Erinayo Oryema, and the Chief of Staff of the army, Idi Amin.[6] Now the Bikangaga Plan was shelved. Luwum committed himself to the building of agricultural centres and leprosy hospitals. As a bishop, Janani Luwum was a gifted administrator, scrupulously fair, always ready to reconcile and never taking sides. He viewed division as positively as he could, arguing that polarities properly harnessed could create powerful energy – but also warning that, ungoverned, they could merely create a vacuum of power. For him trust was essential in relationships. No one, it seemed, was afraid to come to his home or office to talk. Luwum managed to combine boldness and courage with a warmth that made people feel at ease in his presence. In controversies he used his engaging character to great effect. He sought never to do for others what they could do for themselves.

But the nation which had been born only four years before was already disintegrating into confusion. Obote ruled increasingly by force. In January 1971 his government was overthrown by a *coup d'état* organized by Idi Amin. Amin, a Muslim, had been made an officer by the British. Now he awarded himself medals and presented a spectacle of jovial bombast and ruthless intimidation. The state that he set out to build was to become notorious for its brutality. The army which he commanded became an unrestricted instrument of oppression and violence. During his years of power, as many as 300,000 people disappeared. This was the terrible context in which Luwum sought to lead the Anglican Church.

Soon after Amin's *coup d'état* in January 1971 the body of the Kabaka was returned to Uganda from England where he had died, allegedly from acute alcoholic poisoning. Bagandan Anglicans accused Archbishop Erica Sabiti of being a traitor and refused him entry into his cathedral church of St Paul, in Namirembe. By October they were threatening to secede from the Anglican Province. This rift between the Baganda and the rest of the Church of the Anglican Province[7] provoked Amin to intercede. At a gathering in Kigezi, in western Uganda, he made his first moves. Then, on 26 November, he summoned all the Anglican bishops and diocesan officers of the Church of Uganda to a meeting at the International Conference Centre. Once inside, he told them not to leave the Conference Centre until they had resolved their church affairs.

Harsh words were spoken. For two days the church leaders remained at odds. Then, according to Bishop Festo Kivengere:

> The Lord gave us a message from Philippians. We saw that we were men going up, each one thinking about his reputation and demanding his rights. But that day, we caught a vision of the Man-coming-down: Jesus, 'Who, being in the form of God … made himself of no reputation, and took upon him the form of a servant, and was made in the likeness of men: And … he humbled himself even [to] the death of the cross.' What a change he made! In the presence of him who came down, our dear archbishop Erica Sabiti, and each of the nine diocesan bishops, went down in confession of the sins which had contributed to the divisions in the church, and a great melting by the Holy Spirit came upon us all.[8]

Amin, not unnaturally, took the credit for the settlement.

But some sensed that a church that was so preoccupied by its divisions must be insensitive to questions of political justice and vulnerable to the rule of an unscrupulous state. Few voices were raised in protest when Amin abruptly decreed on 9 August 1972 that over 50,000 Uganda Asians, 'of Indian, Pakistani, Bangladeshi origin, extraction or descent', be expelled from the country. Opposition came from the National Students of Uganda. A complaint was issued from Utrecht by the World Council of Churches that same August. Bishop Luwum found himself one of a group of four (with an Indian, an African-American, and a Nigerian) who drafted a resolution addressed to the Ugandan government. It read:

> The Central Committee of the World Council of Churches, meeting in Utrecht, the Netherlands, expressed its deep concern over the disturbing situation reflected in the news about Uganda. While we do not presume to prejudge the intention of the Government of Uganda with reference to its internal policies, we call upon the Government of Uganda to refrain from any actions which impair or deny the citizenship of Ugandans of Asian origin. Furthermore, we share a deep concern for other nationalities in Uganda who are being affected by Government decree and other reported pronouncements.

In 1974 Luwum was elected Archbishop of Uganda, Rwanda, Burundi and Boga-Zaire. He could have entertained few illusions about the complexities that he now confronted. The Anglican Church over which he had authority was riven by different tribal loyalties. There existed a traditional rivalry between the Roman Catholics and Anglicans in Uganda. The nation itself was governed by a despotic state and disfigured by intimidation and corruption. But Luwum could now revive the fortunes of the Bikangaga Plan, and it became the central feature of his archiepiscopate. He told his brother bishops that he 'did not want to be the Archbishop of a dead Church, but a live one'. In his foreword to a collection of essays written to mark the centenary celebrations he described his vision for the Anglican Province:

> Many of our contributors have emphasised that our Church needs to grow towards 'spiritual selfhood'. In short, this means that our talented Ugandan men and women who have been imbued with the Spirit of the Living God should begin to express themselves in Music, Art, Drama, Literature and other creative forms in order to revive our valuable cultural and traditional heritage so that the Christian Gospel can be communicated at a level our people can easily grasp. In addition to this the Church must take the training of our clergy seriously, remembering that they are the equippers of God's children so that together we may build a Church worthy of its Name.[9]

In his epilogue he struck a darker note. Those who believed were called to be the salt, the light, the leaven in society. The Church should not allow itself to conform to the powers of darkness but rather it should transform the world for Christ.

It was his desire to 'be perfect as our heavenly Father is perfect' (Matthew 5:43–48) that set Janani Luwum on a collision course with principalities and powers of Amin's Uganda. As archbishop, Luwum found himself drawn further and further into the vortex of political authority. Amin he met often: a photograph exists of the two men talking together. In a conversation in December 1976 I told him that some Ugandan Christians had complained that he was attending too many Government functions. In time, this might make it difficult for him to speak objectively to Amin. Too easily might his enemies accuse him of complicity with a corrupt regime.[10] Luwum simply replied:

> The scriptures bid us to love the President. We must pray for him. He is a child of God too. I do not fear the President. That is reserved for God alone. My real concern is for the Church of Uganda to provide a guiding and steady hand on this erratic government. The Gospel is capable of kraaling the President. John, I do not know for how long I shall be occupying this Archbishop's chair. I live as though there will be no tomorrow. I face daily being picked up by the soldiers. While the opportunity is there, I preach the Gospel with all my might, and my conscience is clear before God that I have not sided with the present government, which is utterly self-seeking. I have been threatened many times. Whenever I have the opportunity I have told the President the things the Church disapproves of. God is my witness as I am his.

Repeatedly, he would recall a saying from his apprenticeship as a hunter: 'The best way to show that a stick is crooked is not to argue about it or to spend time denouncing it, but to lay a straight stick alongside it.' For apart from blunt truth, he saw that our lives sink decadently amid the perfume of hints and suggestions. This meant for him a preparedness to stick to truth, especially against a tide of corruption, deceit and self-aggrandizement. But he always ensured that its correct arena was love. He would say to himself 'God wants me to grow up like Christ in everything: to know the whole truth and tell it in love' (Ephesians 4:15). His favourite Beatitude in this regard was 'Blessed are the pure, clean [*katharoi* – plural – that is in every way] in heart, for they shall see God'.

When Amin carried out acts of brutality and atrocities, especially against the Acoli and Langi, it was Luwum, and not the representatives of the Anglican Province, who pleaded with him. The victims of such violence, the growing number of Acoli and Langi widows and orphans, received little assistance from church agencies. Luwum sought to secure the release of people who had been abducted by the secret police, the State Research Bureau. Whenever he heard of acts of brutality committed by the army he would personally seek corroboration, and then telephone the president himself. Arguably, Amin exploited such frankness. In turn, he would call the archbishop at all hours, and send a car to bring him to his residence for conversations. Luwum's wife Mary often cautioned him not to go, but his desire to plead the cause of the downtrodden prevailed.

On 26 August 1976 the authorities of the Anglican and Roman Catholic Churches met with the leader of the Muslim community, the Sheikh Mufti of Uganda, at Lweza. Their purpose was to discuss how best to respond to the abuses and injustices of the Amin regime. Luwum was invited to chair the meeting.

Afterwards, a detailed letter was sent to the President requesting a meeting. In the eyes of government ministers, it was sufficient to make Luwum appear the leader of a new, vocal movement of opposition. Amin accused him of holding a meeting without his permission. He declared that the archbishop was a traitor who conspired with the World Council of Churches to overthrow the government. In the early hours of 5 February 1977 Luwum's home was raided by soldiers who had been ordered to search for arms and enemies of the state. Luwum was threatened with a rifle. He remonstrated 'There are no arms here. Our house is God's house. We pray for the President. We pray for the security forces. We preach the Gospel. That is our work, not keeping arms to overthrow the government.' Once the search had ended the soldiers asked Luwum to open the gate for them to leave. Mary Luwum retorted that they should walk through the fence that they had knocked down on their way in. But Janani Luwum told her 'We are Christians! We have clean hearts and as a witness to our Lord and Saviour let me open the gate for them.'[11]

The home of Bishop Yonah Okoth was also attacked. The bishops of the Anglican Church proposed that Roman Catholics join them in writing a statement of protest after the raids. But the authorities of the Roman Catholic Church in Uganda offered merely to write a covering letter for the statement. They would not sign a strongly worded rebuke to the President. Luwum personally delivered the document to Amin on 12 February 1976:

> We are deeply disturbed. In the history of our country such an incident in the Church has never before occurred. This is a climax of what has been constantly happening to our Christians. We have buried many who have died as a result of being shot and there are many more whose bodies have not yet been found; yet their disappearance is connected with the activities of some members of the Security Forces.

Anglican and Roman Catholic leaders were again summoned to the Conference Centre in Kampala. There, Luwum was once more accused of aiding and abetting the shipment of arms through Bishop Okoth, on the Kenyan border. Bishop Festo Kivengere, who was standing next to the archbishop, says that when Luwum was named, he made no reply to the charge, but simply shook his head and whispered to him 'They are going to kill me. I am not afraid.'

One by one the other churchmen were dismissed. The first to leave was Cardinal Nsubuga. Only two bishops, Festo Kivengere and Silvanus Wani, remained all afternoon, until they were driven away at gunpoint at five o'clock. As they parted, Luwum said to them 'I can see the hand of the Lord in this'. They never saw him again.

What followed is uncertain. It has been written that he was taken to a torture cell where he met two Christian cabinet ministers. One was Erinayo Oryema, who had attended his consecration as Bishop of Northern Uganda five years before. He prayed for them, placing his hands on their heads. The three men were then driven away. Bishop Festo later spoke of a rumour that Amin himself tried to force Luwum to sign a confession that he was involved in a revolutionary plot. This Luwum would not sign. The archbishop then prayed aloud for his captors before he died. Some claimed that Amin shot him; others saw his corpse bearing bullet wounds in a morgue. Some evidence suggests that he was shot at six o'clock.[12] To this day his body has never been found. He received no Christian burial.

The state of Idi Amin was destroyed by invading Tanzanian forces in 1979. Amin himself fled to Libya and escaped justice. Obote returned to govern, but with little success. Tribal conflicts and then guerrilla wars unseated him a second time. In 1986 a National Resistance Army led by Yoweri Musevani came to power.

Janani Luwum gave to the Church of Uganda, Rwanda, Burundi and Boga-Zaire a new spirit and vitality. His wise leadership had encouraged Christians not to disregard, but to confront issues of church and state in Uganda. That he challenged the authorities of his day publicly, like the prophet Nathan, set him apart from other bishops of the church, whose relations with the state had often been confined to the private sphere. His contribution was also characterized by the confidence of his faith; that the gospel of Jesus Christ could offer eternal values to a violent, unjust and deceitful political power. He sought to shape his province into a distinctive Christian body that cherished its past and its diversity, but one that reached out to what was universal in the gospel. For me, his martyrdom was a defining moment. The day he died I resolved to be ordained.

Notes

1 In this essay I have used extensively unpublished interviews, sermons and 'diaries' of Janani Luwum dating from 1966 to 1976.
2 Margaret Ford describes us in *Janani* (p. 24) as 'a theological student and his wife'. At the time of her writing our identities had to be protected because of our closeness to Luwum, and because it was likely that I would return to Uganda to become Provost at All Saints Cathedral, Kampala. In the event it proved too dangerous to return.
3 Margaret Ford, *Janani: The Making of a Modern Martyr* (London). Margaret Ford was Janani Luwum's secretary for several years when he was Bishop of Northern Uganda, and for a short time while he was Archbishop until he died on 16 February 1977.
4 Margaret Ford in her book uses rather more colourful language of the current 'revival' expressions than the event, as described by Luwum himself, would seem to warrant. They were neither being asked 'to denounce their faith' nor 'tortured'. See *Janani*, pp. 22–3.
5 Archbishop Leslie Brown, who had imaginatively led the Church of Uganda, later including Rwanda, Burundi and Boga-Zaire, from 1953 to 1965, tells with justifiable sadness of an attack made on him. At the reception following the installation of Bishop Dunstan Nsubuga as his successor as Bishop of Namirembe diocese, a leading Mugandan accused

him of not loving the Baganda, unlike the old missionaries. It was because he had authorized the reprinting of the Muganda Prayer Book without the name of the King of Buganda inserted in the section for State Prayers, and left blanks, as the Prayer Book was used in other parts of Uganda. Secondly, he had retired early at a time when no Muganda bishop could be elected as Archbishop – see his own account in his book, *Three Worlds: One Word*, pp. 171ff. I personally believe that Dr Leslie Brown's decision to hand over the leadership to a Ugandan was the right decision. Staying on for a longer time to allow Dr Dunstan Nsubuga to become electable was a pious dream. He was not elected in two subsequent elections, although he was eligible. Indeed he only received one vote. His fellow bishops were all members of the East African Revival and he was not.

6 See Margaret Ford, *Janani*, p. 37.

7 David Apter in his revised 3rd edition of *The Political Kingdom in Uganda: A Study in Bureaucratic Nationalism* suggests how certain recurrent themes and characteristic issues, such as the social problem of Buganda in Uganda, continue to sustain themselves, taking on new and more contemporary significance. His study makes it clear that comparative political theories have for the most part failed to come to grips with the complexities of African political life, with the result that they tend to be thin and lacking in fresh insight.

8 Festo Kivengere, *I Love Idi Amin*, p. 12.

9 In Janani Luwum's foreword, written in November 1976, to Tuma and Mutibwa, *A Century of Christianity in Uganda, 1877–1977*.

10 In *Janani*, Margaret Ford describes me as one of Janani Luwum's critics (p. 25). Indeed I was always in critical solidarity with him because he and I had similar approaches to life although we came from tribes that were often seen as opposites.

11 A more detailed account is given by Margaret Ford in *Janani*, pp. 80ff.

12 Festo Kivengere, *I Love Idi Amin*. I think the circumstances surrounding Janani Luwum's death and the two cabinet ministers who died with him will never be entirely discovered. What most people believe is that he was shot twice, through the mouth and chest. I have found no witness to corroborate the account by Robert Backhouse, from which some of these details are taken. See Robert Backhouse, *Christian Martyrs* (London), p. 289.

Bibliography

Bishop Leslie Brown, transcript of a talk in the series 'Reflections', broadcast by BBC World Service, 15 April 1981.

J. F. Faubel, *African Holocaust* (2nd edn, London, 1965).

Festo Kivengere, *I Love Idi Amin* (London, 1977).

George Ivan Smith, *Ghosts of Kampala: The Rise and Fall of Idi Amin* (London, 1980).

Tom Tuma and Phares Mutibwa (eds), *A Century of Christianity in Uganda 1877–1977* (Kampala, 1978).

The oppression of the people: Archbishop Oscar Romero of El Salvador

PHILIP BERRYMAN

> Christ invites us not to fear persecution. Believe me, brothers
> and sisters, anyone committed to the poor must suffer the
> same fate as the poor. And in El Salvador we know the fate of
> the poor; to be taken away, to be tortured, to be jailed, to be
> found dead.
>
> Archbishop Oscar Romero, 17 February 1980

LIVING IN Guatemala and working as Central America representative for the American Friends Service Committee, I visited El
Salvador regularly after 1976. On the morning of Sunday, 23
March 1980, I had heard Archbishop Oscar Romero conclude his
sermon in San Salvador with an appeal to the soldiers and police not to
kill their own brother and sister peasants. God's law 'Thou shalt not
kill!' had, he insisted, precedence over human orders. 'No soldier is
obliged to obey an order against God's law ... In the name of God, and
in the name of this suffering people ... I beg you, I implore you, I order
you in the name of God: stop the repression!' After mass, I expressed my
amazement at such boldness. The military must have seen such words
as treason. But the Jesuit theologian Jon Sobrino told me that the group
of lay people and priests who regularly met with Romero on Saturday to
help him prepare his sermons had agreed that some such statement
must be made.[1] At noon the next day I found in the street a
mimeographed hate sheet comparing Romero to the Ayatollah
Khomeini. Late that afternoon we were informed that Romero had
been shot. We rushed to the archdiocesan headquarters at the seminary
in the city and then to the emergency hospital, where we learnt that he
had died. Insofar as I can recall my feelings at that moment, I was

stunned that an archbishop could be deliberately murdered in a Catholic country. Yet I found it logical that those who genuinely believed that the country's problems were the result of Marxist agitation, particularly by priests – several had been murdered with impunity – should now see fit to murder an archbishop.[2]

The following Saturday evening I joined the thousands passing to bid their archbishop farewell as he lay in the unfinished cathedral of San Salvador. On Sunday morning I joined 75,000 or 100,000 mostly poor mourners in the plaza. Conspicuous were members of the mass popular organizations, particularly the Revolutionary People's Bloc, which marched around the plaza as the mass was beginning and then went up to lay a wreath on Romero's casket. In the middle of the sermon, I heard an explosion to my left near the National Palace, and saw a column of smoke rising. Another explosion followed, and then automatic weapon fire began somewhere. In confusion and fear, but also with impressive self-discipline, the people in the plaza slowly made their way out by the one street that offered escape. Some fled into the cathedral where they spent a fearful two hours until security forces allowed them to leave. It was estimated that 40 people were killed, primarily trampled or crushed up against the metal fence in front of the cathedral. 'With Archbishop Romero, God has visited El Salvador', said the Jesuit theologian Ignacio Ellacuría at a mass shortly after the archbishop's murder. Ellacuría himself was to be murdered almost a decade later.

Upon becoming Archbishop of San Salvador in February 1977, Oscar Romero adopted the motto *Sentire cum ecclesia* – 'Be of one mind with the Church'. He was known to be conservative, and it was said that the Vatican, the government of El Salvador and the wealthy of that country regarded him as a safer choice than Bishop Arturo Rivera y Damas, who was favoured by those pursuing church renewal along the lines of Vatican II (1962-65) and the guidelines set by the Latin American bishops in Medellín (1968). But only in his first weeks in office it was the murder of a Jesuit, Rutilio Grande,[3] that appeared to convert – the word is often used – Romero to a commitment to social and political justice. No conversion occurs *ex nihilo*, however, and we must know more about the man Romero was before considering who he became.

Born 15 August 1917 in Ciudad Barrios, a mountain town in eastern El Salvador accessible only by animal or on foot, Oscar Arnulfo Romero was the second of seven children. His family grew some crops and his father worked at the local telegraph office. He attended public school for three years and then studied privately with a woman teacher. He also learned to play the piano and other instruments, and so was initiated into a lifelong love of music. At the age of 13 Romero expressed interest in the priesthood, and despite the initial objections of his father, who had at one point had him apprenticed to a carpenter, he went to study at the seminary in San Miguel, the largest city in eastern El Salvador. To study theology he then went to the capital, San Salvador, and, after a year and a half, was sent to study at the Gregorian University in Rome, where he was ordained in 1942. He began studies for a doctorate in ascetical theology, but the Bishop of San Miguel called him home where he returned to a great welcome in January 1944. As a student, Romero was earnest and genuinely pious. He also wrote and published essays and occasional poems.

His first assignment was as a pastor in a rural town, but after a few months the bishop called him down to San Miguel, where he became secretary of the diocese, a post he was to hold for 23 years. His biographer James Brockman has described his energetic activity: he completed the construction of the cathedral; he grew famous as a preacher – according to co-workers, at one time five radio stations in the small city simultaneously broadcast his Sunday morning mass; he visited the countryside and the city gaols; he organized catechism classes and first communions; he promoted a plethora of Catholic associations, the Legion of Mary, the Knights of the Holy Sepulchre, Alcoholics Anonymous, Catholic Action, the Cursillos de Cristiandad, the Apostleship of Prayer, the Guardians of the Blessed Sacrament, the Holy Rosary Association, the Third Order of St Francis, and the diocesan branch of Caritas, which distributes food to the poor.[4]

Toward the end of his time in San Miguel, Brockman finds that Romero was 'the most powerful priest in the city, with virtually all lay movements centered on his parish, besides being the bishop's secretary, rector of the minor seminary, and editor of the diocesan newspaper'.[5] It was out of this activity that he observed Vatican II and the beginnings of the church renewal that it unleashed. Romero felt considerable identity with Pope John XXIII, especially with the ideas and reflections published in his *Journal of a Soul*. He regarded the Council as a call to reform, but of some new developments he was critical. He was not sympathetic to priests who appeared without clerical attire.

In 1967 Romero was made a monsignor and was appointed secretary general of the Salvadoran bishops' conference, and hence he moved to San Salvador. In 1970, he was named auxiliary bishop of San Salvador, at the request of Archbishop Chávez. During his seven years in San

Salvador, Romero was devoted largely to administrative matters, and the impression that he left was that of one who kept to himself. He did not attend the monthly clergy meetings, as did Bishop Arturo Rivera y Damas, the other auxiliary. He also became close to priests of the conservative and secretive organization Opus Dei, attending retreats organized by them and choosing one of them as his confessor. Not only did he remain theologically conservative, but on several occasions he clashed with priests who pressed for a renewal of the church. In June 1970, priests, religious and lay leaders gathered for a Pastoral Week to apply the positions of the Medellín meeting to El Salvador. Although the meeting was national in scope, only Archbishop Chávez and Bishop Rivera y Damas offered genuine support. The other bishops attended portions of it, or not at all. After initially expressing no objections to the gathering, Romero subsequently sided with the other bishops who attacked the event at their July meeting and denied that it was representative of the Church. When a commission was designated to rewrite and tone down its conclusions, Romero and Rivera were members of it. In May 1971, Chávez appointed Romero to edit the archdiocesan weekly *Orientación*, and here his reputation for conservatism was confirmed; its content moved abruptly away from the editorial policy of its previous director, who had been much influenced by the ideas of Medellín. At one point Romero accused the Jesuit high school, the Externado San José, of Marxism and demagogy, perhaps under the influence of some of the parents. The daily papers fanned the controversy, but the archdiocese defended the school.

In 1974 the Vatican appointed Romero Bishop of the rural diocese of Santiago de María, a strip in eastern El Salvador running from the Honduran border to the Pacific Ocean. Here he seems to have reverted to some of the pastoral style he had earlier shown in San Miguel. Brockman observes 'To attend better to the peasantry, he mounted loudspeakers on a jeep and drove to remote settlements to preach, play sacred music, hear confessions, offer mass, baptize and marry'.[6] He founded and edited a diocesan publication. In one issue he wrote of the coffee harvest praising God for the abundance of 'rubies' (coffee beans are red), but lamenting that the labourers were not well paid. He was shocked to learn that plantation owners, whom he regarded as good people, paid 1.75 colons a day when the legal minimum wage was 2.50 (a dollar). When he noticed seasonal coffee pickers sleeping in the public plaza, he set aside church property for them to sleep in.[7]

Romero's years at Santiago de María coincided with a period of rising militancy, especially by organized peasants, and increased repression. In

June 1975, National Guardsmen raided a hamlet called Tres Calles, hacking five peasants to death and ransacking houses. Romero went to Tres Calles to console the people, sent a letter of protest to President Molina, and wrote a report to his fellow bishops on the incident. But although he was willing to criticize specific acts of violence, he also expressed concerns about the politicization of the clergy, something that he blamed on the Jesuits – and especially those who taught at the Central American University (UCA) – and on a liberation theology that he found unsound. He also feared the influence of some training centres that were run by the church, one of which operated in his own diocese.

In 1976 the military government of El Salvador proposed a land reform, which was to begin slowly in two departments. Owners would be compensated for lands taken. Rural tensions were expected to ease as small farmers acquired enough land to make a decent living, and the landholders could transfer their assets into industry. Underlying the scheme was a notion that the country should shift from an 'agroexport' to an industrial economy (sometimes characterized as a 'Taiwan model' of development). The plan failed to garner support, however: most of the left denounced it as a policy that was merely intended to co-opt peasants, and the landholders and business people furiously campaigned against it. The embassy of the United States supported the idea, but within El Salvador only the Communist Party and the Central American University were in favour. The first bombs were set off at the university at this time. Romero consulted his clergy and took their assessment of the plan – a negative one – to the president. Under pressure from landholders the reform was repealed and General Humberto Romero, who had been a rallying point for opposition, was chosen as the presidential candidate of the pro-military party which had won elections for decades, and which would do so again.

When appointed Archbishop of San Salvador, Oscar Romero was 59 years old; somewhat shy, a zealous worker, occasionally combative, and very much devoted to the church and to Rome, where he had studied. His theology remained generally conservative, and he found it natural to accept the dictates of secular authority and the Catholic hierarchical system. Was there more to the Romero of these years than the zealous cleric? Reminiscences, even of those close to him, largely recall his common touch: he enjoyed Salvadoran popular dishes and found circuses irresistible. He had a few friends with whom he could be at ease, particularly Salvador Barraza, a shoe salesman, and his wife. Barraza frequently took Romero to the beach or other sites – and even to Mexico — for rest. Even so, most recollections are precisely of a man who in 35 years as a priest had done his utmost to serve the church.

Following the Sandinista revolution in nearby Nicaragua in mid-1979, a general mood of expectation was in the air in El Salvador. Militant organizations had been growing since the mid-1970s. In order to forestall a revolution, a military faction in El Salvador had pre-emptively staged a coup the previous October, dismissed one group of officers and installed a new junta, many of whose members were respected civilians. This government proclaimed its own intention of making revolutionary changes. In actuality, the most immediate change was a rise in repression from dozens to hundreds of killings every month. Most of the well-intentioned civilians in the government resigned and began to align with the left-wing parties. Romero became Archbishop of San Salvador in the midst of an emergency in a hastily arranged ceremony that took place not in the cathedral, but in the church attached to the seminary. In this context of confrontation, Archbishop Romero repeatedly denounced specific instances of violence, defended the right of the poor to organize, and encouraged the conflicting sides to avoid plunging the country into war. He had been subjected to insults and threats almost since becoming Archbishop of El Salvador, but now they increased.

Those in power — the landholders, the military and the police — felt quite justified in using violence as a political tool in actions that ranged from arrest and unjust expulsion to torture and murder. Such acts were committed against individuals, like the priests Rutilio Grande and Alfonso Navarro, both of whom were murdered, and against groups. On 28 February 1977 a crowd of protesters were attacked by soldiers in the public square of San Salvador. Many in authority blamed priests for rising peasant militancy, an accusation which contained an element of truth: for some years church people had done pastoral work among the rural poor, developing Christian base communities and holding courses, notably at a half-dozen training centres around the country. Peasants who had once been trained by the church were often attracted to the newly forming 'popular organizations', in particular the Federation of Christian Peasants of El Salvador (FECCAS), which had been founded in the 1960s under Christian Democrat auspices and was now being radicalized.

The work of the church in Aguilares, a half-hour drive north of San Salvador, offered a prime example of all that the landholders and authorities found odious. When Rutilio Grande and his fellow Jesuits entered the parish in 1972 they came with a well-formed pastoral plan based on studies of work done elsewhere in El Salvador and in other Latin American countries. After two years of intensive two-week missions, held in one area after another throughout the parish, they had formed 27 rural and ten urban local communities with their lay leadership. Grande himself was quite sure that church pastoral work and peasant organizing should not be fused together and he sought to make their separation clear. He insisted that people should not be pressured into joining FECCAS, while supporting the right of peasants to organize and press their claims. In his preaching, he denounced the greed of those who could hold large tracts of land and deprive others of their right to land, work and food.[8] On 12 March 1977, a Saturday evening, Grande was shot and killed as he was driving to say mass. An elderly man and a boy, who were in the car with him, also died. Romero went that night to Aguilares and stood before the bloodied body of the man who had been master of ceremonies at the celebration of his consecration as Bishop of San Salvador seven years before. While yet having reservations about his pastoral approach, Romero had esteemed and cherished Grande. The Jesuit scholar Jon Sobrino remembers 'I think that, as Archbishop Romero stood gazing at the mortal remains of Rutilio Grande, the scales fell from his eyes. Rutilio had been right! ... If Rutilio had died as Jesus died ... was this not because his life and mission had been like the life and mission of Jesus? ... Ah then, it had not been Rutilio, but Oscar who had been mistaken!' Grande's life and death gave Romero a new direction for his life and the strength to pursue it.[9]

Romero's vision and approach no doubt evolved over the ensuing weeks and months. He heard President Molina's assurance that the crime would be investigated, and found that it came to nothing. (Indeed, the bullets were never even removed from Grande's body for forensic purposes.) The wealthy, whom he had once seen as good people, could accept and justify such use of violence. The media attacked him, and others in the church. His experience with some fellow church leaders was even more distressing. The archdiocesan clergy had agreed that the persecution of the church called for the extraordinary measures of suspending classes in Catholic schools for three days of reflection, and – more shocking for Catholics, in whom Sunday mass obligation had been instilled – the suspension of all masses except one to be celebrated on the cathedral steps. When Romero went to report these decisions to the papal nuncio, Archbishop Emanuele Gerada, he was subjected to 'a fifteen-minute scolding' and called 'irresponsible, imprudent, and inconsistent in his actions as bishop'.[10] After yet another vote from the clergy, and another humiliating lecture at the nunciature, this time given on canon law by the nuncio's secretary, Romero said that he accepted responsibility. Toward the end of March he travelled to Rome and was sustained by the words of Pope Paul VI, who said to him 'Courage! You are the one in charge!' He also found the Secretariat of State supportive. Less sympathetic was the Congregation for the Bishops, where a secretary again lectured him on what he should do and not do.

In May, government troops carried out a military operation in Aguilares, sweeping through the countryside, rounding up peasants, abducting and killing dozens of people, and then occupying the town. The church was turned into barracks, in the process desecrating the sacrament reserved there. Even Romero was unable to enter the town for some time. Saying mass in Aguilares about a month later, he began his sermon by remarking bleakly 'It is my lot to gather up the trampled, the dead and all that the persecution of the church leaves behind'.[11]

On 1 July 1977 General Romero was installed as President of El Salvador. His election had been secured by widespread fraud. In view of government-sanctioned violence, and the failure to investigate the killing of Grande, Archbishop Romero chose not to attend the inauguration, although normally an archbishop would do so. He was overwhelmingly supported by his clergy. The nuncio and two of the other bishops did attend, however. This division between church leaders who continued to support the government and those who did not endured over the next years. Romero found himself in a position of opposition. The killing and disappearance of lay people, even the murder of priests, did not change the minds of his critics.

Further crisis loomed. A militant group, the White Warriors, threatened to kill the Jesuits one by one. But then, surprisingly, the level of confrontation declined. For the next two years it remained high, however. During this period, that is, until the overthrow of the Somoza dictatorship in Nicaragua in mid-1979, virtually no one believed that El Salvador faced revolution. Military-led governments in Central America were seen as a variant of the military dictatorships that had emerged in Latin America starting with Brazil (1964) and most notably with Chile (1973). By the middle years of the 1970s, only four Latin American countries, Mexico, Venezuela, Colombia and Costa Rica, had elected civilian governments. The prevailing political model was what was called the 'national security state'. Archbishop Romero and his collaborators no doubt learned from the response of the Catholic Church under these regimes, particularly the public stances of the

Brazilian bishops, and the work of the Vicariate of Solidarity in the archdiocese of Santiago, Chile, whose priests worked to defend human rights and organize a humanitarian response for the victims of repression and exploitation.

. Within a period of months the new archbishop established his own style of leadership. One distinctive feature was his openness to the poor. Several peasants from the countryside were often to be seen waiting on the benches outside his office door. His willingness to meet with them, without an appointment, set him apart from many bishops who were busy with administration and evidently had little or no time for ordinary people, let alone the poor. Romero also spent a good deal of his time visiting the rural parishes of the archdiocese. More important was his willingness to listen to them, especially when they recounted their problems and the oppression and violence under which they suffered. One observer noted that if a priest or sister arrived with a report on human rights, the archbishop would ask whether their information was first-hand, and would then direct them to the proper agency. If, however, a woman arrived weeping about the abduction of her child, 'he immediately wrote down the name, the place, the information, and he condemned the incident. The woman's weeping was enough, more than enough, as reliable proof.'[12] He encouraged others to work with him. The archdiocesan offices, located in the large and now under-occupied seminary building, became the hub of many activities. He had a small coffee shop installed so that people who came on archdiocesan business could meet and talk. Some of his close collaborators were people whom he had previously suspected of dangerous ideas or practices, including the Jesuits at the UCA and elsewhere, and a loose network of Salvadoran diocesan priests,[13] many of whom were involved in peasant organizing. Romero's Sunday sermons in the cathedral were prepared collectively. Father Rafael Urrutia recalls his practice of meeting 'every week for several hours with a team of priests and lay people to reflect on the situation of the country, and then he put all of this reflection into his homilies'. Sobrino says that Romero would work with his 'scripture commentaries and homiletic aids on his desk, along with other notes of his own and the newspapers of the week'. Urrutia and the sisters at the hospital where he lived saw him well after midnight, often on his knees.[14] These homilies were broadcast over the radio and then, beginning in 1978, transcribed and later published. Because the Salvadoran media were controlled by an oligarchy which allowed no criticism, or even honest reporting of repression, Romero's sermons became an important source of alternative information and a new perspective. Soon he had a larger listening audience than that of any other programme in the country.

His denunciations became newsworthy. Attending the 8 o'clock mass became obligatory for foreign journalists. Romero himself insisted that he did not want his message to be seen as 'the chronicle of the week, or criticism of the government'. It was 'like the light of the gospel hitting those concrete events'. But the main purpose of his preaching was the gospel itself. His homilies typically lasted 45 minutes, most of that time devoted to a systematic and thematic reflection on the liturgical texts, delivered in a measured tone. But his language was striking. He consistently expressed the church's concern for 'earthly liberation', sharing the pain of 'those who suffer, the illiterate, those without electricity, without a roof, without a home', all the while insisting that the church 'wants to lift those demands to a higher plane and free people from the chains that are sin, death, and hell' to lead to 'the freedom of God's children'.[15] Sometimes he directly addressed his radio audience: cab drivers, market women, the poor, the wealthy, and even torturers and torture victims.

A systematic documentation by the church of human rights violations in El Salvador grew out of a particular constellation of events. In Holy Week 1978, in the area of San Pedro Perulapán to the north-east of the capital, a conflict broke out between members of FECCAS and rivals in the National Democratic Organization (ORDEN), a network of informers and enforcers for the landholders.[16] Contrary to media reports blaming FECCAS, an archdiocesan commission found that ORDEN members had attacked FECCAS members and killed some – impaling the head of one of their leaders, Tránsito Vásquez, on a stick. At one point FECCAS members forcibly brought some members of ORDEN to view Vásquez's body and made them ask forgiveness and dig a grave. ORDEN and National Guard troops then attacked FECCAS. The archdiocesan commission reported that six were dead and 14 wounded. Sixty-eight had disappeared. This account was entirely at variance with what the Salvadoran daily newspapers were saying.[17] From this time on, diocesan staff systematically documented human rights violations. Another organization, Socorro Jurídico, established earlier under Jesuit sponsorship, supplied legal aid to the poor in cases of injustice or repression, and now it was brought under the archdiocesan umbrella. These organizations had informal working ties with the Salvadoran Human Rights Commission which also began to operate around this time. The archdiocesan newspaper, *Orientación*, likewise included reporting on human rights alongside church news.

These things generated a reputation abroad. In 1978 Romero was nominated for a Nobel Peace Prize for his defence of human rights. The archdiocese also received support and occasional visits from ecumenical Protestant organizations, the World Council of Churches and the National Council of Churches of the United States, and it participated in ecumenical observances at a time when almost all Salvadorans saw theirs as a 'Catholic' country and 'the church' seemed synonymous with Roman Catholicism. In fact, in the late 1980s surveys revealed that 16 per cent of Salvadorans were Protestants.[18] The Emmanuel Baptist Church in particular saw Romero as one who spoke for them: in 1980 I saw copies of *Orientación* being distributed at the Sunday service there.

But Romero aroused the ire of the military and landholders, and of private business in general. In late 1978 I was shown a dossier of dozens of recent newspaper attacks on the church and on Romero himself, in biased reporting, relentless columns and paid advertisements from organizations, some of them non-existent. Flyers reading 'Be a patriot! Kill a priest!' achieved notoriety in the press abroad. Priests continued to be murdered. In January 1979 Fr Neto Barrera and Fr Octavio Ortiz were killed; in August Fr Rafael Palacios and Fr Alirio Macías lost their lives. After the killing of Palacios, Romero observed 'It would be sad if in a country where murder is being committed so horribly, we were not to find priests also among the victims. They are the testimony of a church incarnated in the problems of its people.'

How to account for such viciousness? At the end of the twentieth century, where a capitalism that is symbolized and encouraged by the United States enjoys hegemony, it is increasingly difficult to appreciate the fanatical anti-communist righteousness that existed in Latin and South America in the 1970s. In 1978, the executive director of ANEP (National Association of Private Enterprise) told me 'To understand what is happening in El Salvador, you have to begin in Moscow'. Under the influence of an ideology of national security, the military and the wealthy of many societies in the region genuinely believed that they lived in a state of war, a war in defence of Western Christian civilization. In such a conflict ideas were as dangerous as bullets. Neither unarmed peasants nor university teachers were civilians. Priests and sisters who worked with the poor, and particularly Jesuits, were widely suspected as agitators. Implicit in this conviction was a notion that the poor could not think for themselves, and that if they acted it must be at the instigation of other powers. People like Romero, who defended the rights of the poor, and especially their right to have their own organizations, were condemned and threatened as traitors.

In the United States the administration of President Carter had made human rights a major theme of its foreign policy. Many believed that such a concern was not directed at El Salvador.[19] Arriving at the time of President Romero's inauguration in 1977, the American ambassador, Frank Devine, told the press that he would make up his own mind about the issues that faced the country. He said little until 1979. Early in 1978, the Under-Secretary of State for Inter-American Affairs, Terence Todman, met with Archbishop Romero and urged him to have a less confrontational and more constructive relationship with the government. According to an eyewitness, Romero finally told Todman that both he and his government did not understand what was happening: 'The problem is not between Church and government, it's between government and people ... It's not the church, much less the archbishop!' If the government improved its treatment of the people, 'we will improve our relations with the government'.[20] Although the majority of the clergy of his own archdiocese supported him, Romero continued to inspire opposition from his fellow bishops. One of the four who most firmly criticized him, Bishop Alvarez of San Miguel, served as a military vicar, sometimes appearing in uniform. Only one, Rivera y Damas, his auxiliary, was supportive. In an entry in his journal in April 1978 Romero recorded one meeting of the bishops:

> I was subjected to many false accusations by the bishops. I was told that my preaching was subversive and violent. That my priests were stirring up the climate of violence among the peasants and that we should not complain of the assaults that the authorities are making. The archdiocese is accused of interfering in other dioceses and causing division among priests and disturbing pastoral work in other dioceses. The archdiocese is accused of sowing confusion in the seminary ... I preferred not to answer.[21]

According to a journalist, at a press conference in Puebla in 1979, Bishop Pedro Aparicio blamed Romero 'for everything that was happening in El Salvador: for placing bombs, for kidnapping people for training children for the guerrillas. He went so far as to say that the "disappeared" were actually individuals who went into hiding to damage the government.'[22] In May of that year Romero went to Rome to speak to the newly elected Pope John Paul II. Vatican officials saw little reason for urgency in arranging a meeting, but by approaching the Pope personally at his Sunday public audience, he obtained an appointment for the next day. He then arrived with seven folders of documentation, including detailed human rights reports by international organizations. When he took out one of these folders the Pope said there was no time for it. Romero apologized. But, he continued, he had hoped that the Pope could have it read and summarized because he ought to have an accurate idea of the degree of persecution that existed in El Salvador. He mentioned the murder of Fr Ortiz, the first priest Romero had ordained. The Pope's response was to say that rather than making specific denunciations, it was better 'to stick to principles'. Romero persisted that when injustices are very specific, like the killing of Ortiz, the response has to be specific. Invoking his own experience in a politicized situation in Communist Poland, John Paul II stressed that the bishops must be united. Such union, said Romero, could not be simulated, but had to be based 'on the gospel and the truth'.[23] Far from finding support, Romero faced the threat of displacement. An official investigation commissioned by the Vatican had recommended that the Archbishop of San Salvador be given a coadjutor bishop, who would formally be his assistant, but would really be in charge.[24] Against Romero, observes Jon Sobrino, stood 'the oligarchy, the government, the political parties, the army, the security forces, and later, the majority of his brother bishops, various Vatican offices, and even the US government'.[25]

In July 1979, the Somoza regime was toppled in Nicaragua. In its place was now the first revolutionary government to appear in Latin America for twenty years. The level of confrontation and conflict in El Salvador itself rose. A group of officers there carried out a coup on 15 October and formed a new administration, but one which contained few true reformers. They spoke and acted publicly while the hardline majority consolidated its positions. A number of respected civilians were then invited to join the cabinet, and even to head major government agencies, and they included several professors from the UCA. But at the same time repressive actions by official forces and death squads increased. Human rights organizations documented the killing of 281 people in December alone.[26]

The organized left, the guerrillas and their allied popular organizations, denounced the coup from the outset. Their marches, demonstrations and occupations were stepped up, and intended to push the new government to reveal its true repressive nature. To the displeasure of the left and of some of his clergy, Romero argued that the new junta should be given a chance to prove itself. At the same time, he stated that it should halt the violence. One test, he said, would be whether it could account for approximately 275 people who had 'disappeared' under previous governments. If these people were being held, he said, charges should be brought or they should be released. If they were dead, their families should be notified. If the new government was unable or unwilling to resolve these matters, it could not claim to be bringing reform.[27]

At year's end the civilians of the government had resigned, having become convinced that they were merely presenting a facade behind which the military moved to eradicate the left and prevent a revolutionary uprising. Romero regretted but understood their decision. At this point the popular organizations, which had been feuding bitterly for several years, united in a coalition. Romero still insisted that the church did not endorse any single party, but he condemned both reformers and revolutionaries for their violence. On 22 January 1980 the popular organizations held a march that stretched several kilo-metres along a main artery of San Salvador, where they were strafed with crop-dusting planes and then attacked by sharpshooters when they reached the centre of the city. Even as the country seemed to be moving inexorably toward insurrection, the archbishop repeatedly called for peaceful approaches to end the conflict. At the same time, he was encouraged by what he heard of the first steps taken by the new revolutionary government in Nicaragua and he made plans to visit that country to see for himself what was happening there.

When newspapers reported that the government of the United States was preparing to send military aid to maintain the El Salvadoran government in power, Romero prepared a letter to President Carter and then read it in his Sunday sermon before sending it. Far from bringing justice and peace, such aid would 'undoubtedly sharpen the injustice and the repression suffered by the organized people, whose struggle has often been for respect for their most basic human rights', he wrote. If President Carter truly wished to defend human rights, he should not send military aid, but guarantee that his government would not intervene, 'directly or indirectly, with military, economic, diplomatic, or other pressures, in determining the Salvadoran people's destiny'. This letter upset the Vatican Secretariat of State. Representatives from the embassy of the United States came to Romero with a letter from their Secretary of State, Cyrus Vance, which recognized that security forces had 'occasionally' gone too far and asserted that the present Christian Democrat government offered the El Salvador the 'best prospect for peaceful change toward a more just society'. It also expressed concern that a civil war might break out. Romero countered that Vance's political assessment was open to discussion and that 'reasonable solutions' still remained alternatives to civil war.[28]

As the political stakes rose, death threats against the archbishop became even more common. Some killings were intended plainly to intimidate. The attorney general, Mario Zamora, was gunned down in his house, days after he had been called a 'communist' on television by a former major, Roberto D'Aubuisson, who was now the major spokesperson for the right and an organizer of death squads. At a memorial mass for Zamora, Romero commended Zamora's wife for her public commitment to bring up her children to follow their father's footsteps. Thanking him, she replied that his words had deepened her commitment. 'It's time for all of us to commit ourselves to one another more each day, don't you think?' he said. Shortly afterwards, a priest found hidden behind a saint's statue a briefcase with 75 sticks of dynamite, enough to have blown up the church, the worshippers, and even surrounding houses. The government did nothing to solve Zamora's murder, but it said it had discovered a death list on which the first two names were those of Zamora and Romero.[29] An army colonel, Guillermo García, came to the hospital where Romero lived to tell him that he had heard rumours that he was to be killed, and to offer him a bulletproof car. 'As long as you are not really protecting my people', Romero responded, 'I cannot accept any protection from you. ... Why don't you use these bulletproof cars and give security to the families of the disappeared, and the dead, and those in prison?' García became angry and abruptly left.[30] As a bishop Romero had employed a driver; now he tended to drive his own car to avoid jeopardizing another life.

On his last retreat he wrote in his personal diary of his fear of assassination: 'It is not easy for me to accept a violent death, which is very possible under present circumstances; in fact, the nuncio in Costa Rica warned me of imminent danger for this week ... I place my entire life under God's loving providence and I accept my death, no matter how difficult it may be, with faith in Him.'[31] One day early in March, a journalist for the Mexican newspaper *Excelsior* recorded these words:

> I have often been threatened with death. I must tell you, as a Christian, I do not believe in death without resurrection. If I am killed, I shall arise in the Salvadoran people. I say so without boasting, with the greatest humility.
>
> As a shepherd, I am obliged by divine mandate to give my life for those I love – for all Salvadorans, even for those who may be going to kill me. If the threats are carried out, from this moment I offer my blood to God for the redemption and for the resurrection of El Salvador.
>
> Martyrdom is a grace of God that I do not believe I deserve. But if God accepts the sacrifice of my life, let my blood be a seed of freedom and the sign that hope will soon be reality. Let my death, if it is accepted by God, be for the people's liberation and as a witness of hope in the future.

You may say, if they succeed in killing me, that I pardon and bless those who do it. Would, indeed, that they might be convinced that they will waste their time. A bishop will die, but God's church, which is the people, will never perish.[32]

On 24 March 1980, as Archbishop Romero began the offertory in a late afternoon mass in the chapel of the hospital where he lived, a marksman took aim through the doorway, and fired one shot. It hit the archbishop in the heart. He fell at the altar and was rushed to an emergency room where he died.

The Salvadoran legal system made no significant investigation into the murder. Three days after the murder, two men attempted to kill the judge to whom the case would be assigned and he fled the country. Some evidence pointed towards the group led by D'Aubuisson. It was alleged that the marksman was Hector Antonio Regalado, and that he was abetted by a driver, Amado Antonio Garay, who was known to be the chauffeur of Captain Alvaro Rafael Saravia, and who was close to D'Aubuisson.[33] But in asking who killed Romero, the specific individuals are of lesser importance than the kind of political, geopolitical and ideological climate that for years could have justified the sacrifice of dozens, then hundreds, then thousands of people in the name of anti-communism or national security.[34] Two months later, a large group of people – some said 600 – were slaughtered by Salvadoran troops as they sought to cross the Sumpul river into Honduras; 10,000 or 12,000 were killed in 1980. The abduction, murder and rape of three American nuns and a lay volunteer in December 1980 by National Guardsmen caused a temporary suspension in aid from the United States. Almost a decade later, in November 1989, a number of Jesuits were killed by the Atlacatl battalion, an élite brigade trained by advisers from the United States. The American government repudiated the El Salvadoran regime. By then the Communist governments of Europe had fallen and the Cold War between East and West had ended. The hectic affairs of Central America were no longer seen as a threat to the security of the United States.

In his last letter, dictated but left unsigned, Archbishop Romero had written to Bishop Pedro Casaldáliga of Brazil to thank him for his support. He had been 'a great inspiration to us as we strive to keep on with our mission of expressing the hopes and anguish of the poor, in a spirit of joy at being accorded the privilege of running the same risks as they, as Jesus did by identifying with the causes of the dispossessed'.[35] The day after the murder, Casaldáliga made his reply to El Salvador itself:

All the Americas and the world, the whole church, and especially the poor
have their eyes on El Salvador and Central America. For us you are a
living gospel, an Easter witness ...Thank you for your witness, thank you
for the blood of Archbishop Romero. His presence, now risen, will be a
new 'subversive memory' for our church. Romero is a new martyr of
liberation, a new saint for us in the Americas.

With immediate intuition Casaldáliga grasped that Romero had become
'Saint Romero of the Americas', as he later called him in a poem.[36]
Within El Salvador, however, the murder was at first seen to be effective.
Romero had been silenced. Nothing seemed beyond the power of
violence. Public expressions of opposition, such as street demonstrations, virtually ceased. Activists went underground, and over the next
several years many priests and other church leaders were forced to leave
the country. By 1982 one writer had estimated that 40 per cent of rural
parishes had no resident priest and that the archdiocese had lost 35 per
cent of its priests and religious.[37]

The Vatican appointed Bishop Arturo Rivera y Damas, the only
bishop who had supported Romero, to succeed him. From the outset
Rivera sought to position himself as a mediator in the conflict, moving
away from Romero's sympathy, albeit critical, with the popular
movements. It was a stance that reflected both his own temperament
and his assessment of the situation. An insurrection took place in El
Salvador in January 1981 and led neither to a popular uprising nor to a
defeat of the guerrillas, who then withdrew to a number of rural regions
of the country. Rivera went to Europe and then the United States
seeking support for a negotiated solution, but in Washington he was
rebuffed by the new Reagan administration. By 1981 the rector of the
Central American University, Ignacio Ellacuría, who was sympathetic to
the left, was also advocating a negotiated settlement.[38]

How Romero's own position would have evolved had he lived is
impossible to determine, but his memory remained controversial. When
preparations were made for Pope John Paul II's visit to El Salvador in
1983, the UCA printed 20,000 copies of a poster bearing a photograph
of the Pope and Romero together. Bishop Rosa Chávez ordered that
they be removed, reportedly after two women from Roberto D'Aubuisson's party, ARENA, had complained to the nuncio. However, some
posters had already been distributed, and people brought them to the
public meetings. On the Pope's schedule was found no visit to the
cathedral of San Salvador where the body of Archbishop Romero lay.
But then, on its way to the main public event of the visit, the Pope's
motor car turned unexpectedly towards the cathedral. He went inside

and prayed at Romero's tomb. When he spoke later to the crowds who had been waiting for him, John Paul II mentioned 'a zealous and venerated pastor, the archbishop of this flock Oscar Arnulfo Romero, who tried, like his brother bishops in the episcopacy, to bring about an end to violence and re-establish peace', and the crowd responded with sustained applause. Romero's memory, he announced, must 'always be respected and ... no ideological interest seek to take advantage of his sacrifice as a pastor committed to his flock'.[39]

A little over a year later, on the anniversary of Romero's death, 300 members of CoMadres, an organization of mothers and relatives of those who had disappeared under repression, marched through the streets to the cathedral where they attended a mass. Although few bystanders joined them, many watched, particularly a large number of journalists who were in San Salvador to cover an election. It was the first street demonstration in almost four years. Within weeks a group of workers went on strike, and over the next two years protests became common and an increasingly militant opposition to the state spread. Some of the organizers no doubt saw Romero primarily as a rallying symbol, and ignored non-political aspects of his message. Indeed, Romero himself might have been willing to be adopted in this manner, if those who invoked his name served a just cause and used suitable means to pursue it. It is no unusual phenomenon to find the lives of religious figures exploited by political movements.[40] If in life Romero was criticized for being political, it is not surprising that his legacy has some untidiness about it. Some declared that Romero had been a simple man who had been manipulated by others (often, it was said, by the Jesuits). I once heard President Duarte of El Salvador say that Romero had preached two kinds of sermon, 'the one he wrote and the one they handed him'.[41]

Romero was instantly called a martyr, even though he was not murdered in defence of any article of faith – or indeed of the faith as a whole, confessionally. Images of him went up on the walls of humble homes in El Salvador and elsewhere. Organizations and conferences were named after him. Within a few years there appeared several books of his writings, an important biography, a film in 1989, and even an opera. Today, some in El Salvador resent this veneration and question whether Romero was truly a martyr. Such a discussion had arisen in Romero's own lifetime, that is, whether the Christians then being murdered should be so regarded. Romero had said that for him they were martyrs not canonically, but in a 'popular sense' and 'in the basic sense of the word': 'They are genuine human beings, who have gone to the limit of danger, where the UGB [the White Warriors Union death squad] lurks, where someone can "finger" you and you die. This is how Christ died.'[42] The figure of Christ that Romero had seen in those being killed around him we now see in him. It is the likeness of his own life and death to that of Christ and his explicit repeated preaching of the gospel and hope in the resurrection, that make him so clearly a martyr (a 'witness') in the late twentieth century. During his own lifetime, many Salvadorans and others saw in the travail of that tiny country the birth pangs of liberation. They hoped that Nicaragua, then El Salvador and then other countries, would be able to forge a new kind of society, one that would no doubt be austere but where meeting the needs of all would have precedence over satisfying the wants of a few. This was not to say that revolutions like that of Nicaragua would take place in the larger Latin American countries and in the Third World, but that it could still be possible for a small country to chart its own course. God's reign on earth may not be realized, but perhaps a meaningful step toward it might be made. Romero shared those hopes. 'How beautiful will be the day', he exclaimed a few weeks before he was killed, 'when a new society, instead of selfishly hoarding and keeping, apportions, shares, divides up, and all rejoice because we all feel we are children of the same God.'[43]

A peace agreement between the warring parties of El Salvador was signed early in 1992. It is now criminal, not political, violence that people fear there. The conflicts of earlier decades, which arose as Salvadoran peasants struggled for more land, have receded. At the end of the twentieth century almost half of El Salvador is an urban society, and as much as a fifth of Salvadorans now live in the United States. Their dollar remittances to their homeland are a more important source of income than coffee. The origins of some youth gangs in San Salvador can be traced to Los Angeles.

Archbishop Rivera y Damas died in 1995. The Vatican appointed Fernando Sáenz to succeed him. Sáenz cut a quite different figure in the archdiocese; he agreed to accept the rank of brigadier general in the army after he had been named military vicar by the Vatican. He dismissed critics with the assertion that whatever abuses of power had taken place in El Salvador in the past were the work of individuals rather than the military institutions.

But Romero is still much remembered. Jon Sobrino, whose theological reflection has repeatedly drawn on the life and teaching of Oscar Romero, has written of him 'I should have to say that what impressed me most was his thoroughgoing *consistency* in following his chosen path — his *fidelity* to that path. The basic principle of this consistency was his option for the poor.'[44] This was a theological principle, an ecclesiological principle, and a prudential principle. For myself, I will simply say that having spent hours reconsidering Romero in what is plainly a different day, I am left discontented and feel pressed to discover what such a fidelity must mean in my own life and for that of others who still cherish the ideals to which Romero witnessed to the end.

Notes

1 I was in El Salvador with a delegation representing Catholic, Protestant and Quaker bodies in the United States. After mass we observed Romero's press conference and then met with him and about a half-dozen of his close advisors.

2 In Guatemala where I was living several priests had likewise been murdered and were regarded as martyrs. Attending a memorial mass in 1978 or 1979 it suddenly struck me that the liturgy was coming to mean observances for those who had given their lives in the struggle. Jesus' own life and words had provoked conflict, as Latin American theologians were reminding us, and I was now seeing this drama re-enacted around me in protagonists I knew.

3 The film *Romero* supports this version, inasmuch as two-thirds of it takes place in the early phase of his episcopacy around the murder of Grande, and then it leaps to the final period of his life. James Brockman's superb biography also begins during this period, and then sketches his earlier life: James R. Brockman, *Romero: A Life* (Maryknoll, NY: Orbis Books, 1989), revised version of *The Word Remains: A Life of Oscar Romero* (Maryknoll, NY: Orbis Books, 1982).

4 Brockman, *Romero: A Life*, p. 40.

5 Ibid., p. 42.

6 Ibid., p. 58.

7 Ibid., pp. 58-61.

8 Cf. Philip Berryman, *The Religious Roots of Rebellion: Christians in Central American Revolutions* (Maryknoll, NY: Orbis Books, 1984), pp. 106-9. On Grande, Rodolfo Cardenal, *Historia de una Esperanza: Vida de Rutilio Grande* (San Salvador: UCA Editores, 1985).

9 Jon Sobrino, *Archbishop Romero: Memories and Reflections* (Maryknoll, NY: Orbis Books, 1990). Two Passionist priests have written an entire book to document their conviction that Romero's conversion began in the mid-1970s when he was Bishop of Santiago de María: Zacarías Diez and Juan Macho, '*En Santiago de María me topé con la Miseria*': *Dos Años de la Vida de Mons. Romero (1975-1976) ¿Años del Cambio?* (211 pp., no publication data). Their purpose is evidently to combat simplistic views of an instantaneous conversion. Even if the change can be traced to Santiago

de María, it was the situation he encountered as he became archbishop – and especially Grande's murder – that brought that change into the open.

10 Brockman, *Romero: A Life*, pp. 12-18.

11 Ibid., p. 62.

12 Juan Bosco Palacios, quoted in María López Vigil (ed.), *Piezas para un Retrato* (San Salvador: UCA Editores, 1993), p. 196.

13 The group had no official name, but they often referred to themselves as *la Nacional*, thus indicating their Salvadoran identity in some tension with foreign priests, who made up about half the clergy. The fact that the clergy was even half Salvadoran (as opposed to Guatemala, Honduras, Nicaragua and Panama whose clergy was around 80 per cent foreign) reflected the work of Romero's predecessor, Archbishop Luis Chávez y González, who over his long tenure (1939-77) did much to develop a Salvadoran clergy. Chávez was also supportive of socially active priests in the post-Medellín era.

14 Urrutia from López Vigil (ed.), *Piezas para un Retrato*, pp. 210-11; Sobrino, *Memories and Reflections*, pp. 51-2.

15 Quotations from Oscar Romero, *The Violence of Love: The Pastoral Wisdom of Archbishop Oscar Romero*, ed. James Brockman SJ (San Francisco: Harper and Row, 1988), pp. 185, 156.

16 The organization had been founded in the 1960s by Gen. José Medrano, who later claimed to have had help from the CIA.

17 Berryman, *Religious Roots of Rebellion*, pp. 130-2.

18 Instituto Universitario de Opinión Pública, 'La Religión para los Salvadoreños (Una Encuesta de opinión pública)' (mimeograph, 1988).

19 It may be noted that in the first half of 1977, the US ambassador, Ignacio Lozano, a Republican newspaperman and political appointee of the Ford administration, did pursue an activist human rights policy. He and his political attaché became *personae non gratae* and left the country on the eve of General Romero's inauguration. (Author's interviews in US embassy, 1977.)

20 Roberto Cuellar and José Siman, cited in López Vigil (ed.), *Piezas para un Retrato*, pp. 213-14.

21 López Vigil (ed.), *Piezas para un Retrato*, pp. 215-16.

22 Julian Filochowski, in López Vigil (ed.), *Piezas para un Retrato*, p. 225.

23 This account is from Romero's diary, *Mons. Oscar Arnulfo Romero: Su Diario del 31 de marzo de 1978 al 20 de marzo de 1980* (San Salvador: Imprenta Criterio, 1990), pp. 178-9.

24 In his diary Romero describes his meeting with the Pope as 'not entirely satisfactory' but 'useful'. María López Vigil, who spent several hours with Romero two days later as he was in transit in Madrid, presents a harsher view of the encounter: *Piezas para un Retrato*, pp. 282-5.

25 Sobrino, *Memories and Reflections*, p. 9.

26 Legal Aid Office, Archdiocese of San Salvador, *El Salvador: Del genocidio de la junta militar a la esperanza de la lucha insurreccional*, p. 36.

27 A week after the 15 October coup, I attended an evening meeting

organized by Socorro Jurídico where Romero publicly posed this challenge to the new government.

28 Text of letter in Rodolfo Cardenal *et al.* (eds), *La Voz de los Sin Voz: La Palabra viva de Monseñor Oscar Arnulfo Romero* (San Salvador: UCA Editores, 1980), pp. 263–4; account in Brockman, *Romero*, pp. 227–9.

29 López Vigil (ed.), *Piezas para un Retrato*, p. 356.

30 Ibid., pp. 369–70.

31 Quoted in López Vigil (ed.), *Piezas para un Retrato*, p. 355.

32 Brockman, *Romero*, p. 248.

33 In an appendix to *Romero* Brockman summarizes what could be known of the murder in the late 1980s. Three days after Romero was killed two men entered the house of Atilio Ramírez Amaya, the judge to whom the case would be assigned, and shot at him. He repelled them with his shotgun, and left the country. The justice system moved very slowly in taking testimony and in the mid-1980s the case was shelved. Hector Antonio Regalado became head of security at the National Assembly when D'Aubuisson was its head, and was active in death squads. The driver Garay observed that his passenger had fired 'a kind of rifle' from the back seat but only after hearing news reports did he realize that Romero had been killed. Three days later, he saw Saravia tell D'Aubuisson 'We did what was planned – killed Archbishop Arnulfo Romero'. When D'Aubuisson complained that he had acted too soon, he replied 'We did it as you ordered'. Although at one point extradition proceedings were begun against Saravia, who had moved to the United States, the ARENA party was able to block the action. Romero's murder, like that of the tens of thousands of others, remained unsolved.

34 Carolyn Forché reports that a highly placed Salvadoran source dismissed as a myth the generalized belief that Roberto D'Aubuisson was behind the killing, by noting that being able to say 'D'Aubuisson did it' was very useful because it prevented questions from being raised about the landowners, the military high command and the US embassy: 'Oscar Romero' in Susan Bergman (ed.), *Martyrs* (San Francisco: HarperSanFrancisco, 1996), pp. 76–7.

35 Sobrino, *Memories and Reflections*, pp. 39–40.

36 Bishop Pedro Casaldáliga, *In Pursuit of the Kingdom: Writings 1968–1988* (Maryknoll, NY: Orbis Books, 1990), pp. 193–4; poem, pp. 207–9. The somewhat unusual wording 'St Romero' (rather than St Oscar Romero) reflects the fact that the Spanish word *romero* means both 'religious pilgrim' and 'rosemary'.

37 Iván D. Paredes, 'Evolución de la Iglesia salvadoreña, 24 de marzo 80/28 de marzo 82', *Estudios Centroamericanos*, nos 403–404 (May–June 1982), p. 446.

38 Interview with Ellacuría in Managua, July 1981. Even though Ellacuría could not safely return to El Salvador at this time, he did not believe that the FMLN guerrillas had a realistic chance to take power.

39 Philip Berryman, *Stubborn Hope: Religion, Politics, and Revolution in Central America* (New York: The New Press, 1994), p. 73. Only the journalists observed the Pope since troops had been stationed to keep people away from the cathedral area and so prevent any spontaneous rally. Against all evidence the Pope sought to tie Romero to the other bishops who, with the exception of Rivera y Damas, opposed him while he was alive and ignored him in death (never citing him, for example, in their joint statements).

40 To cite an example I observed, in 1980 Mother Teresa was scheduled to visit Guatemala. CONFREGUA (Conference of Religious of Guatemala) warned of the danger that the military and government, which by then had killed several priests, and dozens of lay church workers, would use the visit for their own legitimation, and they urged that the visit not take place. The upper-class groups organizing the visit ignored the request, and indeed her presence was exploited by the military and government.

41 Delegation, including US congressional representatives, in presidential palace, April 1985.

42 Quoted in Sobrino, *Memories and Reflections*, p. 47.

43 Romero, *Violence of Love*, p. 222.

44 Sobrino, *Memories and Reflections*, p. 32.

Bibliography

The indispensable work is James Brockman, *Romero: A Life* (Maryknoll, NY: Orbis Books, 1989). Brockman's *The Violence of Love: The Pastoral Wisdom of Archbishop Oscar Romero* (San Francisco: Harper and Row, 1988) is a chronological selection of quotations from Romero's sermons and writings. Jon Sobrino, *Archbishop Romero: Memories and Reflections* (Maryknoll, NY: Orbis Books, 1990) combines personal observation and theological reflection. Among sources in Spanish: María López Vigil (ed.), *Piezas para un Retrato* (San Salvador: UCA Editores, 1993) gathers oral testimony from many people; Rodolfo Cardenal *et al.* (eds), *La Voz de los Sin Voz: La palabra viva de Monseñor Oscar Arnulfo Romero* (San Salvador: UCA Editores, 1980) is an especially valuable collection of the archbishop's words; *Monseñor Oscar Arnulfo Romero: Su Diario* (San Salvador: Taller Criterio, 1990) is a day-to-day record of Romero's contacts and activities; *Mons. Oscar A. Romero: Su Muerte y Reacciones* (San Salvador: Arzobispado de San Salvador, 1982) presents 600 pages of reports on his murder and funeral from sources around the world.

Index